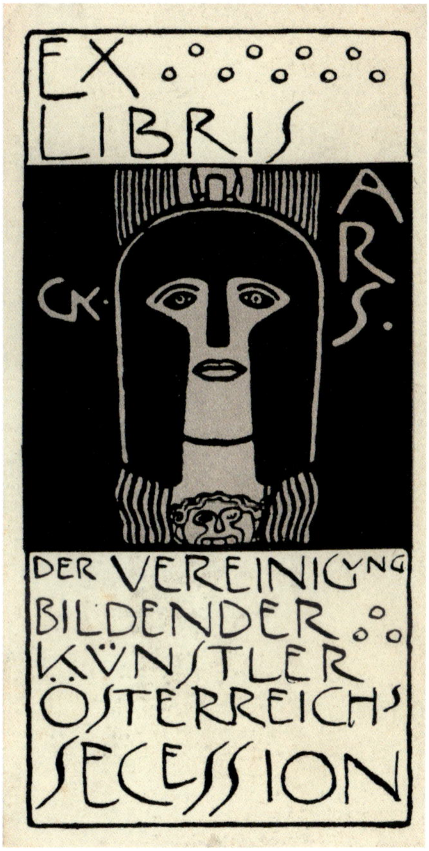
EX LIBRIS
ARS.
GK.
DER VEREINIGUNG BILDENDER KÜNSTLER ÖSTERREICHS SECESSION

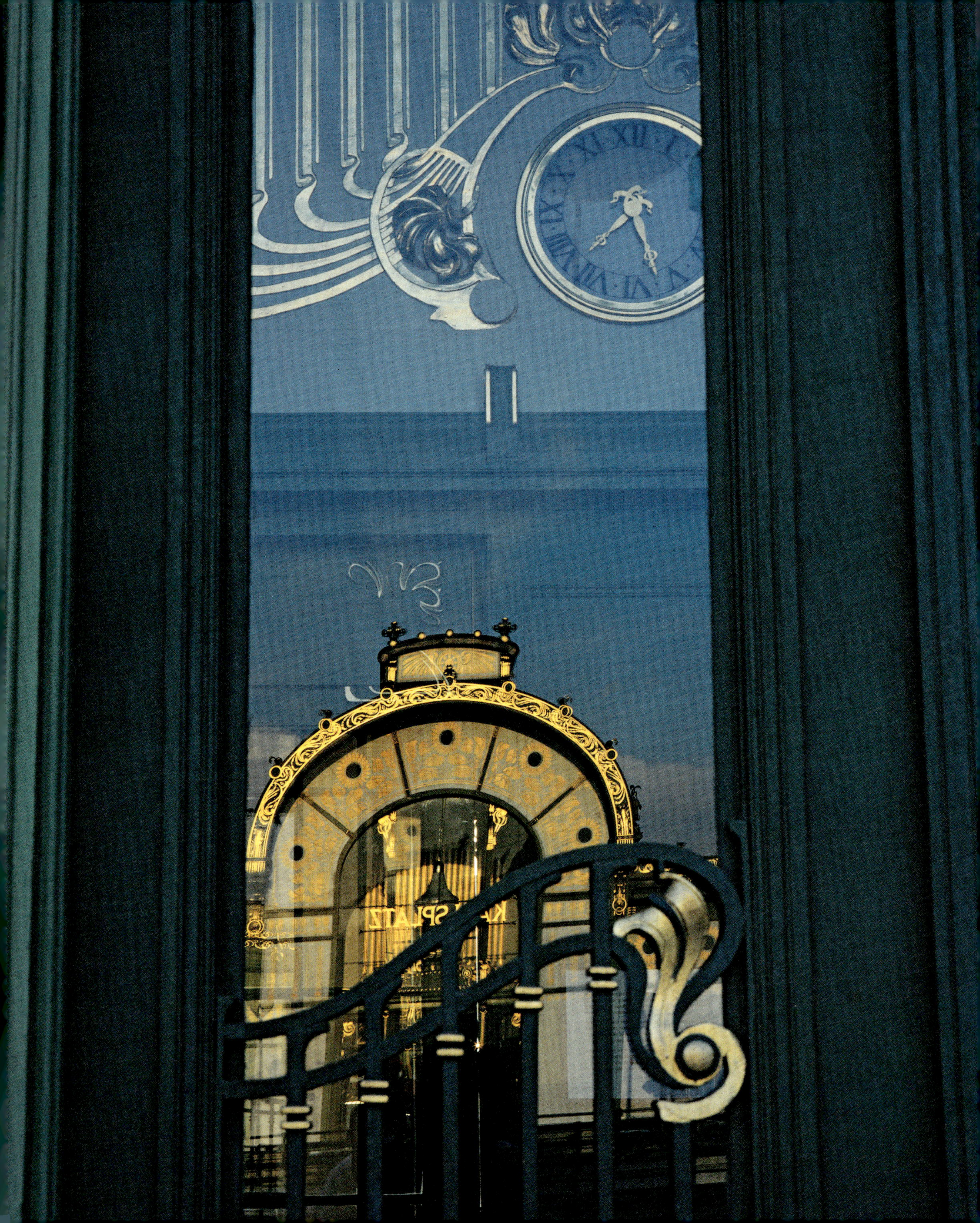

Rainer Metzger (ed.)
Daniela Gregori
Maik Novotny
Thomas Trenkler

Vienna 1900

TASCHEN

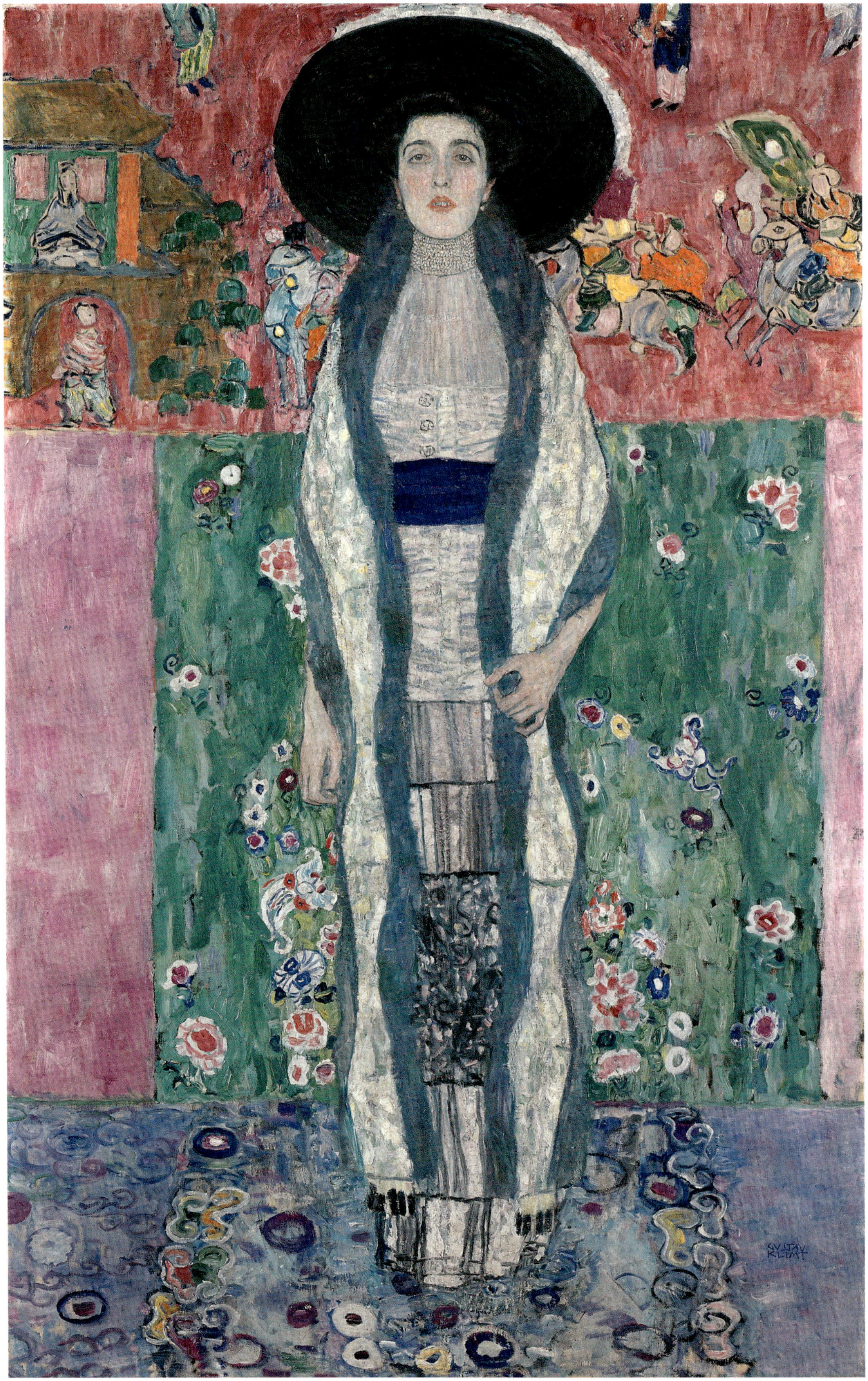
GVSTAV
KLIMT

Contents

6 **Ugly Facts in Pretty Guises**

32 **Gustav Klimt** — Auditorium in the Old Burgtheater

34 **Joseph Maria Olbrich** — Vienna Secession Building

36 **Alfred Roller / Josef Maria Auchentaller** — Cover and decorative page for *Ver Sacrum*

38 **Otto Wagner** — Buildings on Linke Wienzeile

40 **Karl Kraus (ed.)** — *Die Fackel*

42 **Adolf Loos** — Café Museum

44 **Wilhelm Gause** — Court Ball

46 **Max Fabiani** — Artaria House

48 **Josef Hoffmann** — Overdoors in the Beethoven exhibition of the Secession

50 **Jože Plečnik** — Zacherlhaus

52 **Koloman Moser** — Armchair

54 **Otto Wagner** — Postal Savings Bank

56 **Josef Hoffmann** — Palais Stoclet

58 **Moriz Jung** — Nocturnal Conversation

60 **Bertold Löffler** — Poster for the Cabaret Fledermaus

62 **Carl Otto Czeschka** — Wittgenstein Vitrine

64 **Richard Gerstl** — Nude Self-Portrait

66 **Oskar Kokoschka** — Pietà

68 **Ditha Moser** — Calendar for the year 1910

70 **Adolf Loos** — Haus am Michaelerplatz

72 **Arnold Schönberg** — Gaze

74 **Egon Schiele** — Seated Male Nude (Self-Portrait)

76 **Emil Mayer** — Onlookers at the Prater

78 **Josef Hoffmann** — Glass Collection Bronzite Series B, Lobmeyr

80 **Max Oppenheimer** — Portrait of Tilla Durieux

82 **Egon Schiele** — Cover of the magazine *Der Ruf*

84 **Mauritz Stiller** — Das fremde Mädchen [The Strange Girl]

86 **Emilie Flöge** — Reform dress

88 **Oskar Kokoschka** — The Bride of the Wind

90 **Gustav Klimt** — Death and Life

92 **Madame d'Ora** — Emperor Charles I of Austria with His Family

94 **Egon Schiele** — The Family (Cowering Couple)

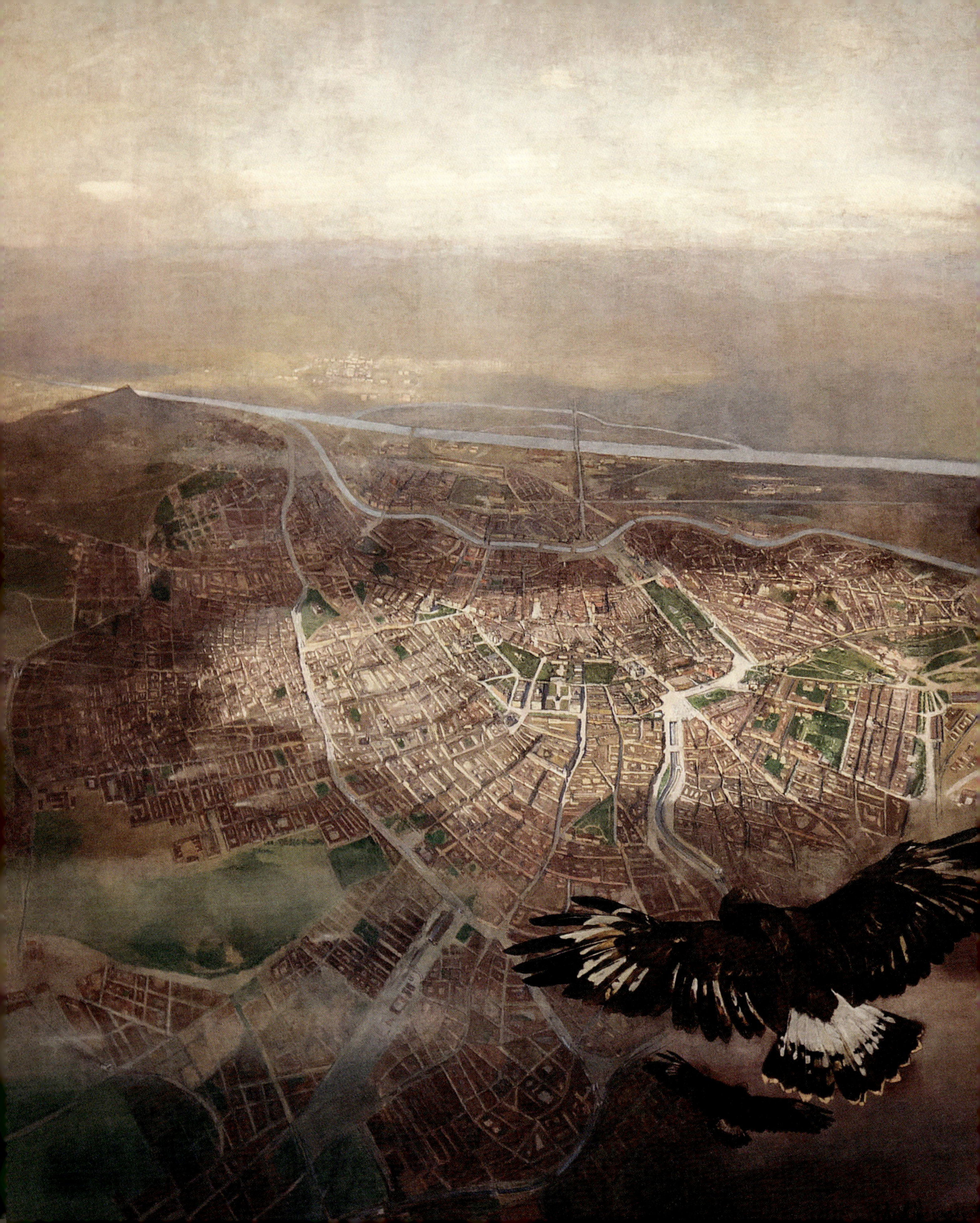

Ugly Facts in Pretty Guises

Rainer Metzger

This is how we act our parts out,
Acting plays of our own making,
Early-ripe and sad and tender,
The commedia of our spirit,
What we feel as time slips by us,
Ugly facts in pretty guises,
Smooth-tongued speeches, coloured pictures,
Half-felt feelings sensed in secret,
Agonies and episodes…

— HUGO VON HOFMANNSTHAL, PROLOGUE TO ARTHUR SCHMITZLER'S *ANATOL*, 1892

Two eagles are circling over the city. We can look over their shoulders, so to speak, at a height of 3,000 metres. The city is the capital of the Habsburg Empire, the Danube Monarchy, the realm of Austria-Hungary. That there are two majestic birds of prey might tempt us to recognize a heraldic reference, which would be the two-headed eagle, as it soars over a prominent section of its territory. The city, therefore, is Vienna. In the play of light and shade we can recognize lines above all: those marked in a bluish colour in the background indicate the Danube and a number of whitish accents apparently delineate streets, squares and traffic areas (ill. p. 6). The artist who created the painting is particularly concerned about these flowing places, areas of transition and diverse life. Carl Moll (1861–1945) recorded the status quo in 1898 in his panorama, shown literally from a bird's-eye view. He obviously made use of materials like the latest maps and plans, whose rigorous two-dimensional view is nonetheless transformed here into three-dimensionality. In this way he lends his artwork something of the dynamism that was basically a matter of course in most metropolises on the cusp of the 20th century.

Moll's painting had been presented in the spring of 1898 at the central celebration of the year, the great jubilee exhibition which was staged to mark the 50th anniversary of the accession of His Majesty Franz Joseph I (1830–1916; ill. p. 44). On the rotunda area of the Prater, the site of the World Fair of 1873, everything the empire had to offer by way of dignitaries, honourable and respectable citizens was assembled (ill. p. 7). Art, of course, was also represented. Like the World Fair, which flopped as a result of the economic crisis and the epidemic, the Imperial Jubilee Exhibition was ill-fated. On 10 September, the Empress was assassinated by an anarchist. The famous Elisabeth (1837–1898), known by the nickname "Sisi", was more of a myth than the Mother of the Nation. No one was interested in celebrating after that. But the Emperor would keep a stiff upper lip through 18 further years in office. He would ensure that the centrifuge which his realm

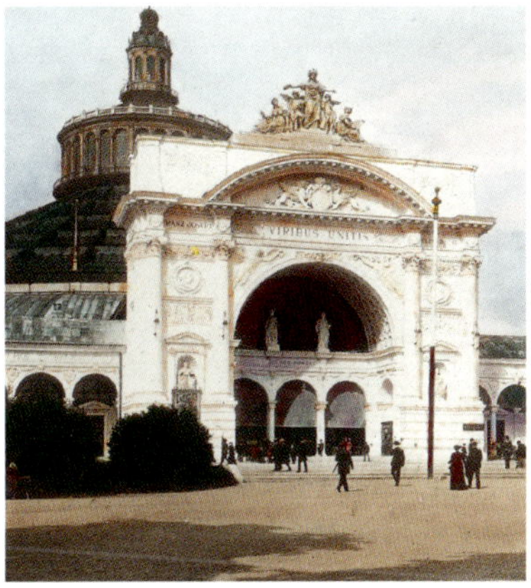

Karl von Hasenauer
The South Portal of the rotunda in the Wiener Prater
Hand-coloured lantern slide, c. 1890

Carl Moll
Panoramic View of Vienna, 1898
Tempera on canvas,
324 x 260 cm (127½ x 102¼ in.)
Vienna, Hofpavillon

PAGE 1
Gustav Klimt
Ex Libris, 1899/1900
Colour lithograph,
29 x 37 cm (11½ x 14½ in.)

PAGE 2
Reflection on a glass door – Otto Wagner, Stadtbahn station at Karlsplatz, 1998/99
Photograph by Keiichi Tahara

PAGE 4
Gustav Klimt
Portrait of Adele Bloch-Bauer II, 1912
Oil on canvas, 190 x 120 cm (74¾ x 47¼ in.)
Private collection

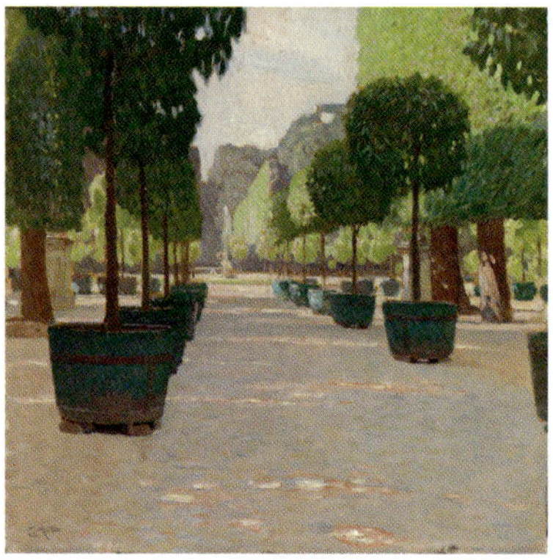

Carl Moll
The Park of Schönbrunn Palace, 1910
Oil on wood, 35.6 x 35.3 cm (14 x 14 in.)
Amsterdam, Van Gogh Museum

had long since become would at least retain a centre around which it could rotate. This middle – if not vacuous – was at least difficult to balance out. Perhaps we can read here the sovereign's instructions for use; perhaps it explains his persistence and his perseverance. His remoteness meant that each individual could envision his own emperor. The stuff of which the dreams of subjects were made consisted of tradition, ceremony and constancy. Not even the hot-headed avant-garde doubted the sense and the guarantee of safety offered by His Majesty.

For Moll's bird's-eye view things would go further too. To this day the picture is still in its intended location – in the Pavilion of the Imperial and Royal Supreme Court, which had been built in the vicinity of Schönbrunn Palace so that the Emperor and his entourage could use the Stadtbahn (city railway), which was in the process of being built. Like all the stations of this most modern link in Vienna's transport system, the "Kaiser-Pavillon" (ill. p. 8 bottom) had also been planned in the office of Otto Wagner (1841–1918). Wagner was considered the most modern of all architects in Vienna around the turn of the century; his projects acted as catapults in the upswing which construction would shortly experience. In the case of the station for His Majesty, Wagner and his chief draughtsman Joseph Maria Olbrich (1867–1908) exercised considerable restraint. The latter had also designed the eye-catching building for the Secession (ill. p. 35) around the same time. Contrary to all ideas of functionality, the station is surmounted by a cupola with oval windows – a clear reference to the rotunda of the Karlskirche, whose Baroque style heralds the imperial predecessor, the name-giving Karl VI. Wagner's chosen motto was "Artis sola domina necessitas" – "necessity is the only mistress of art". In this case, however, the moral of the material was subordinated to the dignity of the effect.

Moll's painting can be understood as a sort of signpost to the routing of the Stadtbahn, corresponding more or less to today's underground lines U4 and U6. Directly

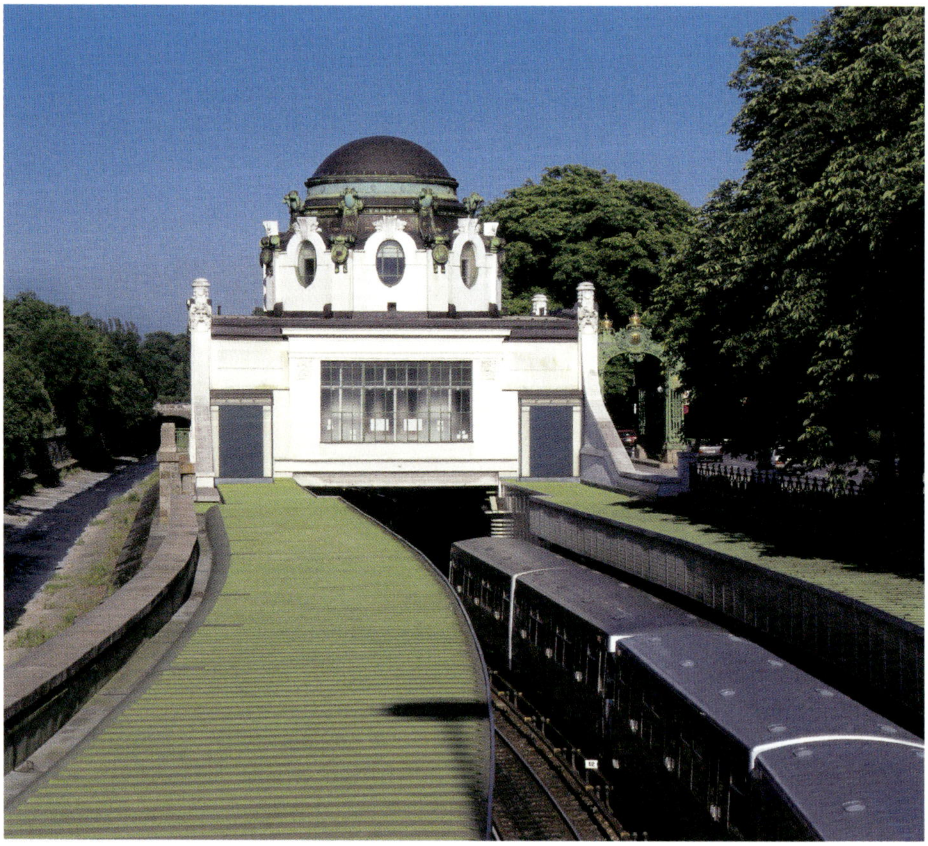

Otto Wagner
Hofpavillon station in Wien-Hietzing, 1899

The so-called Kaiser-Pavillon was erected near the Schloss Schönbrunn so that the imperial house could use the Stadtbahn.

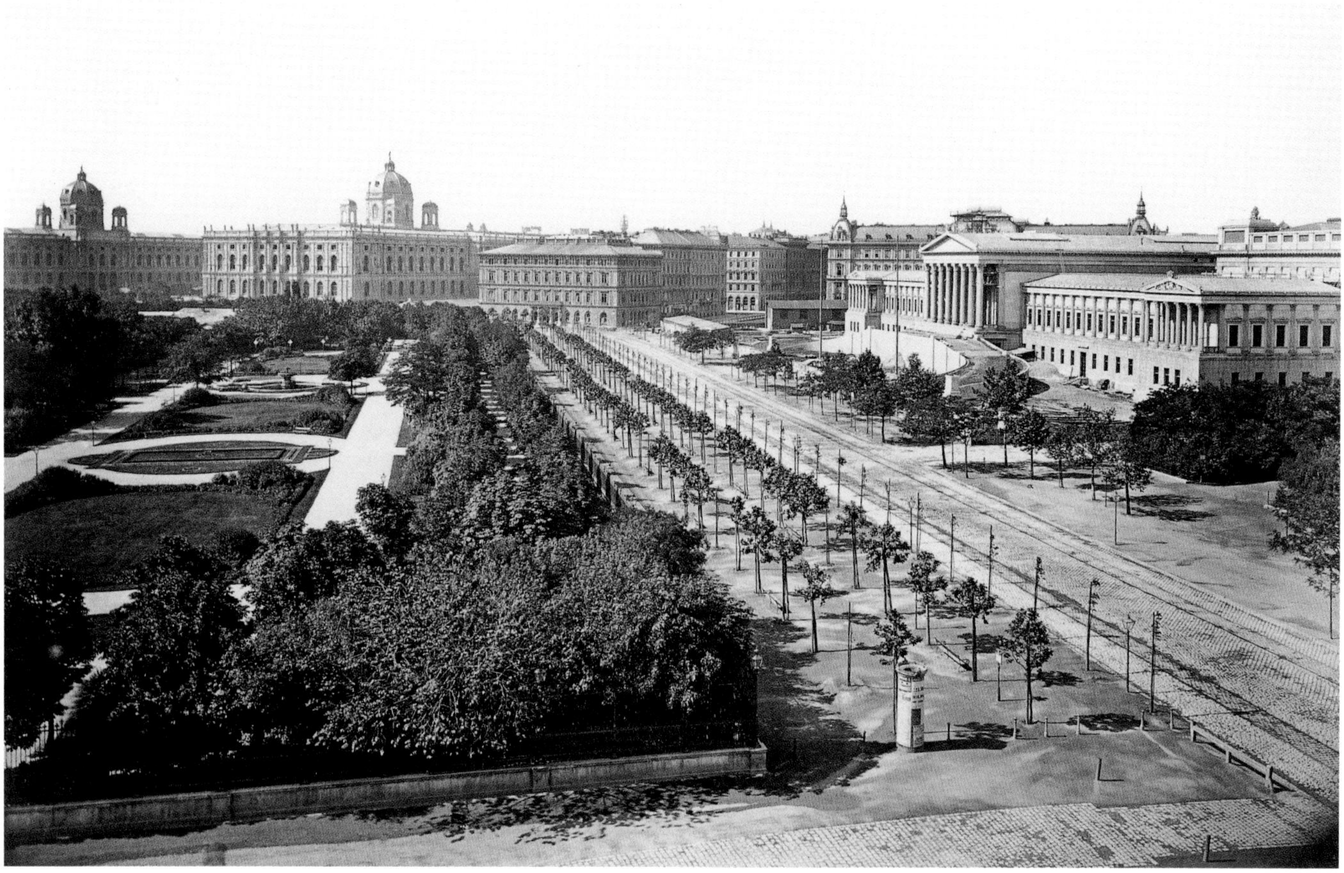

View of the Ringstrasse, c. 1890

beneath the two heraldic creatures we can make out the Schönbrunn Palace (ill. p. 8 top) and park; from there, a white ribbon winds its way towards a lightly occupied middle ground. This is where the new trains run. Another ribbon runs downwards from top left, marking the second Stadtbahn line. Opposite these two routes, along the Wien River and Gürtel, Moll's picture pays little attention to Vienna's real sensation of town planning. The Ringstrasse, planned in the 1850s, lining up signature buildings like the Opera, the Burgtheater and the University side by side and now, still unfinished around the turn of the century, can at best be recognized as a faint hint of radial movement (ill. p. 9). But if we try, in the painting, to make out an actual piece of architecture, we must look at the lightest part which highlights the Karlsplatz, where the Wien valley intersects with the straight arterial road heading south-east. Here we can recognize a circular accent, the newest of the new – the Secession. It is the exhibition building of the artists' association of the same name. Carl Moll had been one of the founding members in 1897.

The Stadtbahn was hardly a roaring success. It was intended to relieve the Viennese community but failed to achieve the planned results. The city had grown in the meanwhile to two million inhabitants and occupied fifth place on the list of metropolises worldwide. In line with the radial structure of Vienna, it travelled around the centre rather than actually reaching it with a line directly into the heart of the city. Despite the beauty that Wagner had given them with his purism and his desire for geometry, the stations (ill. p. 10 top) were too large, too inaccessible and thus, quite simply, too impractical. Above all, however, the trains were still steam locomotives. And from that point of view they had arrived on the scene too late. But on the other hand, measured by the possibilities offered by electricity, which would soon become available, they had arrived on the scene too soon. The Stadtbahn was not the only thing in Vienna which was a complete anachronism.

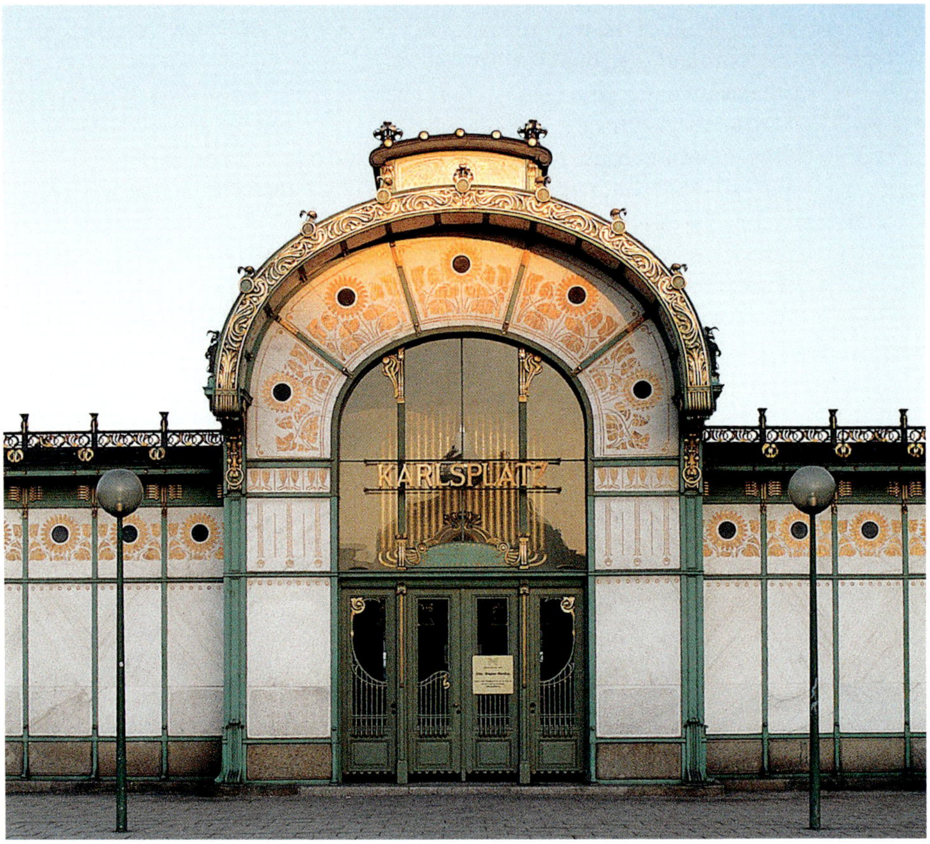

Otto Wagner
Stadtbahn Station at Karlsplatz, Vienna, 1896–1899

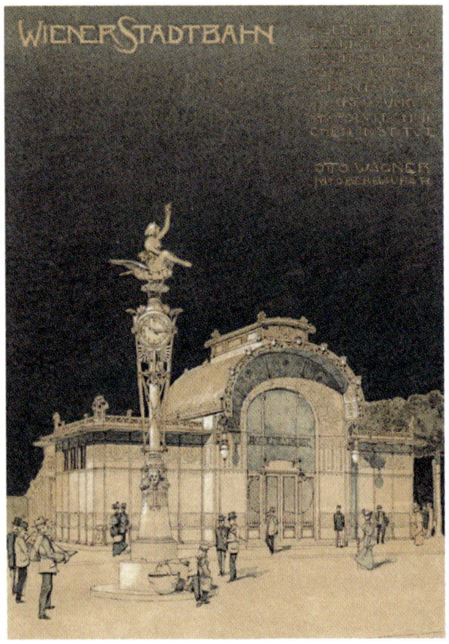

Otto Wagner
Presentation illustration of the Stadtbahn (detail), 1898
Pen and ink over pencil sketch
Vienna, Wien Museum

The Emperor used his pavilion twice. His two visits on 16 June 1899 and 12 April 1902 were for representational purposes. Indeed, for what else? Since the idea that an emperor would mix with the people – on their terms, at their level and completely without the ceremonial framework – was too crazily progressive at that time. But it was, in fact, the representative function the architect who planned the pavilion, Otto Wagner, had in mind in the first place. The pavilion was photographed, published and engraved on a medal. It was the stone incarnation of the complicity between the monarchy and the modern age. It was here that venerability and the contemporary world encountered each other.

In August 1899, when Wagner had just joined the Vereinigung Österreichischer Künstler (Union of Austrian Artists), the Secession magazine *Ver Sacrum* (ill. p. 37) dedicated an extensive, inevitably eulogistic article to this showpiece that fused the demands of contemporary aesthetics with the expectations of the imperial court. The Vienna of around 1900 frequently took place in a similar interference of time layers in which the various epochs appear firmly embedded. It was a characteristic of the modern age that it wanted to take off into the sky. It was a characteristic of Viennese Modernism that they left it up to the imperial eagle to execute these flights of fancy; Moll's painting shows this in an almost emphatic manner. With the eagle in front, the artists also took off.

And so the exponents of Viennese culture always play-acted a little. They were precocious, delicate and melancholy. Even if they were only just 18, they knew that ugly things lurked behind the pretty guises. At times they asserted these things as agonies, but they were also happy to remain mere episodes. When Hugo von Hofmannsthal (1874–1929) compiled his four-footed trochees in 1892 in order to place them in front of Arthur Schnitzler's (1862–1931) melodramatic play *Anatol*, he was still at grammar school.[1] When he appeared on the literary scene at the age of 17 he was regarded as the sensation of the season. And so the words of the wunderkind proclaimed the truth. Hofmannsthal was extravagant, exquisite and precious. The exponents of Vienna around 1900 were no less so. Hofmannsthal was young, very young, in his ivory tower. An aesthetic programme which refers like the Secessionists to the *Ver Sacrum*, the "Sacred Spring", finds its willing embodiment there: it would happen youthfully, virginally, in purity. At the same time people knew only too well about the burden they carried around, a burden of tradition, education and duty. And physicality.

"Squander the inheritance" is the opening of Hofmannsthal's *Lebenslied* (The Song of Life) from 1896.[2] The poet saw himself as an "heir", and he considered that what he was expected to do with his talents would "squander" them. Hofmannsthal belonged to the generation of the grandchildren – nor was he the only one. The grandfather had built it up, had arrived from the provinces and had founded a company, a bank and a consortium. The son had expanded it and had achieved prosperity. When economic influence had become sufficiently prominent he had been granted an aristocratic title. The grandson would now transfer these possessions into the realm of culture, to that place where the obligation to a certain other-worldliness overlaid the smell of money, to which it owed its existence, with preciousness. Hofmannsthal invested his inheritance for his own artistic production. Many others of his generation were active as supporters, collectors and patrons. Here they displayed a commitment that linked the Vienna of around 1900 more strongly than elsewhere to the close circle of the assiduous – to the point of self-denial. This circle was much more important than just a mere audience. In many cases it was Jewish in origin. This lineage is also a part of a mentality of self-denial. And so in many respects Viennese culture was a sort of cover-up. There was no shortage of ugly facts. People met them with pretty guises. And the Emperor wielded power above all of it.

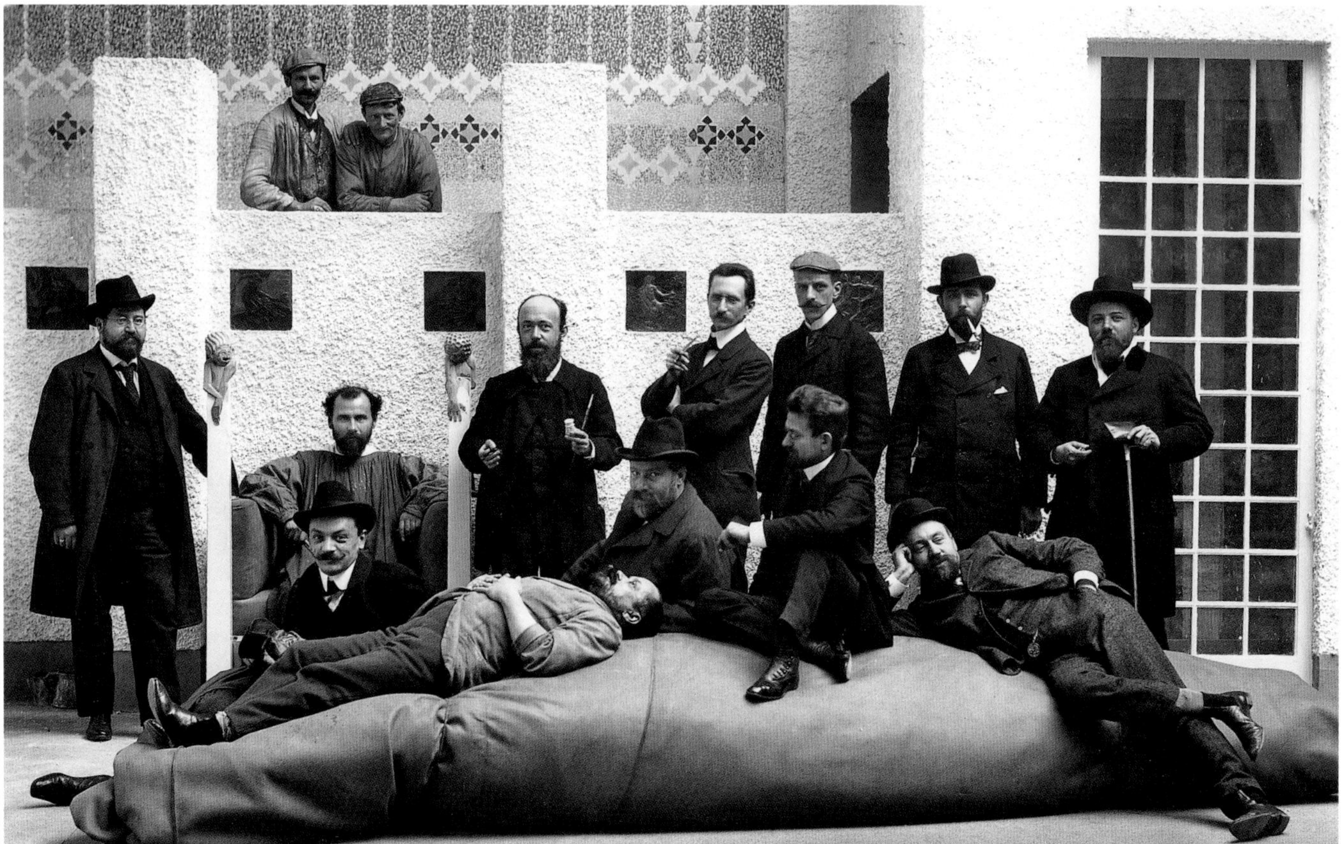

Group photo of the Secession artists, 1902
Back row from left to right:
Anton Stark, Gustav Klimt, Adolf Böhm, Wilhelm List, Maximilian Kurzweil, Leopold Stolba and Rudolf Bacher
Front row:
Koloman Moser, Maximilian Lenz, Ernst Stöhr, Emil Orlik and Carl Moll
Photograph by Moritz Nähr

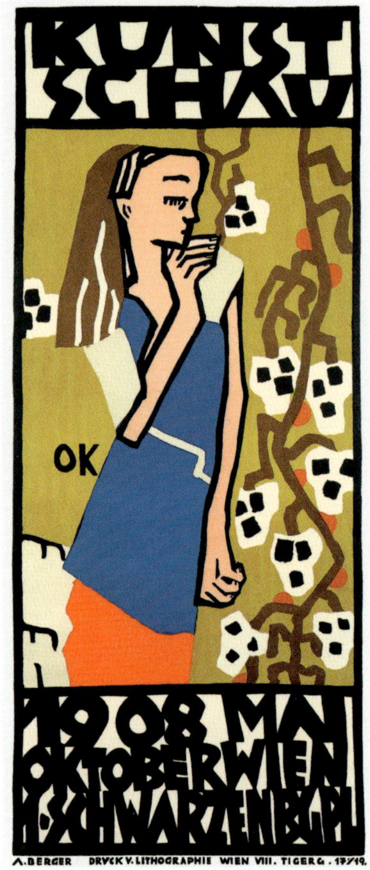

Oskar Kokoschka
Poster for the ***Vienna Kunstschau***, 1908
Colour lithograph, 96 x 38 cm
(37¾ x 15 in.)

The ideal society

"And so", mused Hofmannsthal in the local jargon in 1893, "we go around in this city, the royal guards of the sunken kingdom, the last knowledgeable representatives of noble blood… We! We! I know quite well that I am not speaking about the entire vast generation. I'm talking about a few thousand people scattered across the great cities of Europe."[3] What we describe with expressions like "Fin de Siècle", "Décadence", "Art Nouveau" or "Jugendstil" is an exclusive affair: an idiom of the initiated which at best uttered a few quiet murmurs in the staccato of changes with which the modern age afflicted every major city demographically, socially and economically.

But it is a long time since the Vienna of around 1900 as a whole had started to be noticed as a high point of cultural history. This highlight is so pronounced, but it was only attributed to the city around 1980, when many of the aesthetic accents, which had once been set, became in demand again. Postmodernism raised questions about the significance of ornamentation, about the exuberant staging of the *Gesamtkunstwerk* (total work of art), about a modern age which now seemed to have been outgrown. Not to forget the fondness for the catastrophic which had obsessed the early 1980s. It was a milieu which Karl Kraus (1874–1936; ill. p. 41) described in 1914 as the "experimental station for doomsday."[4] Hermann Broch (1886–1951) called it a "merry apocalypse"[5] in his book about Hofmannsthal, which found its mirror image decades later. One exhibition devoted to Vienna around 1900 was staged by the Hamburger Kunsthalle in 1981. It was correspondingly infatuated with the idea of the end of the world and bore the title *Experiment Weltuntergang* (Doomsday Experiment).

The enthusiasm reached its zenith with *Traum und Wirklichkeit* (Dream and Reality), an exhibition in the Künstlerhaus in Vienna that Hans Hollein (1934–2014) designed, one of the grand masters of postmodern architecture. No fewer than 622,106 entrance tickets were sold ensuring that it was the biggest success of all time of any exhibition in Vienna. And it was, moreover, an exhibition about Vienna. Since then, all the presentation spaces in the city have attempted a repeat performance by competing with each other, always with the same topics. In 2012, to mark the 150th anniversary of his birthday, visitors could admire Gustav Klimt (1862–1918) simultaneously in the Kunsthistorisches Museum, the Wien Museum, the Leopold Museum, the Albertina, the Theatermuseum and the Künstlerhaus. We can draw at least one conclusion from this list of colourful rivalry: Vienna around 1900 enlivens calculations, and they are not necessarily developed only in order to gain new historical insight. The reconstruction of the past is always also a construction of the present.

In this confusion of different periods of time we can also recognize the overlapping of spaces. The culture of Vienna around 1900 wanted to close ranks with the phalanx of the avant-garde and to open up toward trends surging forward from the centres of the spirit of the times – from Paris first and foremost, but also from Munich. Belgium, too, and especially Great Britain had also been hard at work. It was not least for this reason that the Vienna Secession was founded in 1897 (ill. p. 11). Klimt (ill. pp. 33, 91) was the founding president, supported by a battalion of soon-to-be grand masters, all of them young and correspondingly ready for action. Before long their names stood for all that were refined, sensitive and noble: Josef Hoffmann (1870–1956; ill. pp. 14 bottom, 49, 56, 57, 78, 79), Koloman Moser (1868–1918; ill. p. 53) and Olbrich supplied everything that was to be desired by good taste, which itself was established for the first time as a result. They saw themselves as the Secession, and they had formed by means of a split. Their departure from the Wiener Künstlergenossenschaft (Vienna Society of Artists), from their imprisonment in the artistic canon and their clannish insider economy, happened in a demonstrative manner. The Secession was to become a label, a brand, and the house in which they presented themselves was the exclamation mark. The result speaks for itself: the specifically Viennese version of those international reform movements that brought a breath of fresh air into turn-of-the-century aesthetics was known as the Secession Style (ill. p. 34).

Despite this new openness, cosiness and homeliness were not to be ignored either. Hermann Bahr (1863–1934) was the impresario of cultural life in Vienna around 1900, the man who discovered Hofmannsthal and the mentor of the young men of letters – the personification of the latest trends and one of those figures who epitomized the scene, not so much for his originality as for his organizational talent. Bahr had the following message for the newly formed Secession: "But to give us art is more than the finest exhibition of the most modern pictures can achieve. You must be great magicians. You must show us in lines and colours everything that we Viennese have in our souls by way of subtle joys, heartfelt and delicate wishes and restless hopes. You must create what has not yet existed: you must create an Austrian art form for us. If you cannot do that it would have been better if you had let us continue to sleep peacefully. You have aroused our longings. Now fulfil them! An Austrian art form! Each one of you feels what I mean. When you walk along our old, gentle streets or when you see the sun shining on the grating in front of the Volksgarten, while the lilac wafts its perfume and the little Viennese girls skip playfully, or when the strains of a waltz echo as you pass a courtyard, then you experience a curious feeling and no one can say why your heart is so full of happiness that you want to cry, and yet you simply smile: That is Vienna! And this 'That is Vienna' is what you have to paint."[6]

It was a unique mixture of provincialism and broad horizon, of the notorious "know-all" mentality of the dyed-in-the-wool Viennese citizen and the exposure to a fragile refinement at work here which created these works. Marie Herzfeld (1855–1949), the

Vienna Kunstschau, 1908
The Room for "Advertising Art"
From: *Deutsche Kunst und Dekoration*, vol. 23, 1909
Photograph by Bertold Löffler

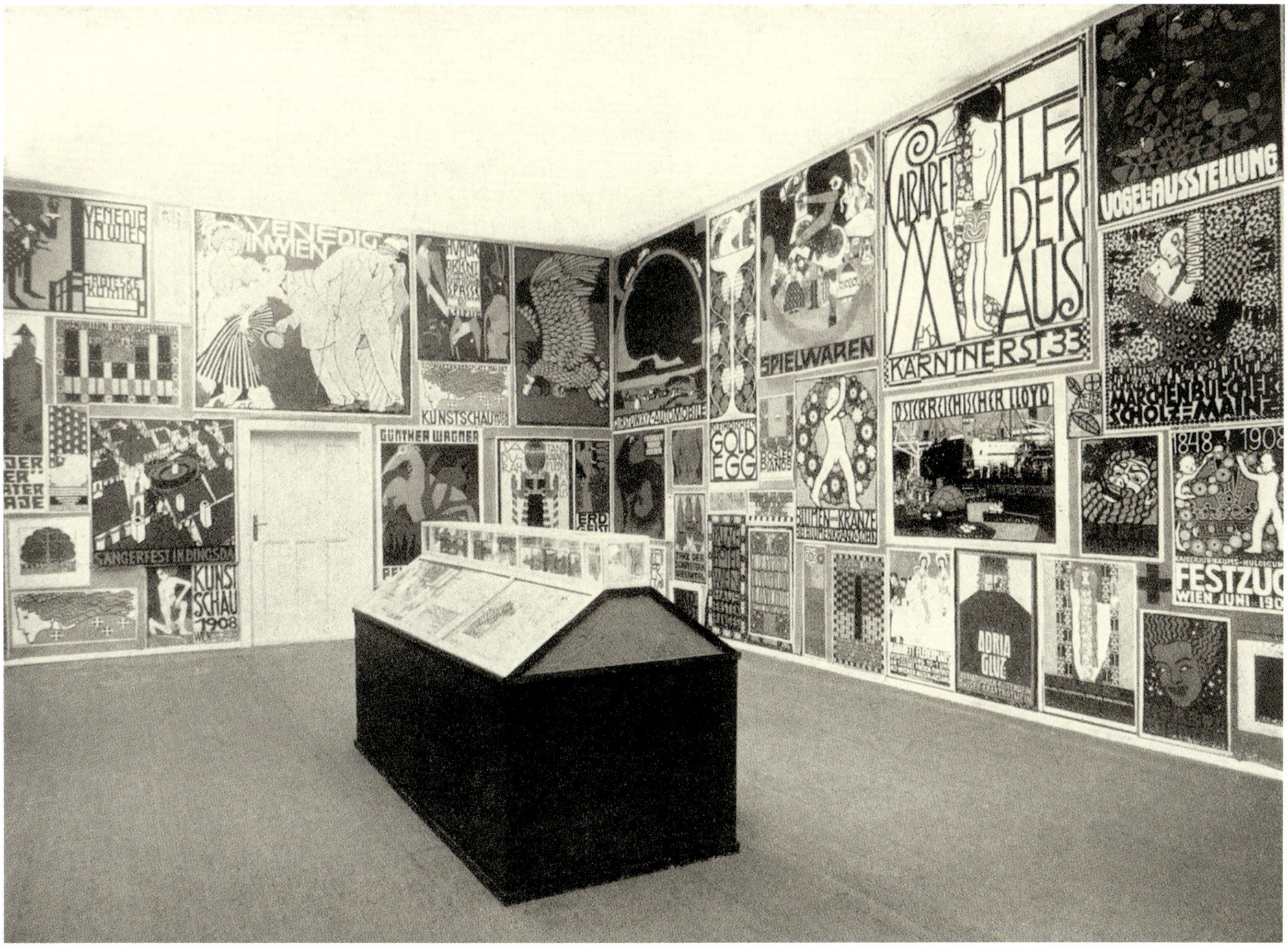

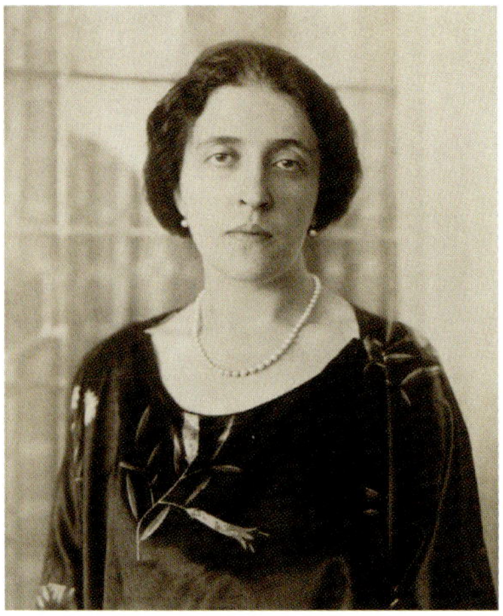

Adele Bloch-Bauer in a dress by the Wiener Werkstätte, c. 1910

essayist and translator, had moved to the city from the provinces, like so many in Vienna around 1900. She found words back in 1891 which describe the soul of this special aesthetic constitution, even though they applied specifically to Bahr: "Regardless of how he disguises himself, Hermann Bahr always remains an Austrian… An Austrian in his ability to assimilate everything, to fuse with the environment he is, in each case – to feel German with the Germans, French with the French, Russian with the Russians and then suddenly to withdraw and to be nothing but the old Austrian who discovers his Wien River by the Manzanares and a Lerchenfeld everywhere – a Lerchenfeld where he can let himself go with a certain coarseness to recover a little from the arduous task of being refined."[7] Letting oneself go and refinement: it was in this balancing act that the regional character could unfold with all the qualities of a world culture. Ultimately, that was also Hofmannsthal's motto: Ugly facts and pretty guises conform with the uniqueness.

The *Kunstschau* exhibition in 1908 was one of the central events of Vienna around 1900 (ill. pp. 12, 13). It was staged on what was then a wasteland where the Konzerthaus now stands, and it was intended that it should be a model event for all the virtuosity and masterly achievements of the last decade. The Emperor had provided them with another anniversary of his accession, this time the 60th. The Klimt group, named after its most prominent representative, had not fully absorbed what had been launched as the Secession Style. They had moved out of the headquarters in 1905 in a secession from the Secession following a dispute about the aesthetic direction. The Stylists had taken up positions around Klimt; they were opposed by the Naturalists. The question as to how far one could promote exclusivity was unanswered. Those who wanted to push it further, Klimt and his allies, left the association. The Kunstschau would now demonstrate what had transpired since by way of stylization.

Klimt gave the opening speech on 1 June 1908. This contribution on the opening day of the exhibition would become his most detailed text document that has survived. In addition to the usual words of thanks and reminiscences it included the following remarkable passage: "We define the term 'artist' as broadly as we do that of 'artwork'. Not only creative people, but also [art] lovers, call us that – the ones who are capable of experiencing with emotion and appreciating what has been created. For us the 'artistic

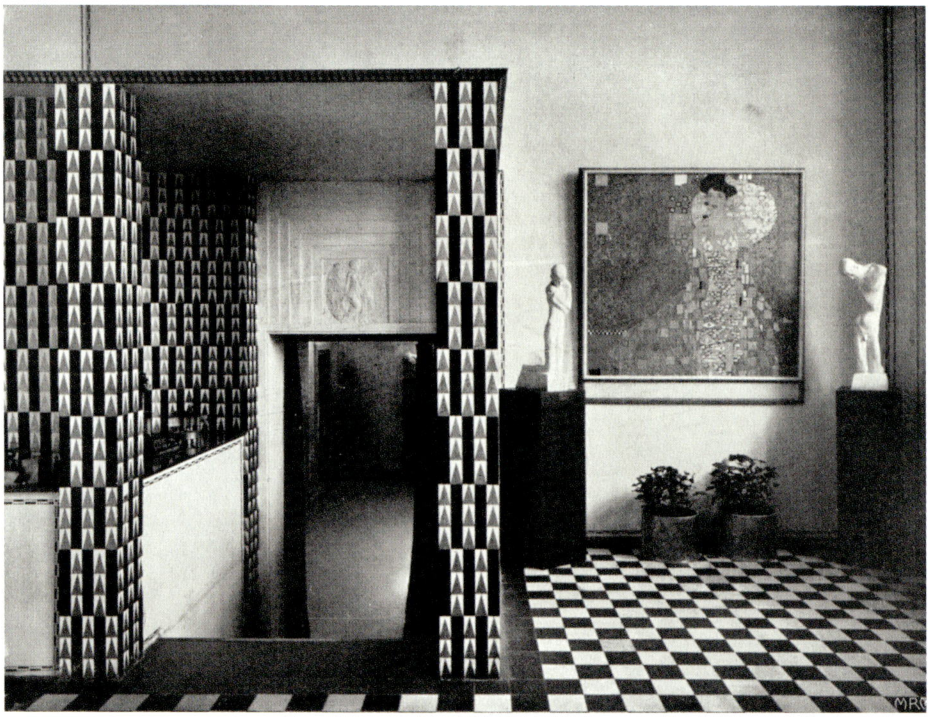

Josef Hoffmann
Room of the Wiener Werkstätte, 1907
International Exhibition in Mannheim, with the *Portrait of Adele Bloch-Bauer I*
From: *Deutsche Kunst und Dekoration*, vol. 20, 1907

Gustav Klimt
Portrait of Adele Bloch-Bauer I, 1907
Oil and gold leaf on canvas, 140 x 140 cm (55 x 55 in.)
New York, Neue Galerie

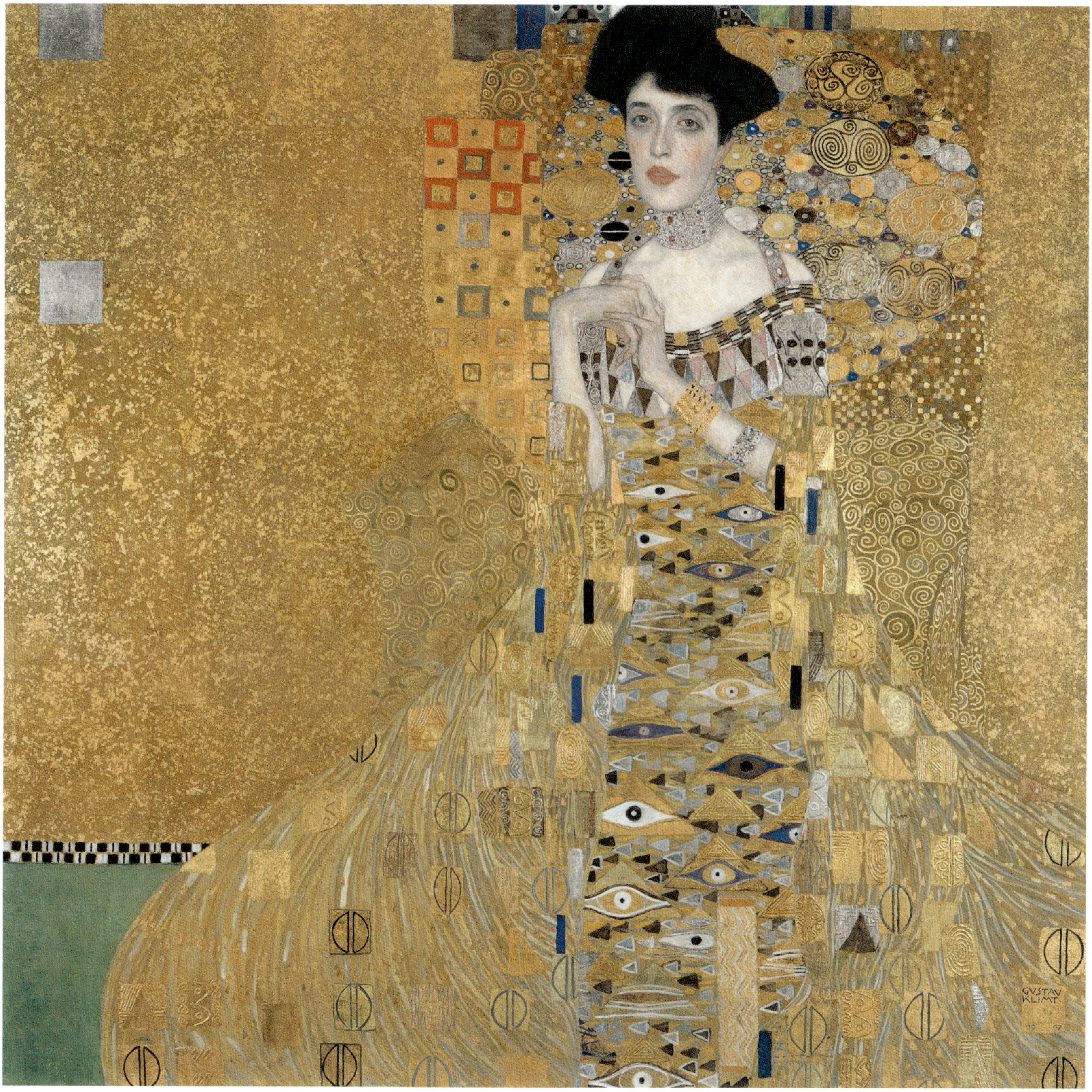
GUSTAV
KLIMT

community' is the ideal community of all who create and all who enjoy their creations."[8] Thereby he had marked out the arc around the circle of the "happy few". It was the small group of those who had the right taste and the conviction that they could afford it. An ideal community: in order to stylize it, it was necessary to abstain from a great deal. It was foreseeable that this would not be the end of the matter.

Exterior and interior

"… and I was staggering / when I recognized my flesh / and all-loving / when I spoke with a girl": these are the final lines of a special publication which the Wiener Werkstätte had presented in 1907 (ill. p. 17). The "House for Everything Decorative" had been founded in 1903 entirely in the spirit of the Secession. Unity, entirety, totality was to be demonstrated here in detail and as an overview, in a word: the possibilities of the *Gesamtkunstwerk*. This was the place where Oskar Kokoschka (1886–1980; ill. pp. 27, 30, 31, 67, 89) also staggered forth towards world fame. It was here that his mentors worked – Kokoschka names in his autobiography Alfred Roller (1864–1935), a stage decorator at the Burgtheater at that time, Josef Hoffmann, Koloman Moser and Carl Otto Czeschka (1878–1960; ill. pp. 62, 63), in whose class he had studied at the Kunstgewerbeschule (College of Applied Arts). It was from the Wiener Werkstätte (ill. pp. 14, 22, 78) that he received his first commissions for artist's postcards, which formed a not unimportant business area for the establishment.

Kokoschka's 24-page brochure entitled *Die träumenden Knaben* (The Dreaming Boys; ill. p. 17) appeared as a harbinger of his main work. It consisted of eight lithographs, a title vignette and one dedicated to Gustav Klimt. It was published in a print run of 500 copies. The work looks like a children's book, or at least a fairy tale. The scenes that appear on the pages do indeed reveal a playful other-worldliness. They are projected as dreams and show, in their planarity typical of the Secession Style, paradisiac constellations of people alone, in groups and especially as single couples reclining in insular remoteness in somnambulistic settings. The figures wallow in

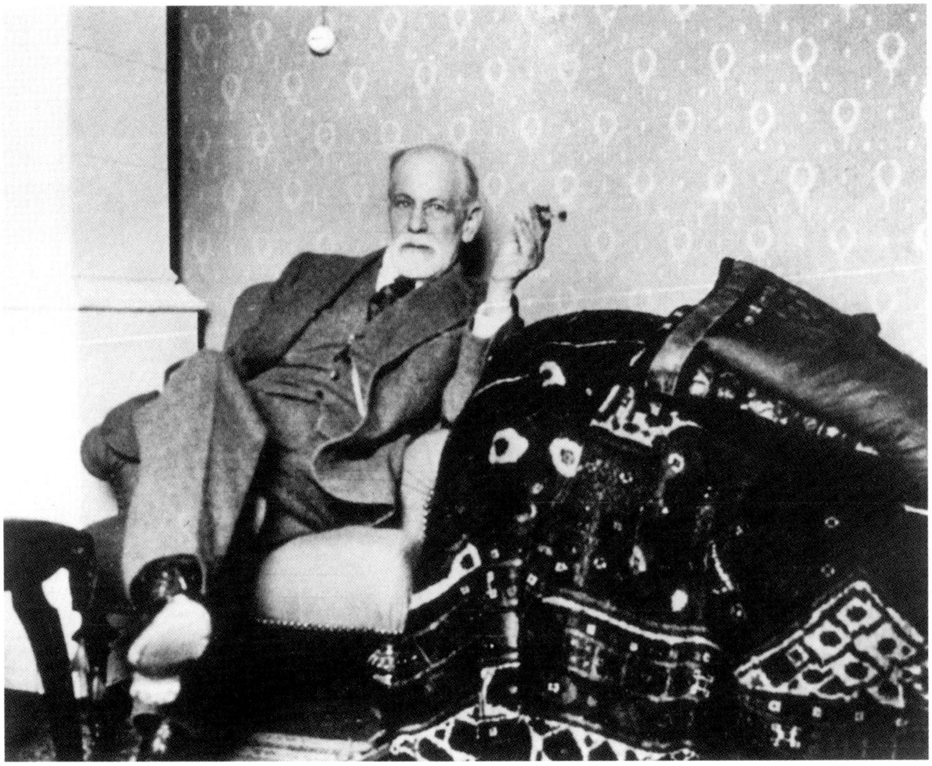

Sigmund Freud beside the couch in his consulting room
Vienna, Berggasse 19
Photograph, c. 1935

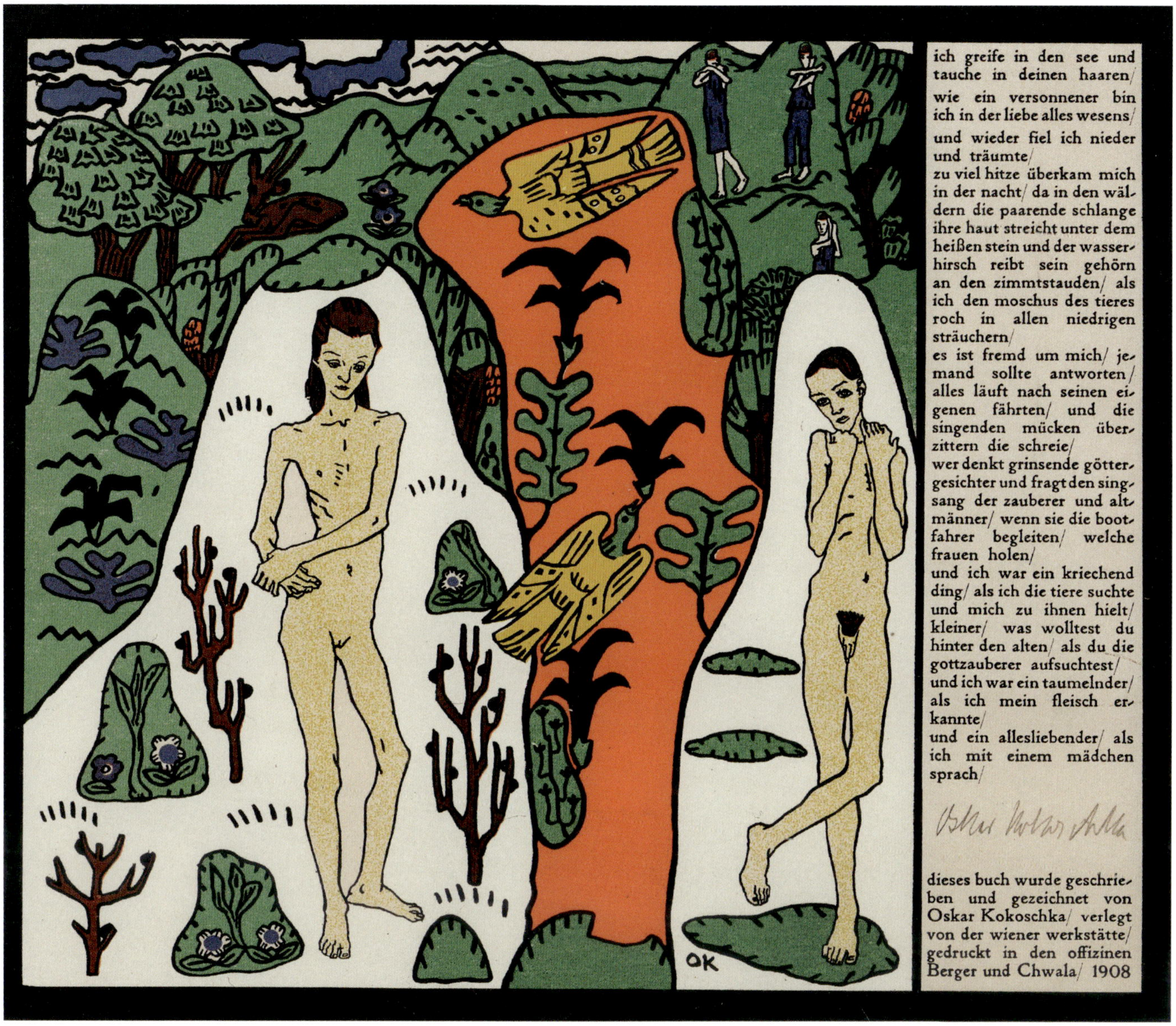

Oskar Kokoschka
The Girl Li and I
From: *The Dreaming Boys*, 1907/08
Colour lithograph no. 8, 24 x 29.3 cm
(9½ x 11½ in.)

paradoxical pleasure in their existence, presenting themselves in the best *Lebensreform* manner and in innocent nakedness. They clearly seem to be waiting for a signal, an *élan vital* that, according to the standards of the time, would come from inside, from the body and its hormones.

In this respect the text that accompanies the pictures in a column along the margin sets a clear accent. It invokes the "flesh", the naked, exposed, revealed, gaping flesh. It expresses a particular physical awareness. We could call it Expressionistic, and Kokoschka would be one of the very first representatives of this approach. Another section of the lyrical offerings of the *Dreaming Boys* goes as follows: "my unbridled body / my body heightened with blood and paint / creeps into your arbours / swarms through your villages / creeps into your souls / festers in your bodies". It is now the task of the pictures to externalize this festering and this swarming as it rumbles internally. In an essay from 1890 about *The Modern* Age Hermann Bahr had formulated it the other way round: "We have nothing but the exterior to internalize."[9] The exterior and the interior: around 1900, Vienna was orbiting a worldview in which these two spheres kept each other in suspense; exterior and interior, body and soul, skin and brain, the façade and the interior

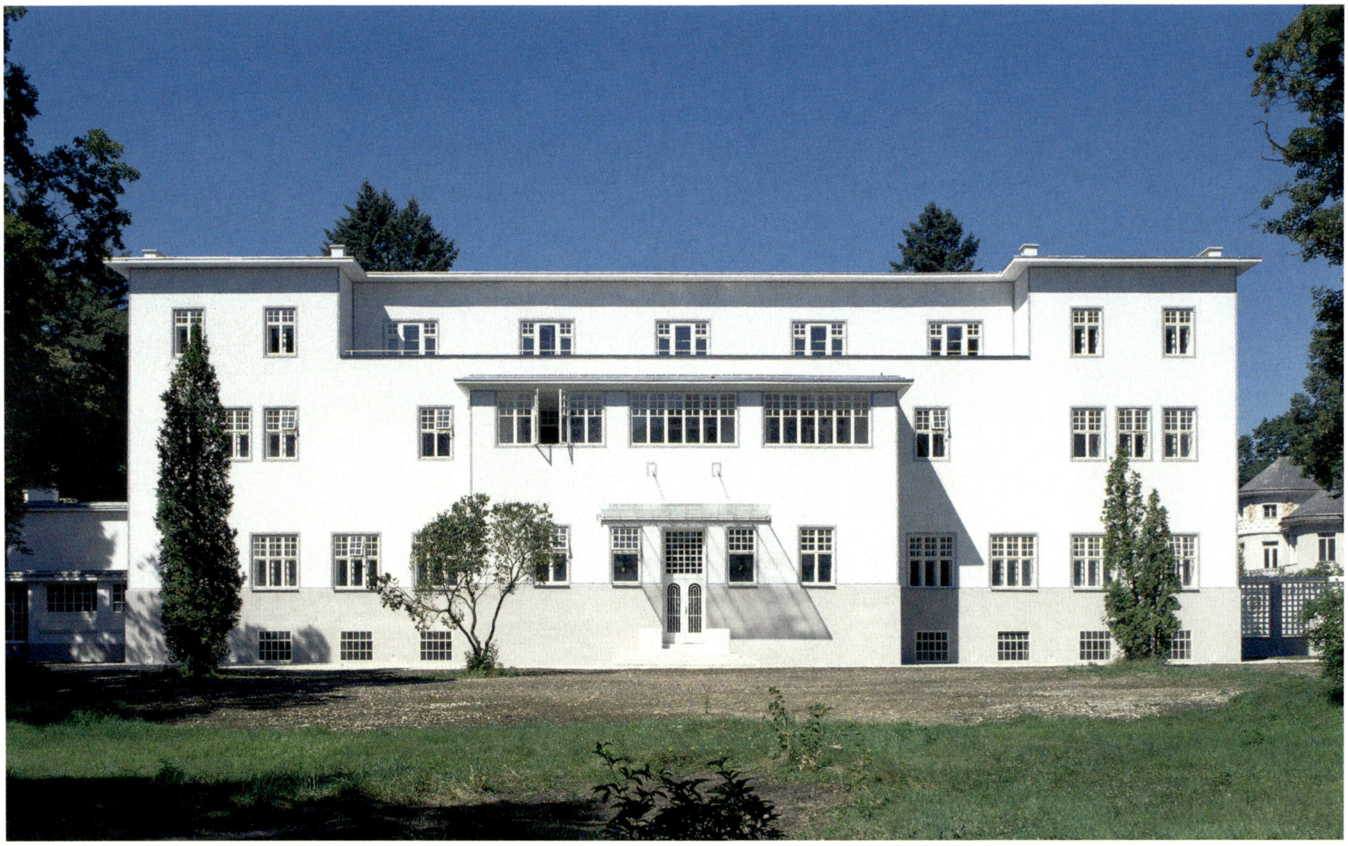

Josef Hoffmann
Purkersdorf Sanatorium

architecture, the dignified and the abysmal being physical states in which the aura of life was expressed.

In 1906, one year before Kokoschka, Robert Musil (1880–1942) attracted attention with his first work. His novel *The Confusions of Young Törless* follows close on the heels of a young cadet. In his youthful career the military drill, daily rituals and education with strict discipline conceal with difficulty the lack of restraint, violence and tendency to torture as an end in itself. The exterior and the interior – Musil lets his hero Törless explain it thus: "Then it was also possible that the bright everyday world which was the only one he had known so far, contained a gateway leading to another, dull, surging, passionate, naked, destructive universe. That there is not just a crossing between those people whose lives move back and forth in a regular manner between office and family as in a transparent and solid building of glass and iron, and others who have been cast downwards, bloody, dissolute and soiled, lost souls wandering in confusing corridors full of a hubbub of voices, but that their boundaries collide secretly and at close quarters and can be crossed at any moment."[10]

The instrument for sounding out the interference, this overlaying of the dark and the light, is the one to which Kokoschka's *Dreaming Boys* also succumbs: the dream. Sigmund Freud (1856–1939; ill p. 16) had published *The Interpretation of Dreams* in 1900. This was probably the key work if one were to search for a singular expression of Vienna around 1900. The book was not successful initially; fewer than 400 copies were sold during the first six years. But the design advisor par excellence of the human doorkeeper of the unconscious, the inventor of psychoanalysis, through which all forgetting, all losing and all incomprehension lost their innocence, knew from the beginning what his work contained. When *The Interpretation of Dreams* was published Freud imagined that "one day" a plaque would be mounted on his house at Berggasse 19 with the inscription: "Dr. Sigm. Freud revealed the secret of the dream here…"[11] In Grinzing, where Dr Freud

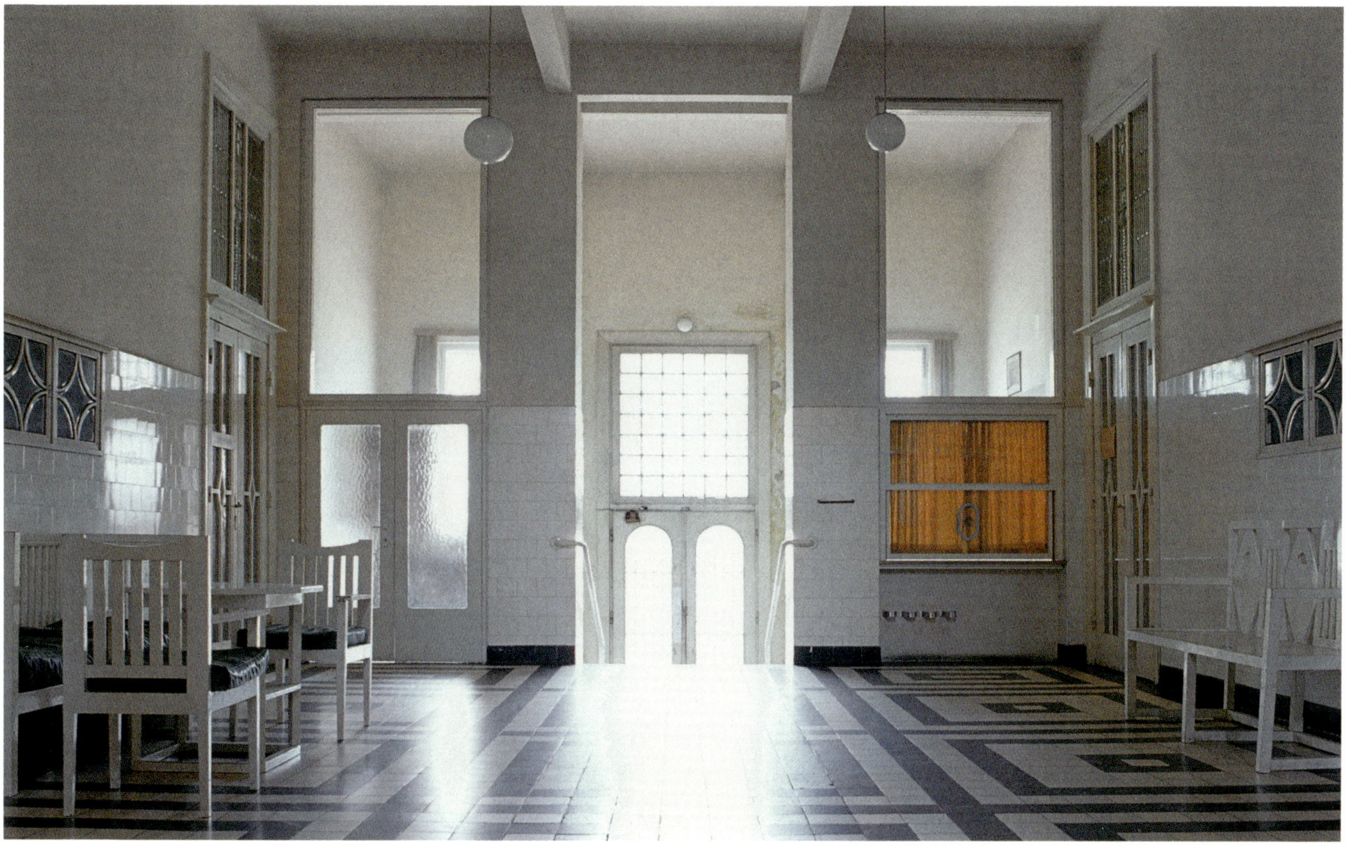

Josef Hoffmann
Purkersdorf Sanatorium

The sanatorium in Purkersdorf is one of the first highlights of Josef Hoffmann's architectonic and artistic development and at the same time a manifestation of the principles of the Wiener Werkstätte.

regularly stayed during the summer, this plaque was indeed installed with this text – in 1977. Freud, showing his education as he always did in his writings, took the motto of his book from the *Aeneid* by the Roman poet Virgil: If he were unable to make the gods above relent, he would move Hell.

Above all, the loftier beings should maintain in constant contact with those below. It was in dreams that sexuality was expressed, and here Freud had nothing less than his very own tunnel vision. This sexuality had to seek its own medium through which it could speak up because it was banished to the realms of the degenerate, the literally unspeakable, that which had to be swept under the carpet. The one was unthinkable without the other, as we must admit, thanks to Freud. It was now a matter of the programme, of the taste or the individual's attitude as to how clearly the one – the taboo subject – was allowed to resonate, to be heard or taken into account within the other – the permitted. One of the most forthright was Arthur Schnitzler (ill. p. 58). In 1906, Freud wrote the following effusive comment about that man of letters: "I have often wondered to myself where you could have acquired this or that secret knowledge which I have acquired through arduous research into the object, and eventually I found myself envying the poet whom I had previously admired."[12]

Viennese culture is recognizable in the way it reveals or obscures things, and especially in the sophisticated staging of all the activities in between. Freud marks out the field when he defines his paramount expression as follows: "The dream is a (disguised) fulfilment of a (suppressed) wish."[13] The wish-fulfilment which the dream allows against the prevailing order is "disguised"; Freud places the explanatory adjective in brackets. Thus a level of significance becomes available which is fruitful for many creations of Viennese culture. Disguised: that has to do with clothing, with dressing and undressing, with materials we use to make ourselves visible or – preferably – invisible. In fact, Viennese culture is particularly sensitive when it comes to its use of textiles.

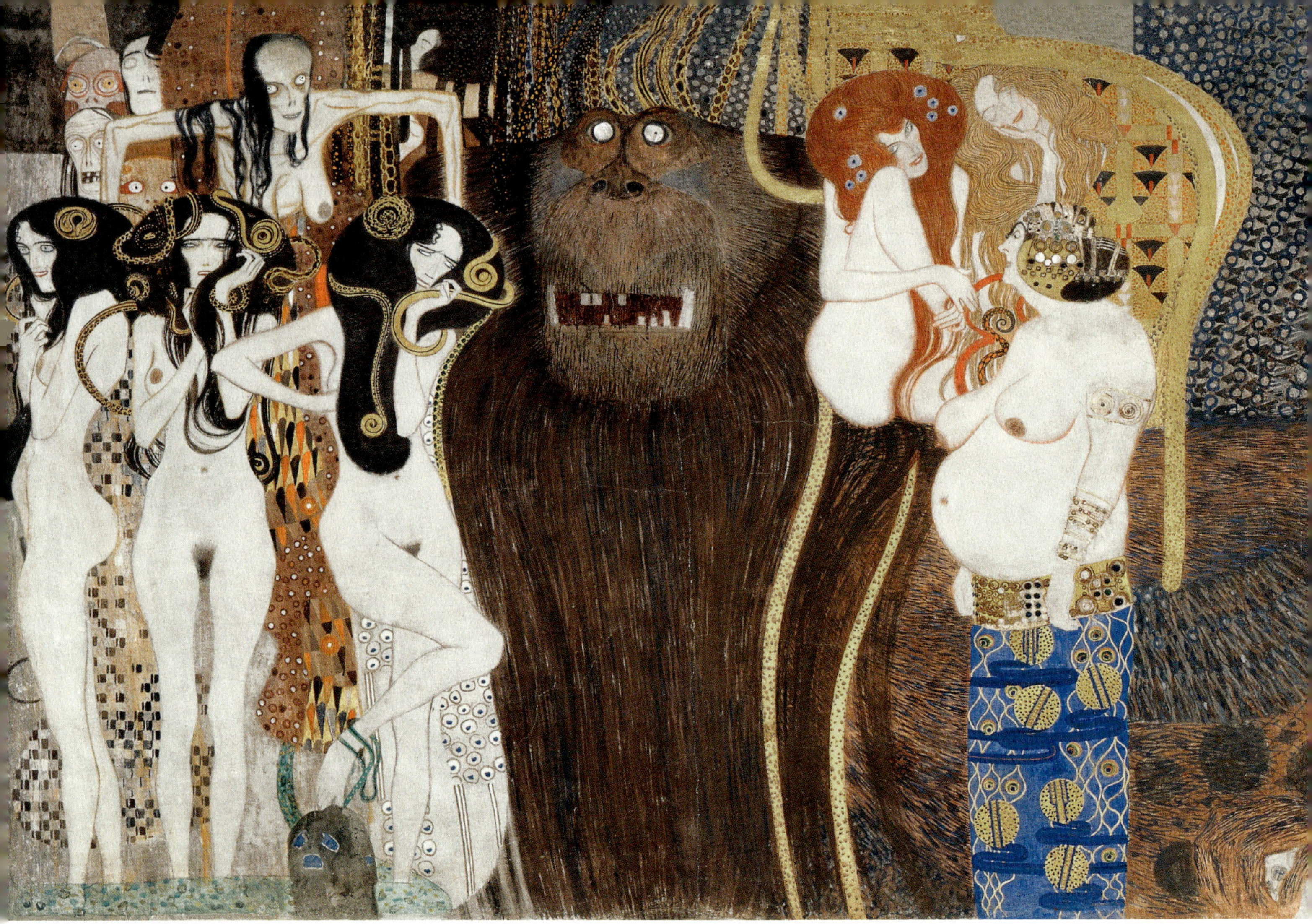

Gustav Klimt
Beethoven Frieze (detail), 1901/02
Short wall
Charcoal, graphite, black and coloured chalk, reddle, pastels, casein paints, gold- and silver-plating, gilded applied stucco, appliqué on plaster
Long walls each 13.92 x 2.15 m (45 ft 8 in. x 7 ft),
short wall 6.30 x 2.15 m (20 ft 8 in. x 7 ft)
Vienna, Secession; on loan from the Belvedere

Golden Adele: Klimt's gem, executed from 1906 and presented for the first time at the Kunstschau in 1908, allows for the possibilities of the material (ill. p. 15) in a particularly exquisite way. The portrait depicts the figure of the wife of a sugar manufacturer exemplarily accustomed to money and boredom. Adele Bloch-Bauer (1881–1925; ill. p. 14 top) is still young, but we can see her jaded attitude, a certain addiction to the circumstances, a *décadence* in which the knowledge of the lateness of her contemporaneity and the bodies which embody it is reflected. We can recognize it in those parts of the portrait that show the flesh: the skin of face and hands, on which life has left its mark. Beyond that, the woman exists in a cocoon of precious materials. She has been fitted into a repeated pattern. Ornamentation, decoration, application imprison her, what is more, in the ancient, venerable, provocatively anachronistic formula of a gold background. The picture brings together the block-like and the rampant, the casing and the inner world, the hieratic and the here: the anorganic-crystalline and the vital-physical are fused in a communion which seems to be not of this world. Artificial to the extreme, Klimt's test-tube work looks as if it should offer everything art has to offer in order to keep this figure, her desires and her abysses in shape.

Perhaps this attitude is the result of the most important cultural legacy that the 19th century bequeathed to the 20th in Vienna: the Ringstrasse (ill. p. 9). It was constructed here like a vast theatre of drapery. People regarded themselves as highly cultured and progressive, building museums, the opera house and educational institutions. They saw themselves as liberal, and erected edifices like the parliament and the university,

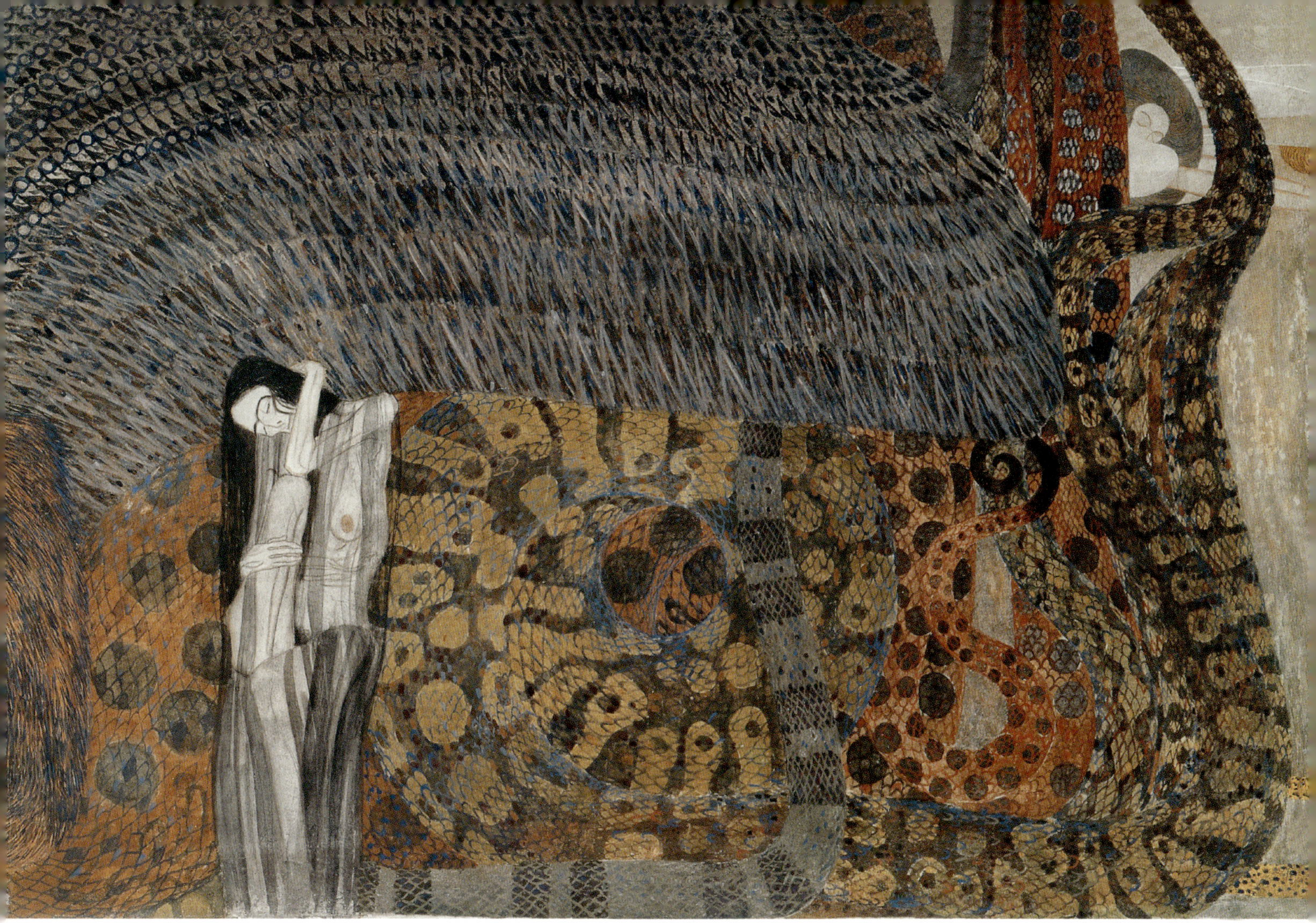

which did not really want to honour the spirit of democracy that they had conjured. Above all, they presented themselves as emphatically aware of their history – those who do not trust the future, want at least to command the past. And so the buildings which were thought of as institutions were draped with historical forms: with elements of the Classical, the Gothic, the Baroque and anything else that the stock of styles had to offer.

Gottfried Semper (1803–1879), who had designed the so-called Imperial Forum of the Ringstrasse and, above all, the Burgtheater together with Carl von Hasenauer (1833–1894), developed a sort of theory for this. As Semper recorded in his somewhat confused, difficult to understand texts, the beginnings of architecture lay in the fact that people had draped some type of textile around the rough framework of a shelter, thereby making it into a dwelling. The original hut consisted of four posts to form a frame and a piece of fabric to provide the *Bekleidung* or cover. Put in a somewhat simplified form, this arrangement formed the basis of Semper's *Bekleidungstheorie*.

Viennese architecture made this into a programme. It started with the covers of the Ringstrasse's historicism and its freely available folding in the form of the styles of various eras; it continued with Otto Wagner's adaptation of the historical with plant-based designs in the pattern (ill. p. 2) repeats of pure ornamentation or in the rivets, seams and fittings of his façades (ill. p. 39). The programme culminated in the varied attempts of his students, by Max Fabiani (1865–1962; ill. pp. 46, 47), Jože Plečnik (1872–1957; ill. p. 50, 51) or Olbrich (ill. p. 35), to understand the master architect and to compete with each other. Finally, the proclamation came in the end of all covers through the eversion of the

Max Klinger
Beethoven Statue
in the 14th exhibition of the Vienna Secession, 1902

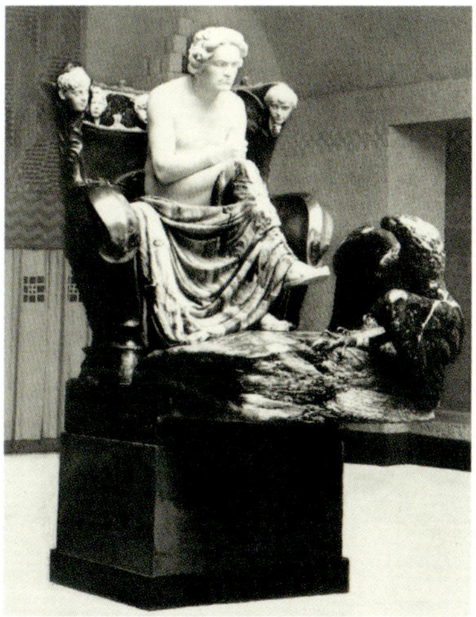

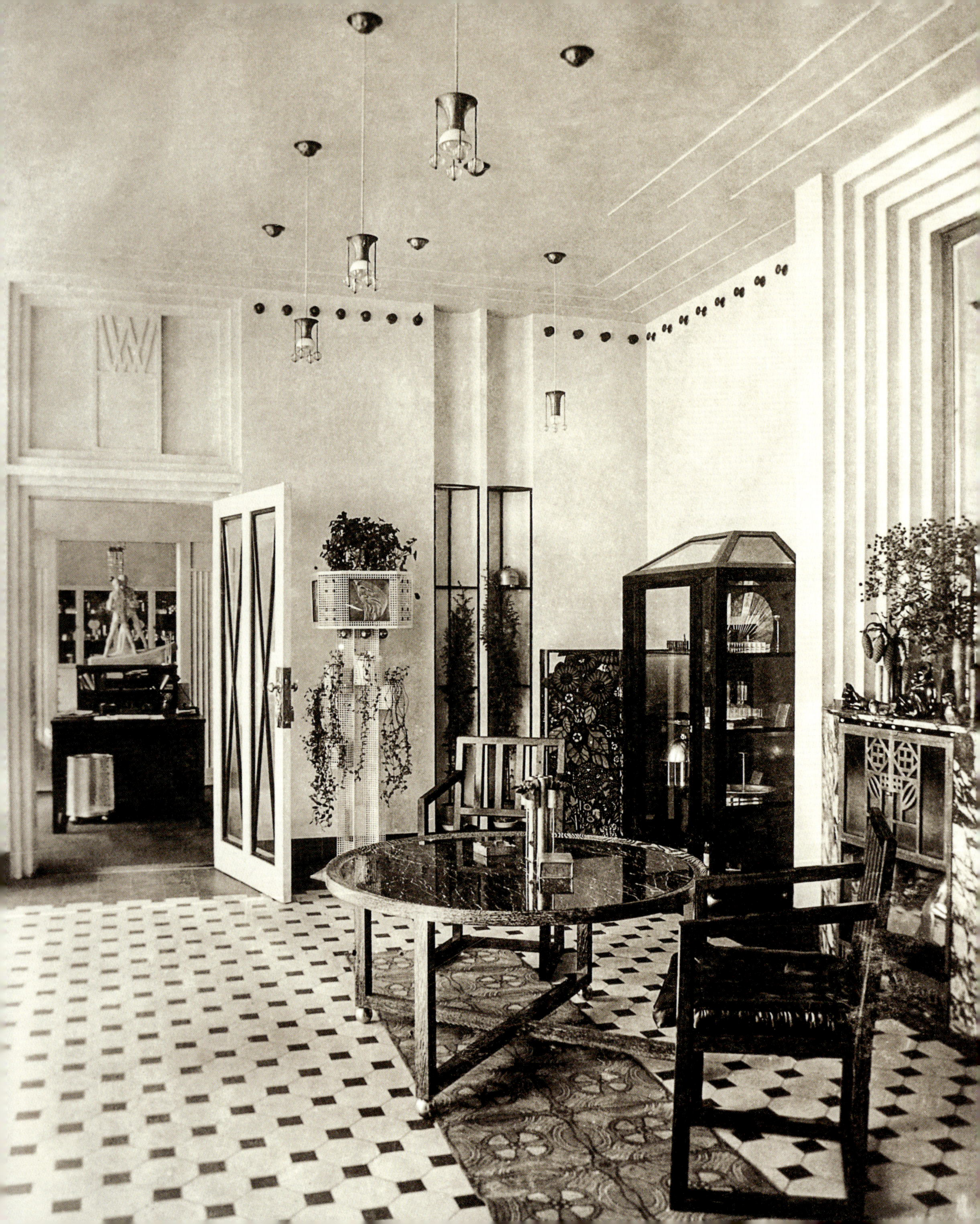

interior which was Adolf Loos's (1870–1933; ill. p. 43) aim. Vienna gave rise to what the architecture of progressive Modernism has produced since the 1920s under the attractive, equally textile-related expression of the curtain wall – a façade in its own right and with its own weight, which is then literally suspended in front of the body of the building.

There is a shell and there is a core; the inevitable third element alongside the exterior and the interior was the wallowing in decoration. The Secession Building was devised as the earliest example of the "white box" of the exhibition business – the functional shell that could then be refitted anew with every new presentation. Each event thus was given its own special setting, its ensemble; all purism of pure neutrality was enriched with decoration. The *Gesamtkunstwerk* was what everyone swore by. The conceptualizers, the planners, designers and decorators worked together to create the all-inclusive, overwhelming, total impression: the individual arts, each of them responsible for a specific task, interacted as if they had always performed together in the hymn to the great whole. Seen thus, they had been providing camouflage. And seen thus, they all contributed to the cult of the emperor. They were focused on the imperial, on the generally responsible, on the uniting of contradictions and contrasts. All focused on majesty. And as in politics, so it was too in the realm of aesthetics; the maintenance of this conviction became increasingly precarious.

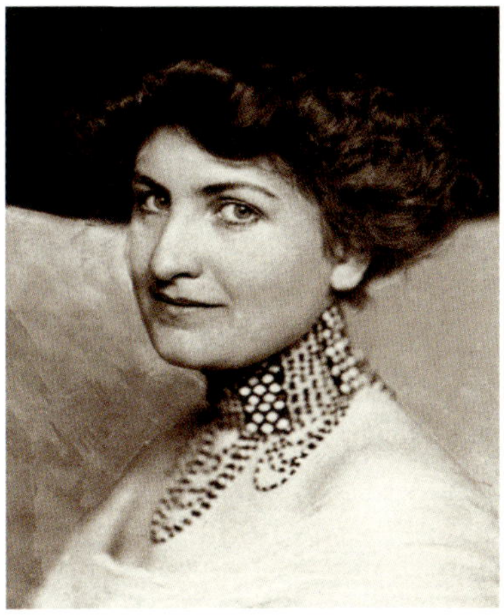

Madame d'Ora
Alma Mahler with jewellery by Koloman Moser, 1904 or 1909

The great inconsequence

In 1910, the city experienced a premiere which demanded the involvement of all its musical resources. Gustav Mahler (1860–1911), Vienna's leading musician, conducted his *Eighth Symphony* for the first time with no fewer than 858 singers and an orchestra with 171 players. Mahler enjoyed what was perhaps his greatest artistic success. In return, during the following year the city's greatest man of letters made him the hero of one of his most famous novellas: Thomas Mann (1875–1955) immortalized Mahler as Gustav Aschenbach in his *Death in Venice*. Thomas Mann? Yes, because Mahler's triumph took place in Munich. He never experienced a premiere of one of his symphonies in Vienna, his own city, which had appointed him Director of the Court Opera in 1897 (only his last, the *Ninth Symphony*, had its premiere there in 1912, but sadly posthumously). All told, Mahler suffered much misfortune in Vienna – so much so that in 1907 he relinquished his prestigious post and moved to New York. The anti-Semitism, one of the ugliest side-effects of the modern age, which started out not least in Vienna, had afflicted him from the start – and not only him.

Mahler is one of the figureheads of the cult of art as it was expressed in the ardour of totality and the intimations of eternity. The cult had what was probably its most sensational appearance in 1902. The Beethoven exhibition was presented in the Secession. What occurred here was an act of homage by the artists of Vienna to another artist, Max Klinger (1857–1920). The native of Leipzig had just completed a large-format statue which was to form the centrepiece of the presentation. This enormous sculpture in turn was intended as an act of homage to an artist, this time to Ludwig van Beethoven (1770–1827; ill p. 21). Artists honour an artist who is honouring an artist. In this high point of the cult of art, the automatism of self-referentiality was entirely at one with itself. The fact that it was painters who idolized a sculpture that referred to a composer only served to provide the ultimate confirmation of this hymn to aesthetic delectation. All the arts joined together to demonstrate the one and only universality of art.

It was serious, sometimes bitterly so, and was often totally lacking in humour. But it was focused on quality in a way that had hitherto been quite unknown. Gustav Mahler, in particular, served to guarantee that fact. He had created a paraphrase of the maestro for the Beethoven exhibition. Altogether he was famous for the heightening of impression and expression which he established at his opera house. Mahler was the first conductor to stand rather than to sit during the performance. And he was the first to use both hands when conducting his orchestra. It seems a matter of course to us today, but it had only just begun back then. Art was presented in a more concentrated way than ever

Exhibition Room of the Wiener Werkstätte, 1904

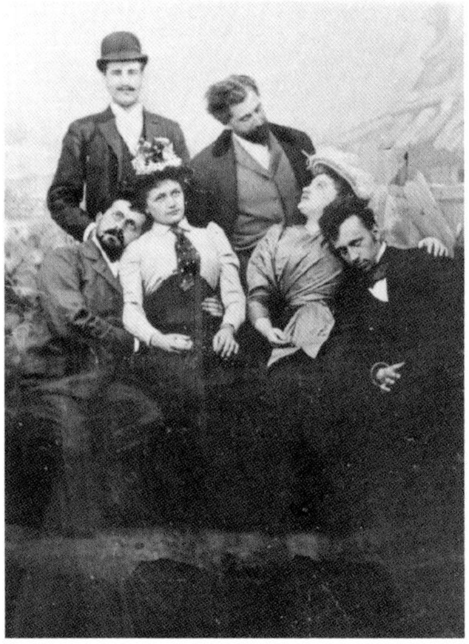

Excursion to the Prater, c. 1894
From left to right:
Hugo von Hofmannsthal and Arthur Schnitzler (standing), Richard Beer-Hofmann and Felix Salten (seated) with unidentified women

before. The works – whether musical compositions, pictures or interiors – definitely profited from the fact that they were associated with a new seriousness in terms of presentation.

It was also in 1902 that Gustav Mahler married. His future wife would also go down in history as Alma Schindler-Mahler-Gropius-Werfel (1879–1964 ill. p. 23, 88) and as the despairing lover of Oskar Kokoschka. Mahler had tried to persuade her of the advantages of togetherness as follows: "From now on you will have only one occupation: to make me happy… You must… make the pattern of your future life in all details inwardly dependent on my needs and desire nothing in return except my love."[14] In these lines too, we can say, Mahler was typical of the state of affairs in Vienna around 1900. There was the influential pacifist Bertha von Suttner (1843–1914); there was the women's rights activist Rosa Mayreder (1858–1938); there was the reform educationalist Eugenie Schwarzwald (1872–1940); and a number of women were employed by the Wiener Werkstätte, especially in the latter years and preferably in the fields of textiles or jewellery. Beyond that, and actually in general, an archetypal patriarchal society prevailed.

Women were models and muses, and at best they were visited and admired if they hosted a salon. They were hostesses, wives and patronesses who channelled the money from their husbands' businesses to culture. As collectors they liked to have their portraits painted by Klimt, and the Wiener Werkstätte furnished their country houses and city apartments for them. Their names were Gallia, Knips, Lederer, Primavesi and Bloch-Bauer. And so they belonged in their own way to the "ideal community" of Viennese culture that extolled Klimt as combining creativity and physical pleasure.

Sometimes they did not even have a name. Then they posed in the artists' studios, allowed them to gaze at the skin between their thighs and allowed those studies to serve as an opportunity in which Klimt, Kokoschka or Egon Schiele (1890–1918) promptly combined masculinity with mastery. It was whispered that Klimt had a real harem at his studio, a horde of girls he called upon when required, to allow them to lounge around in a curious self-referentiality and somnambulism. Schiele, on the other hand, was faced with a court case and investigative custody because of his all-too-youthful models. He was more direct in his representation of sexuality, and, above all, allowed his own sexuality to become part of the event. Klimt swore that it was all of no consequence (ill. p. 4); Schiele forced the entanglement (ill. p. 25). Pornographic elements were involved in the works of both artists. Kokoschka refused, in turn, to allow his girls to sit still (ill. p. 67). Their bodies are thin, almost emaciated, but they are dynamic and they move with great naturalness within the space. The associations of the expressive dance of the kind presented on stage at that time by his good friend Grete Wiesenthal (1885–1970; ill. p. 84) were certainly intended. The bodies clearly experience a compulsion to express themselves; the rebellion appears in contrast purely somatic. The degree of emancipation Kokoschka more clearly granted his models compared with Klimt and Schiele is expressed only in physical movement. It is not a matter of awareness.

In his autobiography *My Youth in Vienna*, Arthur Schnitzler recorded the following dialogue with his father: "During the course of our conversation I felt compelled to ask him what a young person should actually do in order not to contravene the requirements of morality, society or hygiene. Seduction and adultery were prohibited and dangerous; relationships with women of easy virtue and actresses were dubious and expensive; and then there was also a certain type of, so to speak, nice girl who had already deviated from the path of virtue, but by whom even so, as in the case of a seduced woman one might – in the words of my father – 'get caught'; so really the only option was a prostitute, which – even if you knew how to protect your health – invariably meant a pretty sordid affair. And so I asked my father to give me some advice. My father refused to be drawn into the discussion, but made a dismissive gesture and commented simply and darkly: 'You write it off.'"[15] In any case, the parallels of taboo and boundlessness with which women – depending on their social rank – were either idolized or exploited give Viennese culture around 1900 a consistent greatness (ill. p. 24). The term for these conditions is double standards. Or, as the critic Friedrich Michael Fels commented in 1891 in a speech to the public: "You will not be able to refuse us the testimony: that at least we have remained constant in one thing: in our great lack of consistency, in that today we demonstrate social characteristics and tomorrow individualistic ones, and the day after tomorrow a third aspect."[16] The great inconsistency applied not only to sexuality. It applied equally to the disposition towards violence, which was expressed socially in the extravagant enthusiasm for everything military – including a constant willingness to fight a duel – politically, especially in anti-Semitism and in the vulgarization of all forms of decency in the everyday routine of parliament, or educationally, in absurd methods of bringing up and improving children. Under the conditions at that time, the interior and the exterior could not be aligned. An overstrained sense of honour, the willingness to "write it off", as Schnitzler's father put it, the fear of scandal, and the socially strictly graduated acceptance of misconduct created a notorious situation of conflict. The way out of the entanglements of the double standards, which threatened on all sides, was equally notorious: suicide. Agonies, as Hofmannsthal let it be known in his prologue to *Anatol*, come right next to episodes. The city tells a wealth of stories that illustrate the all-too-great proximity of the death struggle and casualness.

Including this one, for example: On precisely 12 September 1908, Richard Gerstl (1883–1908) tackled a full-figure nude portrait (ill. p. 65). Gerstl exposed his entire body to view; totally nude and haggard, he showed himself with his body emaciated and his soul traumatized. The setting was his room, in which he was alone with his anguish. What had trapped him in such a way that his fragile figure cannot be fitted into the picture format, can be seen literally in the centre; what we can see is his lower body, his genitals in dark colours. Gerstl had been so active in this respect in the past months

Egon Schiele
Two Girls, Lying Entwined, 1915
Gouache and pencil,
32.8 x 49.7 cm (13 x 19½ in.)
Vienna, Albertina

One of the two women is portrayed naturally, the other looks like a twisted mannequin.

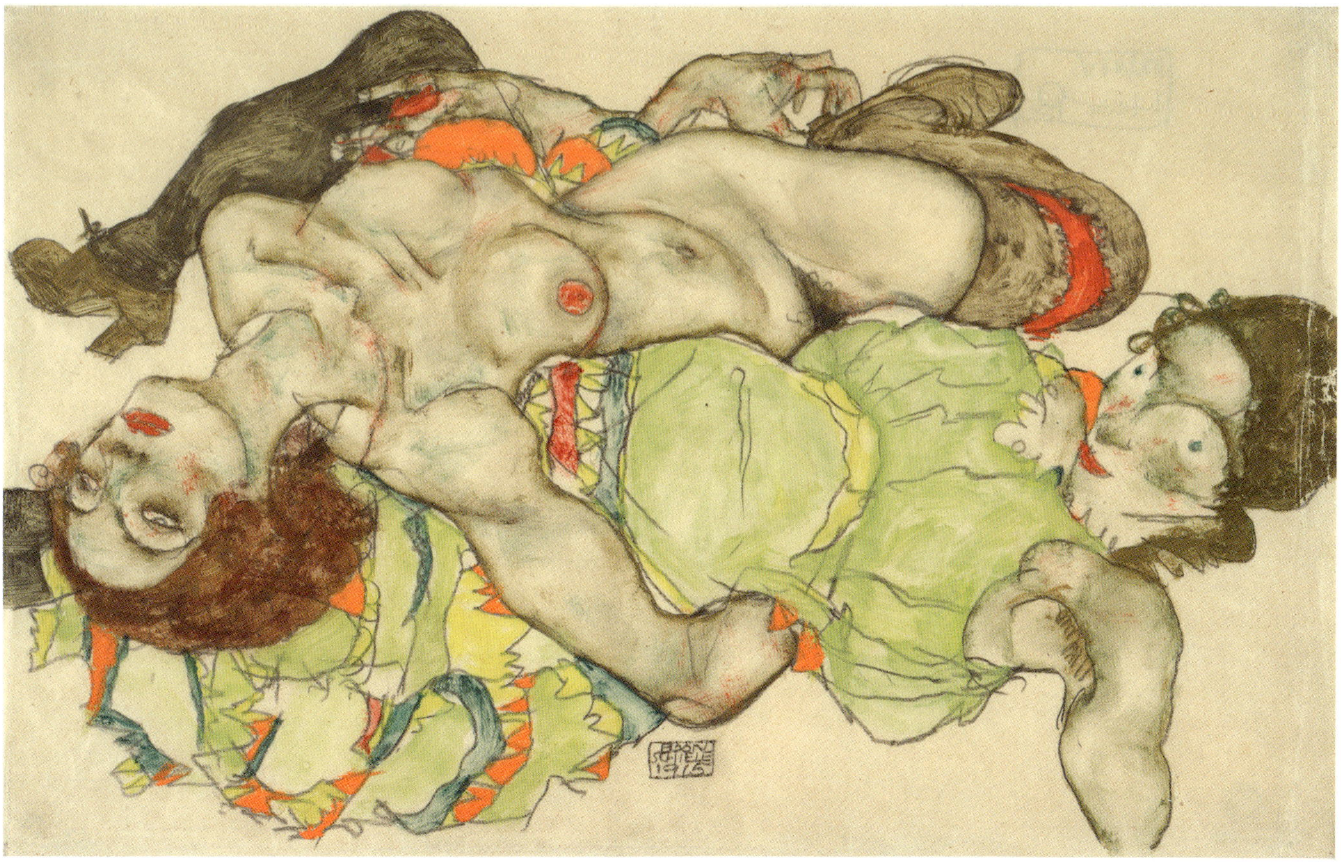

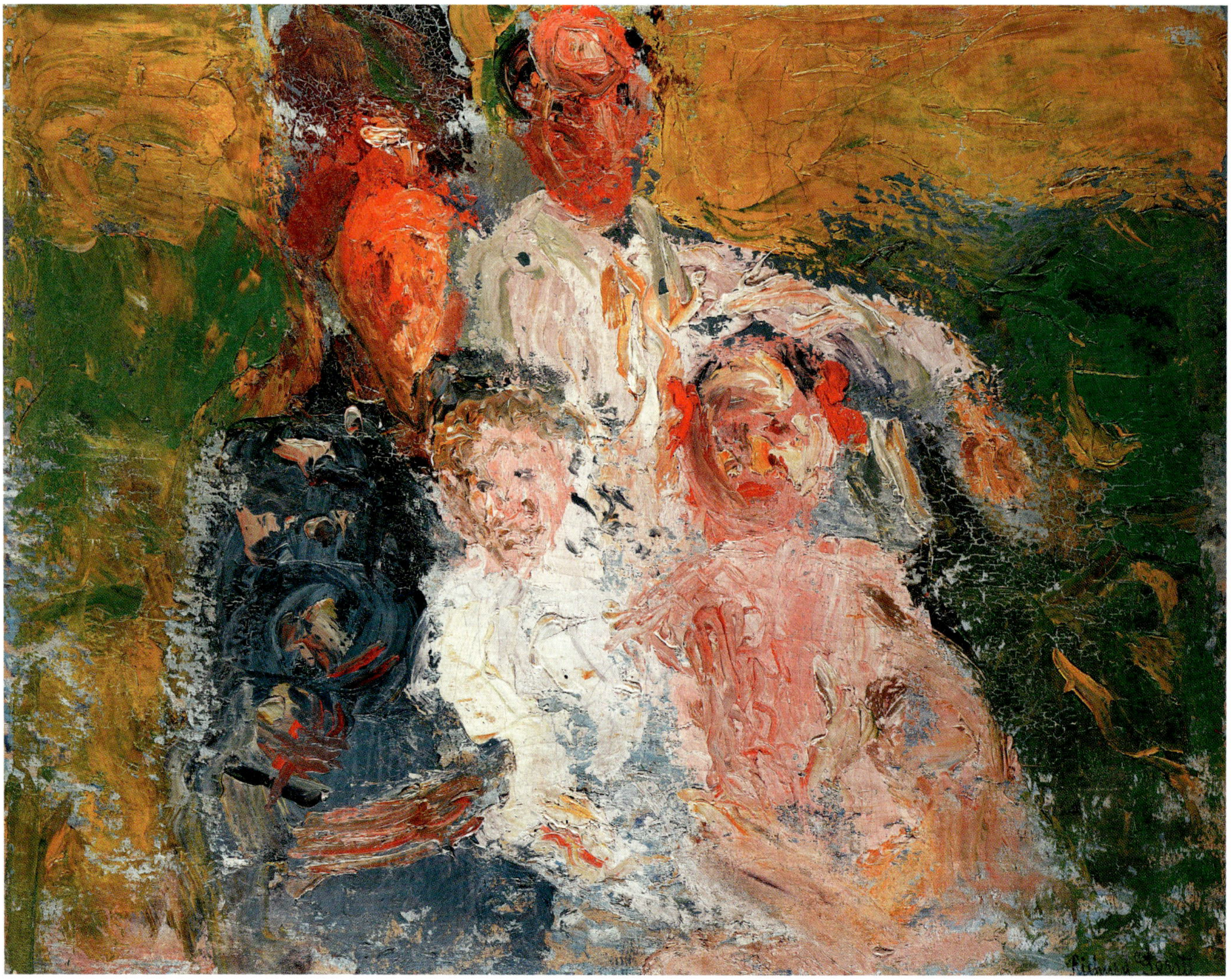

Richard Gerstl
The Schönberg Family, 1907
Oil on canvas, 88 x 109 cm (34¾ x 43 in.)
Vienna, Belvedere

that it had forced him into social isolation. He had had an affair with a married woman. Moreover, her husband was a very important person in Vienna around 1900. Arnold Schönberg (1874–1951) was a composer who had wanted Gerstl to teach him the art of painting (ill. pp. 28, 73). The two became friends and Gerstl was admitted to the exclusive circle surrounding the maestro, so that they spent their summer holidays together (ill. p. 26) and Gerstl painted numerous portraits of fellow contestants and kindred spirits. He became involved in a dalliance with Mathilde Schönberg (1877–1923; ill. p. 29) and the two eloped. Mathilde, however, suffered from pangs of conscience and returned repentantly to her husband and children. Gerstl, unbending, difficult and unmannerly beyond all measure, was left alone. He committed suicide on 4 November 1908, killing himself by hanging and stabbing himself simultaneously.

Or another such story: Heinz Lang (1885–1904) belonged to the city's *jeunesse dorée* together with his brother Erwin (1886–1962) and his sister Lilith (1892–1952). Erwin was Kokoschka's best friend and Lilith the remote goddess, worshipped in immature fashion by the latter's *The Dreaming Boys*. Heinz Lang became entangled in an amour fou with the wife of one of the most important members of the avant-garde of Viennese Modernism. Adolf Loos had married the youthful Lina Obertimpfler (1882–1950), the universally desired beauty and daughter of a café proprietor whose establishment was located in the same building as the fashion studio of Klimt's lifelong companion Emilie Flöge (1874–

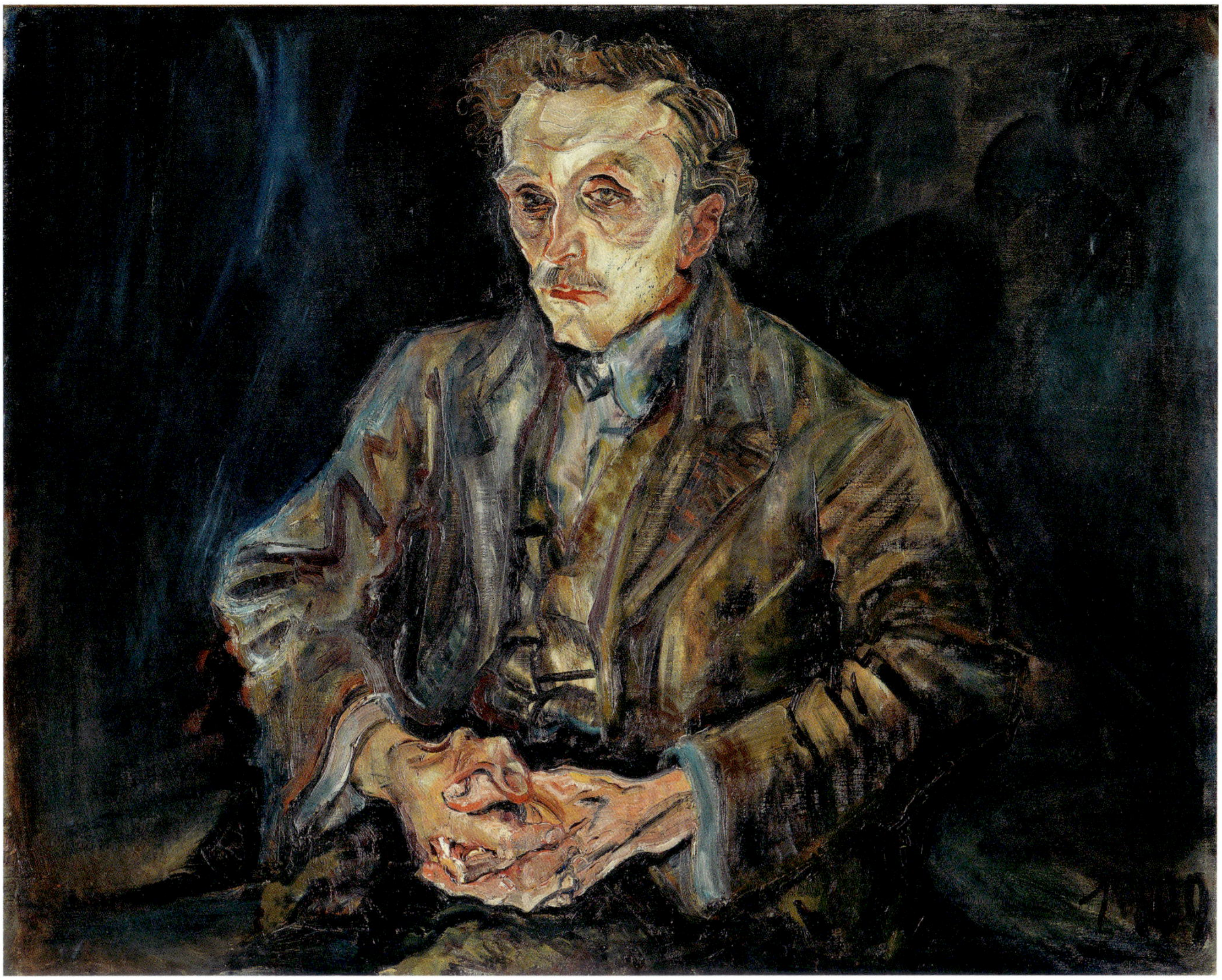

1952; ill p. 87). In the case of Lang's affair with Lina Loos, the connection was so obvious once again within the circle of the initiated that the impossible situation had to be put right. Heinz Lang turned to Peter Altenberg (1859–1919), the columnist, a master of coffee house literature and one of the best friends of Loos and Karl Kraus. "What should you do?" replied Altenberg, "Shoot yourself. And what will you do? Live on. Quietly. Because you are as cowardly as I am, as cowardly as our entire generation, inwardly hollow, a liar like I am."[17] Lang shot himself. He was not what Altenberg described as "a coward". Perhaps it was the curious code of honour which kept only one possible exit route open from the impossibilities brought about by the simultaneous combination of a sense of honour and hormones. Perhaps Heinz Lang was also a representative of a special orthodoxy, a strictness towards himself and a rigour with regard to social requirements. Scandal or not, Lang belonged to the circle of Kokoschka-Loos-Kraus (ill. pp. 27, 30, 31). And this circle contributed a special dogmatism to the culture of Vienna around 1900: supreme consistency in the face of the great inconsistency.

Oskar Kokoschka
The Viennese master builder Adolf Loos, 1909
Oil on canvas, 74 x 91 cm (29¼ x 36 in.)
Berlin, Nationalgalerie, Staatliche Museen zu Berlin – Preußischer Kulturbesitz

The urn and the chamber pot

Vienna's great taskmasters with regard to radical Modernism were Adolf Loos and Karl Kraus. Both were born in the 1870s and both were zealots and purists. For them the first and only premise was the purity of speech, either written and spoken, or encountered in buildings or objects. Karl Kraus summarized their objectives in a wonderfully witty saying: "Adolf Loos and I – he in words and I in language – have done nothing except show that there is a difference between an urn and a chamber pot and that it is only in this difference that culture has the free space it requires. The others, however, 'the Positive Ones', are divided into those who use the urn as a chamber pot and the chamber pot as an urn."[18] This could be read in *Die Fackel* on 15 December 1913, the magazine to which Kraus was the sole contributor because, by this point he was ultimately the only guarantor of the implacability of the topics that concerned him.

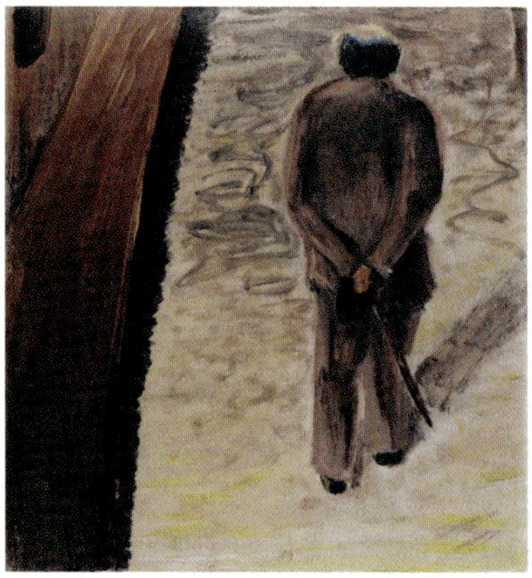

Arnold Schönberg
Self-Portrait, Walking, 1911
Oil on cardboard, 49 x 44.9 cm
(19¼ x 17¾ in.)
Vienna, Arnold Schönberg Center

The urn and the chamber pot: beyond these stood those whom Kraus called "the Positive Ones". He meant the Secessionists in particular, the supporters of the *Gesamtkunstwerk* – those who celebrated embellishment, who mixed and threw off balance, who belonged to the order of "this way and not any other way". They exhausted themselves in decoration, and for him that was a sign of weakness: psychologically, socially and especially aesthetically: "Those who lack spirit", thundered Kraus in the *Fackel* from 9 April 1910, "must have ornamentation. I know a writer who does not dare to write the word 'scandal', and who therefore uses 'scandalum' instead. Because it takes more strength that he has to say the word 'scandal' at the appropriate time."[19] Loos added a real insult to all that. He had given the title *Ornament and Crime* to a text in 1908 which initially only filtered slowly through to public attention, but whose title provoked a furore even before it was heard (ill. p. 70). In the interests of noting the fine distinction, it was the conjunction "and" and not the equation "is" which stood for him between the two terms. Loos permitted ornamentation with regard to the past. In the present it deserved to be incriminated, eliminated, eradicated – and its supporters manifestly with it.

None of Loos's furnishings is as homogeneous and in line with the single style cultivated by the Secessionists. So Loos supplied to an overall decor the alternative to the adaptation. The items were chosen piece by piece, object by object and it had to be decided which would be the best choice in each case. The fact that Loos then modified the design of these perfect furnishings, as the craftsmen noted, can ultimately be explained by the embittered nature of his rivalry. Charged with conviction, he wanted to show his opponents – show them literally through his designs. In retrospect, Loos's superiority lay in the thought, the cool rationalism of his concepts, in – to express it using a word not in use at that time – his coolness.

"You are always right when it comes to your home", he proclaimed to his public in this context, "and no one else."[20] He countered the over-refined and exorbitantly expensive aesthetic of the *Gesamtkunstwerk* with the personal union of persuasive power and knowledge of human nature. He would not be Loos if his explanation did not turn out to be firstly original and secondly polemical: "If someone had a thousand crowns and needed his home furnishing in a way that would look like five thousand crowns, he would come to me. I had become a specialist in that. But someone who had five thousand crowns and wanted to have a bedside table for that price would go to a different architect. Since the first category of customers occurs more frequently than the second, I had my hands full."[21]

In their opposition to any sort of mingling, Kraus and Loos were more or less lone fighters. The demands for tastefulness and individual quality in the furnishing of sentences as well as spaces had to set out from the individual case. The generalized examples of purism and the fighting spirit could then be derived from this unique appearance. They were the coffee house squad. Peter Altenberg was their chief combatant in literary matters, later joined by Kokoschka. The house rules sound quite similar to those of the group surrounding Klimt: they swore like-mindedness and sought support among the collectors of the (haute) bourgeoisie. This occurred in the same way as the "ideal community" which provided Klimt and the Wiener Werkstätte with their special commissions. Loos's clients were often those of Kokoschka's. Their names were Goldman or Ebenstein, and a portrait from the other accompanied the furnishings they ordered from the one. Thus the praxis of these campaigns was not as different as people maintained, although the theory certainly was. With regard to furnishings we could say that the alternatives we see today developed in Vienna initially. Should things fit together or should they be chosen according to the evidence of the individual item? To use the appropriate terms: do you put your money on the *Gesamtkunstwerk* or on aesthetic autonomy?

We could also determine that by studying the different mentalities. In the case of the *Gesamtkunstwerk*'s representatives we can detect a certain suppleness, the frequently invoked Austrian-ness which revels in adaptation to the situation. This is challenged by the supporters of a systematic programme, with its rigour and its tendency towards zealous, slobbering self-empowerment. For 20th-century Modernism, which became increasingly

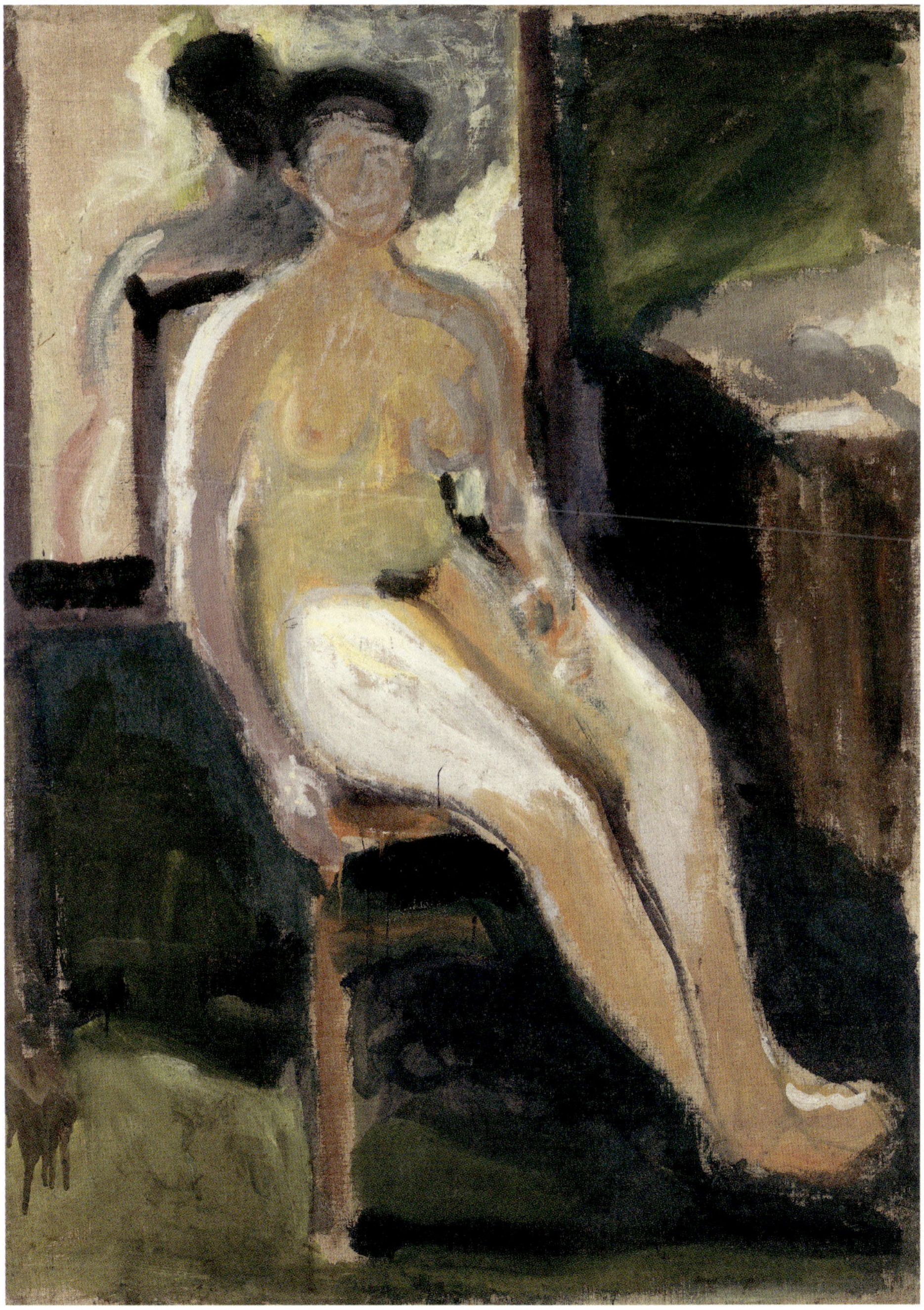

Richard Gerstl
Seated Woman, Nude, 1908
Distemper on canvas,
166 x 116 cm (65¼ x 45¾ in.)
Vienna, Leopold Museum

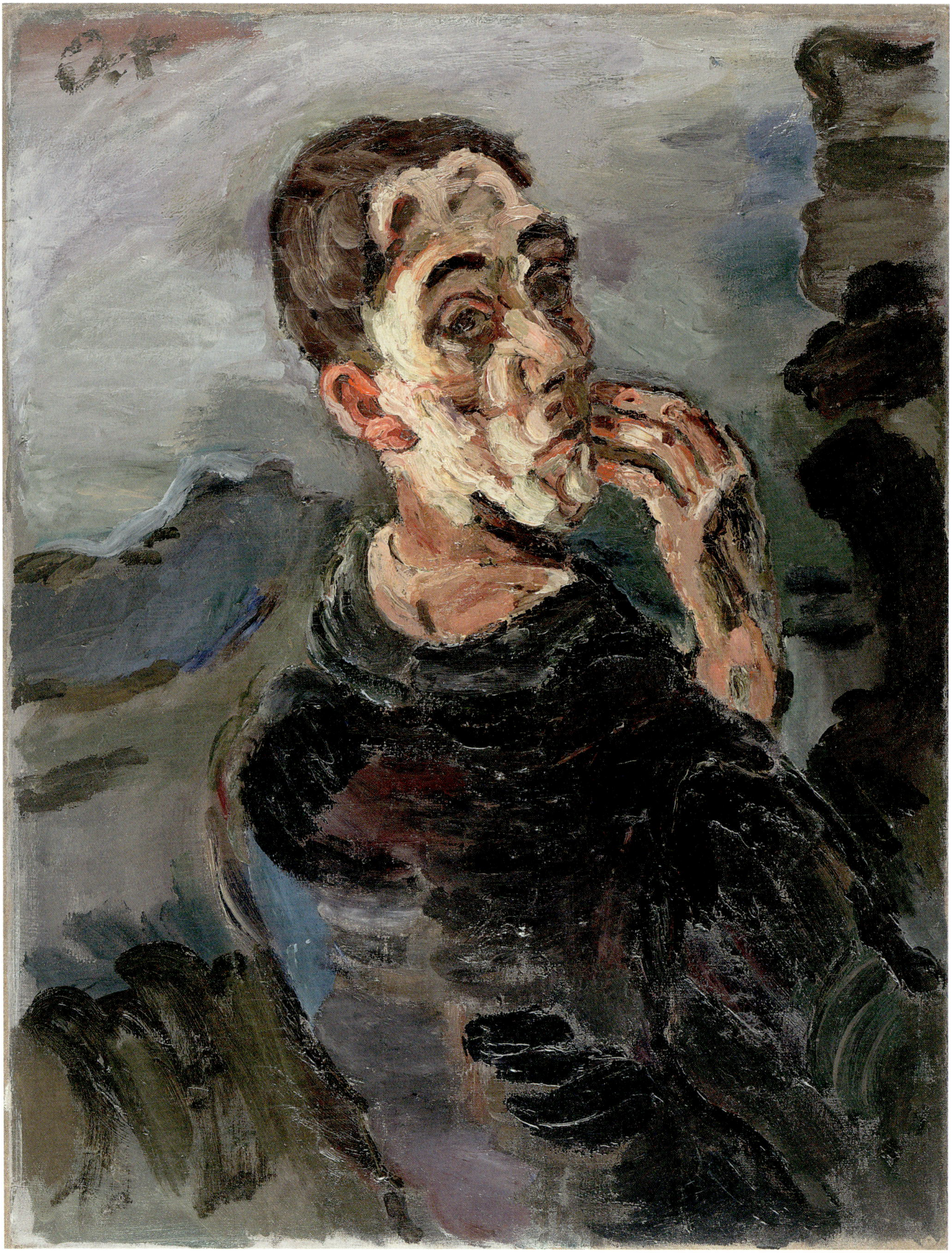

orthodox, it was then evident whose legacies were waiting to be collected. Kraus became one of the ancestors of stylistic criticism and linguistics. Loos became perhaps the most important generator of ideas for Modernist architecture. He was the originator of the free subdivision of interior spaces – across the boundaries of floors and rooms and even including the elements of the façade. Loos called this the "space plan". Kokoschka as a painter would become, in turn, one of the exemplary figures who was driven through the capitals and to emigration, embodying the artistic testimony of an entire century. Another individual who deserves mention from this circle was Egon Friedell (1878–1938). His *A Cultural History of the Modern Age*, published after much preliminary work in 1927–31, was perhaps the most important work of non-fictional literature produced in Vienna.

With the beginning of the First World War, the Vienna of 1900 became caught up in its agony – but without the episodic element. Many of the important artists were young and were accordingly summoned to military service. The older ones laboured indefatigably on, but the community of creative spirits and bon vivants had lost their enthusiasm. Klimt had already left all that was golden behind him at the beginning of the decade and had opened himself up to the new tendencies, especially those surging in from Paris – admittedly from a distance, but with visible efforts. These tendencies were aimed at understanding the picture as paint on a surface, without decoration and without layering (ill. p. 91). Schiele, too, demonstrated certain changes: his ecstatic pictorial language became calmer, smoother and acquired a coolness which heralded the arrival of New Objectivity (ill. p. 95).

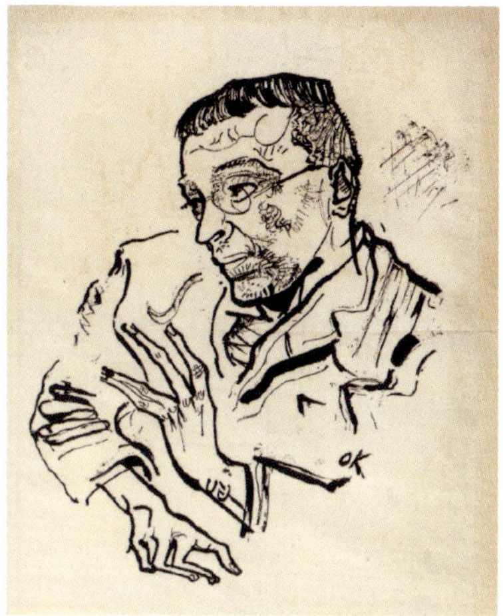

Oskar Kokoschka
Portrait Drawing of Karl Kraus I, 1909
Lithograph

The year 1918 brought it all to an abrupt end. The monarchy disappeared and with it an empire. Its capital became a hydrocephalic, shapeless creature which did not know where it belonged socially, politically or culturally. Prominent representatives of the golden age fell victim to circumstances. Klimt, Wagner and Moser died one after the other and, at the end, supposedly expiring with the words, "The war is over, and I must go", so did Schiele.

Until the bitter end, the culture of Vienna had relied on individualism. The *Gesamtkunstwerk* remained; it could continue to bank on its excesses with regard to the general and the complete, the exquisite and the eccentric. The aesthetics of autonomy of Loos's loyal followers concentrated, in any event, on the individual case. Apart from the urns, chamber pots and the eternal confusion between them, Vienna had been primarily a melting pot. It had had a guarantor until 1918 that the pot would not boil over: the emperor and the "unquestionability" of what he stood for. The strange mélange of the city thus remained unchanged. The danger that totality would shift into totalitarianism remained at arm's length. That, too, would change during the post-war era. After all, it would also become a pre-war era.

In 1921, Sigmund Freud would note a special change in his psychoanalytical point of departure. His work *Group Psychology and the Analysis of the Ego* attempts to open up the doctrine of the soul that had been oriented entirely towards the individual and his very own story, which was thus a very Viennese phenomenon, towards a new, earth-shattering appearance: the masses. In order for it to function, according to Freud, it must be delegated to an entity that arises through a sort of collective will. "The masses" becomes the keyword, the key phenomenon for the era to come. The individual who would steer the collective into the direction he chose in a way which was previously unimaginable, was himself a product of the Vienna around 1900. He, totally lacking in delicacy and being very common, had gotten to know the city and its culture from the other side, from below. But he had gotten to know it all the same. Adolf Hitler (1889–1945) would then come into his very special inheritance. Everything which had hitherto remained in precarious equilibrium would be dismantled with brute force. Its fragile context was nothing less than the trade secret of Vienna's culture around 1900: ugly facts in pretty guises.

Oskar Kokoschka
Self-Portrait with One Hand Touching the Face, 1918/19
Oil on canvas, 83.6 x 62.7 cm
(33 x 24¾ in.)
Vienna, Leopold Museum

Gustav Klimt
Auditorium in the Old Burgtheater, 1888

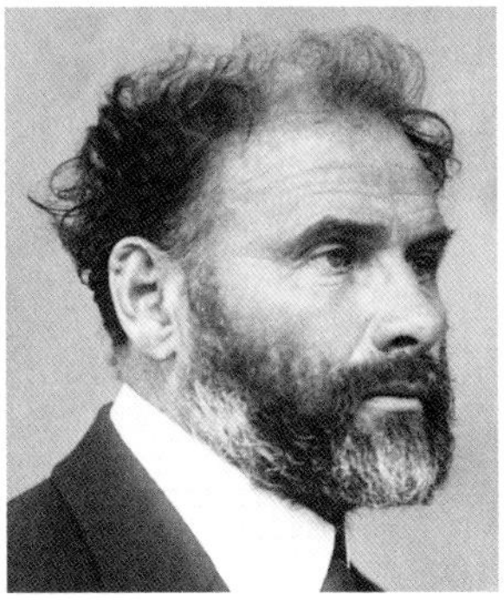

b. 1862 in Baumgarten
d. 1918 in Vienna

Here we see Klimt at the very moment he becomes Klimt: with assiduous attention to detail, he, who wanted to become a master at the age of 26, captures almost 200 portraits on paper. They depicted all of his contemporaries. They had lined up in order to parade past him and provide their likenesses so that he could include them in the large-format genre painting *Auditorium in the Old Burgtheater*. Commissioned by the municipal council of Vienna in December 1886, it was to be a watercolour. The heads thus had to be even closer together.

Although Klimt produced a large number of preliminary studies and sketches relating to this work, he did not do so with the aim of honing his artistic method. It took many drawings to portray the worthy citizens with their ladies, all of whom wished to see themselves adequately depicted, and to position them in the composition. What Klimt focusses on here is in fact a stage – the audience's own stage. They are depicted here with their expectations of the true, the good and the beautiful, and with their knowledge that they represent the social class that supports culture.

The picture shows the old Burgtheater, which was now no longer required. The building is represented in its architectural context with the Hofburg, located on Michaelerplatz in central Vienna. A new Burgtheater had just been completed – that famous theatre within the new, no longer monarchic context of the Ringstrasse which epitomized the entire urban character of Vienna. This was where the museums, parliament building, administrative offices and residential villas were linked together like a pearl necklace to satisfy the most exclusive demands, and it was only here that the national significance of those families and individuals whom Klimt recorded as representatives can truly be seen in its appropriate setting. Klimt, at any rate, fulfilled to perfection his role as the supplier of portraits for the bourgeois aristocracy. When his theatre interior was presented at the annual exhibition of 1890 in the Künstlerhaus in Vienna, it won the recently donated Imperial Prize, together with 400 ducats. Many of those who had been portrayed had replicas of the group portrait made to hang in their homes. And Klimt's proximity to this class, which did not rule the city politically – that was still the preserve of the old aristocracy – but which dictated business and especially culture, would serve him well in subsequent years. When his public commissions dried up, he would recruit clients from this very audience for further, highly priced paintings.

Let us take a look at one group of people from Klimt's overwhelming presentation. In the third box from the left on the third circle, separated by one of the columns supporting the balcony, we can make out three figures: a man in the middle, flanked by two ladies, of whom the right-hand one is wearing a tall hat. She is the youthful Serena Pulitzer (1867–1943) – related to the donor of the Pulitzer Prize – who can be seen here with her aunt and uncle. She was soon to marry the industrialist August Lederer (1857–1936). The Lederers would subsequently be frequent supporters of Klimt. The lady of the house had her portrait painted by him in 1899, and her daughter Elisabeth in about 1915. Lederer stepped in when Klimt was compelled to buy back his pictures for the university, which had become the object of a scandal. And Lederer rescued what was arguably Klimt's most relevant artwork from decay: the *Beethoven Frieze* (ill. pp. 20/21), which had originally been created for the Secession. Lederer and Klimt both knew what they had in each other. RM

Auditorium in the Old Burgtheater, 1888
Watercolour and body colour, heightened with gold, 82 x 92 cm (32¼ x 36¼ in.)
Vienna, Wien Museum

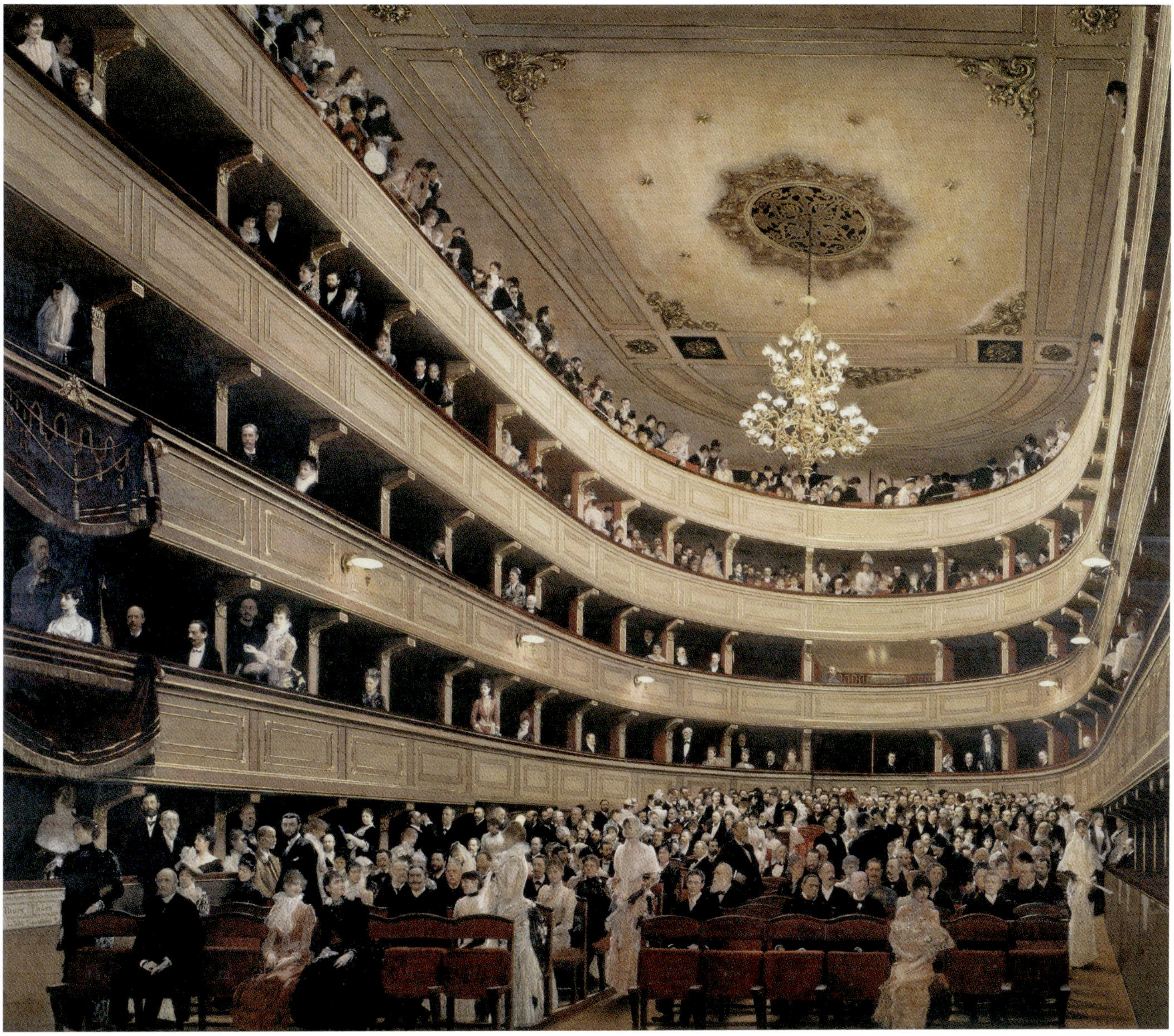

Joseph Maria Olbrich

Vienna Secession Building, 1898

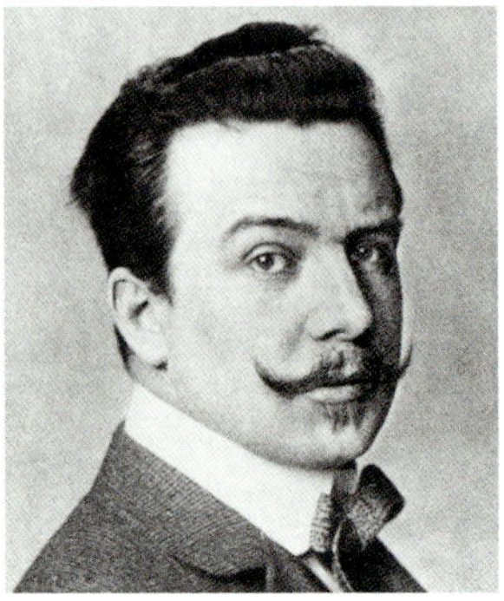

b. 1867 in Opava
d. 1908 in Düsseldorf

PAGE 35
Vienna Secession Building, 1898

Joseph Maria Olbrich
Poster for the second Secession exhibition, 1898
Vienna, Wien Museum

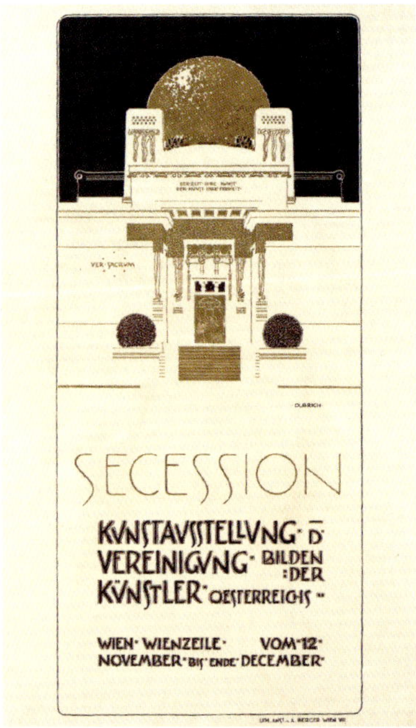

"To every age its art. To every art its freedom", is the inscription in gold above the entrance. It was indeed an act of liberation that had made this building possible. On 3 April 1897 a group of artists and architects that included Gustav Klimt (1862–1918), Koloman Moser and Josef Hoffmann withdrew from their professional association, the Vienna Society of Artists. They made their act of separation into their name, calling themselves the Vereinigung Bildender Künstler Österreichs Wiener Secession (The Union of Austrian Artists of the Vienna Secession), known as the Secession for short. Like many social movements around 1900, the Secessionists were fascinated by the idea of reform. They regarded historicism, which was propagated as an ideal by the Ringstrasse (ill. p. 9) in particular and hence, also by Viennese society, as no more than a hollow façade. Their reform aimed not only to introduce an urgently needed renewal of the concept of art, but also to unite art and life itself.

From the very outset it was clear that the movement would need its own exhibition building. The architect Joseph Maria Olbrich, who was 30 years old at the time and one of the founding members, was to design it. The first plot of land they selected on the Ringstrasse met with little favour from the political circles in Vienna; they did not really want to have the artist rebels in such a prominent location. An alternative site for the building was found at Karlsplatz, and the property was financed by an exhibition as well as by private sponsors, including Karl Wittgenstein (1847–1913), the father of the philosopher Ludwig Wittgenstein (1889–1951).

They were able to open the building just six months later, in November 1898. Olbrich's design looks more like a temple of antiquity than a secular exhibition building: with its white rendering and almost total lack of windows, its symmetry and entrance like that of a sacred building, and its dome of golden laurel leaves as a crown. There was no shortage of symbolism: laurel leaves as the symbol of victory; references to Athene, the goddess of wisdom; figures of owls and tortoises and three Medusa heads bearing the words Painting, Architecture and Sculpture. Olbrich chose the dome form in homage to Johann Bernhard Fischer von Erlach's (1656–1723) Baroque Karlskirche at the other end of the square.

Beside the entrance is the inscription *Ver Sacrum* (Sacred Spring) that refers to the magazine of the same name, which was also founded in 1898, and to the Reformist desire for renewal. Despite all this painterly and sculptural symbolism, the Secession Building remains basically a functional structure – after all, it aimed to provide the art exhibited there with the best possible stage. The main central room behind the dome is relatively plain and is covered by a glass roof which ensures uniform lighting.

For Olbrich, the Secession Building marked the start of a brief international career as an architect. In 1899, he was summoned to Darmstadt by Grand Duke Ernst Ludwig von Hesse (1868–1937), where he was the main designer who transformed the artists' colony Mathildenhöhe into a unique bastion of Jugendstil. Olbrich died of leukaemia in 1908 at the age of only 40. The Union of Artists of the Vienna Secession still exists to this day; the building has long since become synonymous with the movement of which it is the result. It is regarded as an outstanding work of Jugendstil. The fact that the style is known as Secession Style in Vienna is due not least to this building. MN

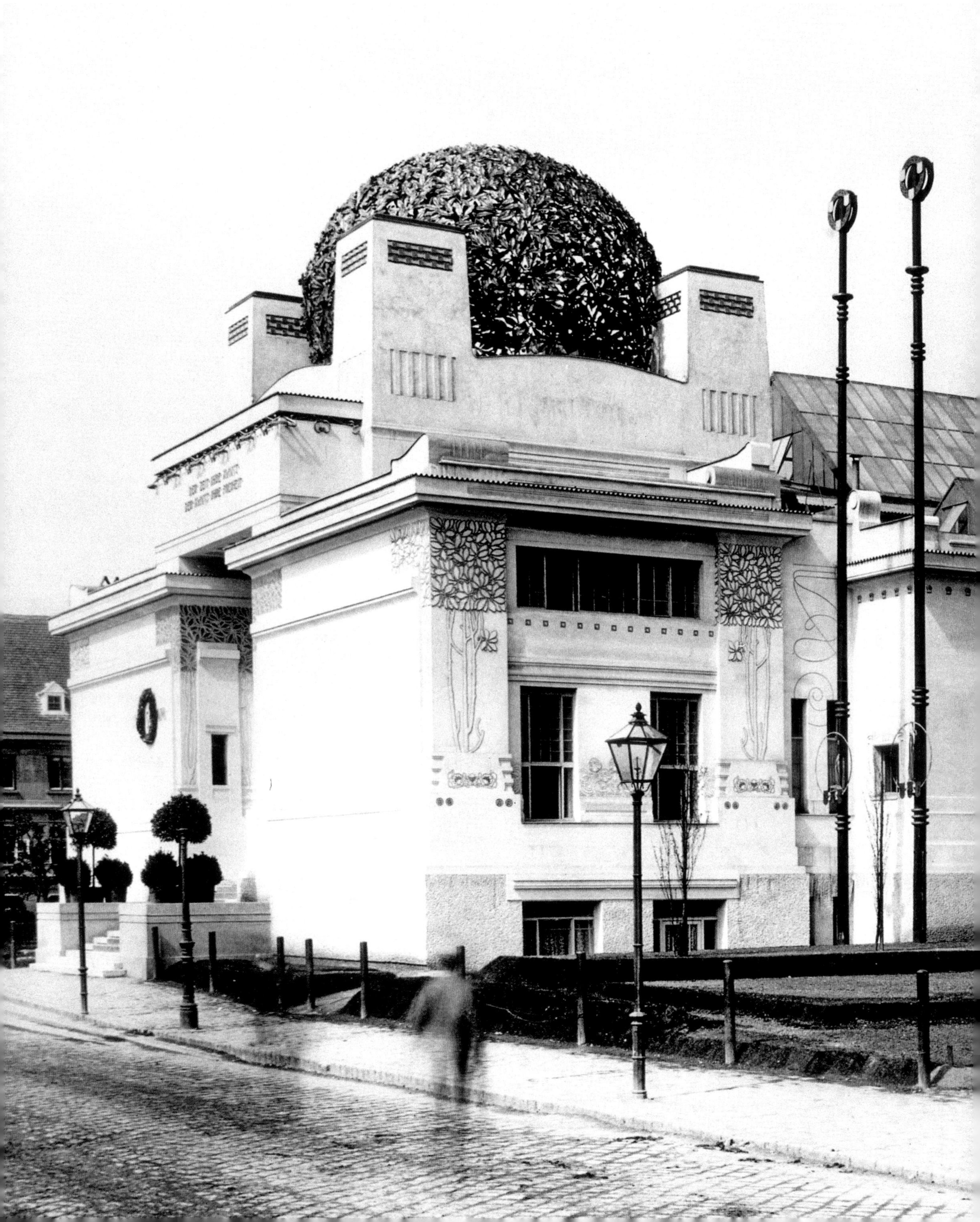

Alfred Roller

Cover for Ver Sacrum, 1898

Josef Maria Auchentaller

Decorative page for Ver Sacrum, 1898

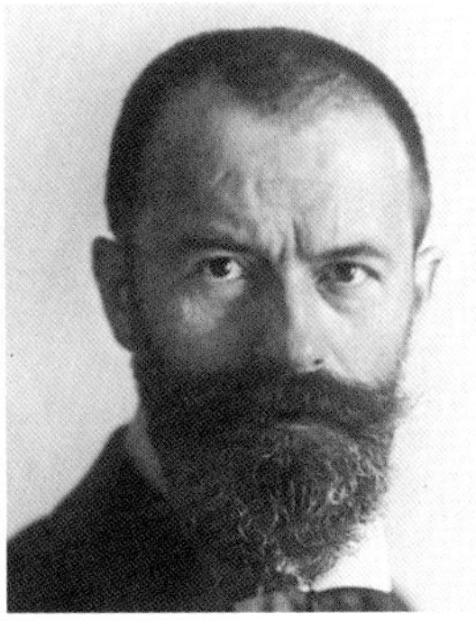

b. 1864 in Brno
d. 1935 in Vienna

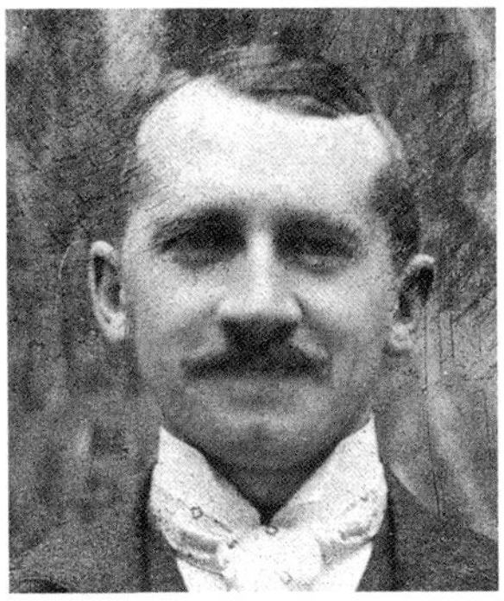

b. 1865 in Vienna
d. 1949 in Grado

"We do not recognize any differentiation between 'high art' and 'craftwork', between art for the wealthy and art for the poor. Art belongs to everyone", was the comment in the editorial of the first edition of *Ver Sacrum*, the magazine of the Vienna Secession, properly named *Organ der Vereinigung Bildender Künstler Österreichs* (Organ of the Union of Austrian Artists), published between 1898 and 1903. Alfred Roller had created a powerful, programmatic image of the sacred spring for the title page of the first issue: the new roots of the young tree in full blossom burst open the wooden tub in which it had been planted (ill. p. 37 top). In the tree's crown three signs can be seen, for painting, architecture and sculpture. In the following years the trio of signs would be repeated on several Secession posters; they recur in the form of three masks on the façade of the building above the entrance portal.

And, indeed, *Ver Sacrum* presented itself as a medium for all, but especially for everything, both local and international. It was also receptive not only to literature but also to photography, which was still very young as an art form. Scattered between the text and pictorial contributions one can find all sorts of vignettes, signets and other ornamental decoration. This art magazine, for which the editorial work lay in the hands of members of the Secession, served all in all as a sample book for two-dimensional art and its wide-ranging applications.

Laid out on a double page is the poem *Ver Sacrum* by the Austrian writer Ferdinand von Saar (1833–1906) in a frame designed by Josef Maria Auchentaller (ill. p. 37 bottom) "Out there in the endless universe it is spring again", is how the verse begins. Correspondingly, the tendrils of the surrounding blossoms seem to reach up into infinity or, at least, far beyond the available format. Over the years, two-dimensional art in Vienna would go on to develop a specific, somewhat more rigorous style, but around the turn of the century the main focus lay entirely on floral Jugendstil that flourished on the international scene. This was no coincidence in the case of Auchentaller, who was born and trained in Vienna, for he was socialized as an independent artist in Munich. Not only was he close to the local Secession there, but he also worked for the magazine *Jugend*, which would, in fact, give its name to the entire era. He was a first-generation member of the Vienna Secession, which he subsequently left in 1905 together with the group surrounding Gustav Klimt. Like Klimt, in the side room on the left, Auchentaller had also created a frieze for the 14th Secession exhibition, the famous Beethoven exhibition. His frieze was designed for the opposite room on the right, which he shared with fellow artist Ferdinand Andri (1871–1956). *Freude schöner Götterfunken*, the opening words of Friedrich von Schiller's (1759–1805) "Ode to Joy", was the appropriate title of his work, which was removed after the exhibition and hence, has not survived. It depicted an airy swirling of draperies billowing around naked bodies, prompting the critic Ludwig Hevesi (1843–1910) to compare it with the dancer Loïe Fuller (1862–1928), who was famous for her dance of the veils.

For family reasons, Auchentaller increasingly withdrew from Vienna to Grado on the Adriatic coast. He concentrated primarily on poster designs; his poster for the seaside resort of Grado on Austria's Coast remains to this day part of the branding of the splendorous former imperial and royal seaside. DG

Cover and decorative page for Ver Sacrum
First issue, January 1898

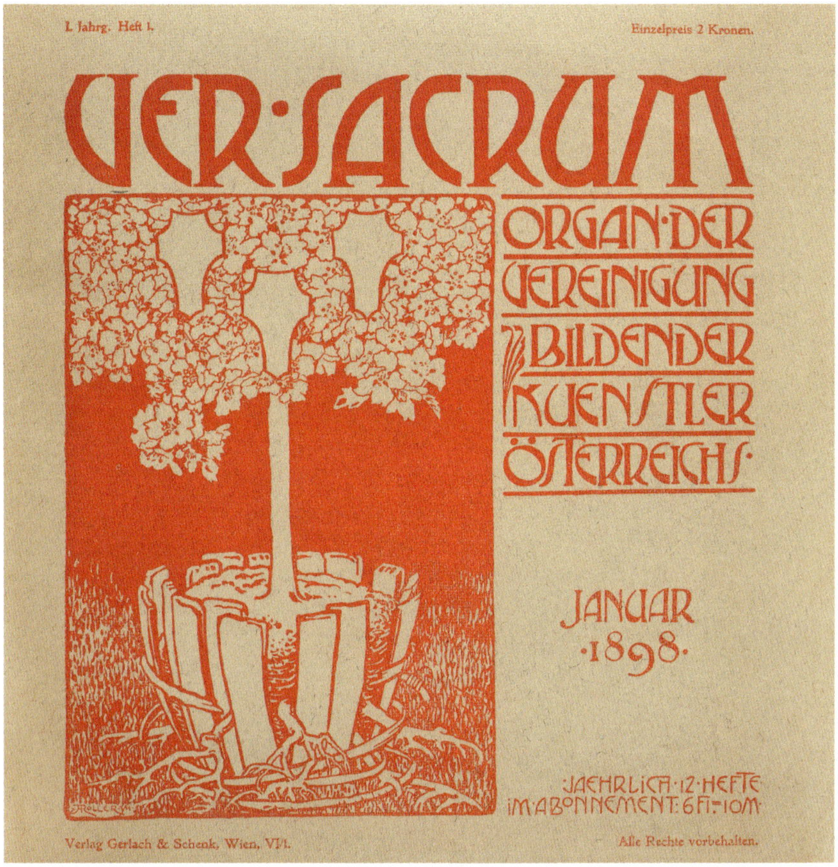

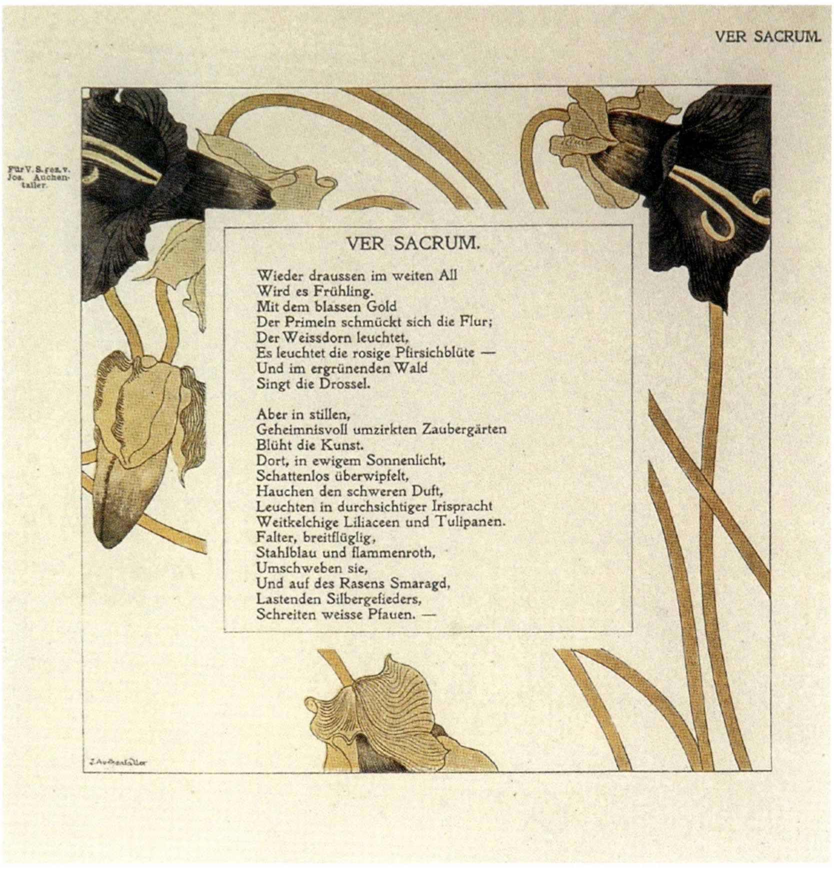

VER SACRUM.

Für V. S. gez. v. Jos. Auchentaller.

VER SACRUM.

Wieder draussen im weiten All
Wird es Frühling.
Mit dem blassen Gold
Der Primeln schmückt sich die Flur;
Der Weissdorn leuchtet,
Es leuchtet die rosige Pfirsichblüte —
Und im ergrünenden Wald
Singt die Drossel.

Aber in stillen,
Geheimnisvoll umzirkten Zaubergärten
Blüht die Kunst.
Dort, in ewigem Sonnenlicht,
Schattenlos überwipfelt,
Hauchen den schweren Duft,
Leuchten in durchsichtiger Irispracht
Weitkelchige Liliaceen und Tulipanen.
Falter, breitflüglig,
Stahlblau und flammenroth,
Umschweben sie,
Und auf des Rasens Smaragd,
Lastenden Silbergefieders,
Schreiten weisse Pfauen. —

Otto Wagner

Buildings on Linke Wienzeile, 1898/99

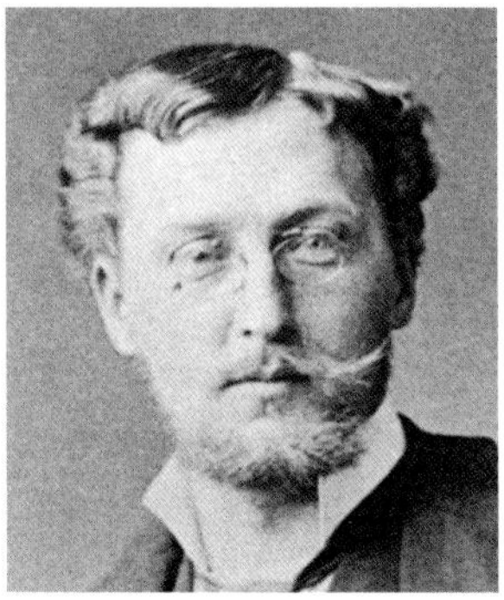

b. 1841 in Penzing
d. 1918 in Vienna

PAGE 39
Façade details of the ***Buildings on Linke Wienzeile***, nos. 40 and 38, 1898/99

Building on Linke Wienzeile, no. 40, 1898/99
Photograph from 1899

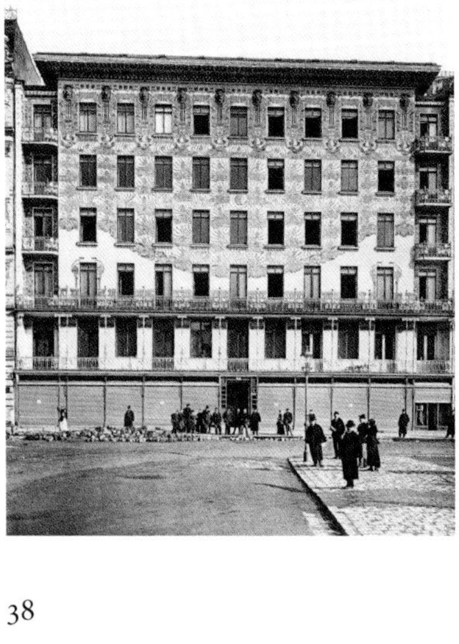

No other modern architect has left his mark on Vienna more effectively than Otto Wagner. As a genius of universal abilities he was an equal master of architecture, town planning and technology; he led 19th-century Vienna, still immersed in historicism, into the modern age and trained a number of talents in his studio who would go on to become the influential architects of the 20th century. The two residences on Linke Wienzeile street, created at the height of his creative career, are fine examples that display his combined, wide-ranging talents. They lie directly beside the Wien River, the regulation of which represented Wagner's biggest infrastructure project to be realized. In 1893, he presented his general regulatory plan for the whole of Vienna, and in 1894 was appointed to the commission for the construction of Vienna's Stadtbahn, or city railway, and the regulation of the Danube.

Wagner was convinced that the time around the turn of the century was an era of technological revolution that would inevitably change the city's countenance. It needed to be planned and in Wagner's view the historicism of the Ringstrasse era (ill. p. 9), which he contemptuously dismissed as "a costume ball of styles", was totally unsuitable for the task. In his essay *Moderne Architektur*, published in 1896, Wagner developed a new practical style as an alternative, whose forms were derived from construction and function. He thus anticipated the "form follows function" of 20th-century Modernism – an approach which exposed him to controversial discussions in the profession and which would also cost him one or two commissions. Nonetheless, he continued undeterred with the practical implementation of this utilitarian style. The stations for the Stadtbahn that Wagner designed (ill. pp. 8 bottom, 10 top) combine technical infrastructure with big-city elegance, and for the two houses on Wienzeile street the integration into the overall design is of elementary importance. Wagner planned a long elegant boulevard along both banks of the river for the regulated Wien valley. Apart from the two residences, built in 1898/99, it has remained unrealized.

Both clearly show the influence of the Vienna Secession, of which Otto Wagner was a member around the turn of the century. Here one will not see the ornamentation of the Gründerzeit executed in an emphatically three-dimensional manner as was customary at the time; instead it is fused with the two-dimensional surface of the façade. In Wagner's later buildings the ornamentation was reduced still further. The three-dimensionality of the building on Linke Wienzeile 38 is entirely optimized towards its effect on the city's appearance from a distance. It is dominated by its tower-like round structure and marks the corner of the street. The Secessionist Koloman Moser decorated it with golden ornamentation. Visible from afar, the roof is crowned by the sculpture *Ruferinnen*, designed by Othmar Schimkowitz (1864–1947). The house immediately next door, on Linke Wienzeile 40, is known as the Majolica House. The surface is clad with coloured tiles whose floral patterns extend across the entire width. Wagner did not choose this design for purely artistic reasons. Thanks to the tiles, the façade was easy to clean. It was washed at regular intervals by the Vienna fire brigade. Characteristic of Wagner's residences is the narrow protruding roof edging which gives the impression of a flat roof when seen from the street. Reduced to the essentials further still is the neighbouring house on Köstlergasse 3, in which Otto Wagner himself lived for a time. MN

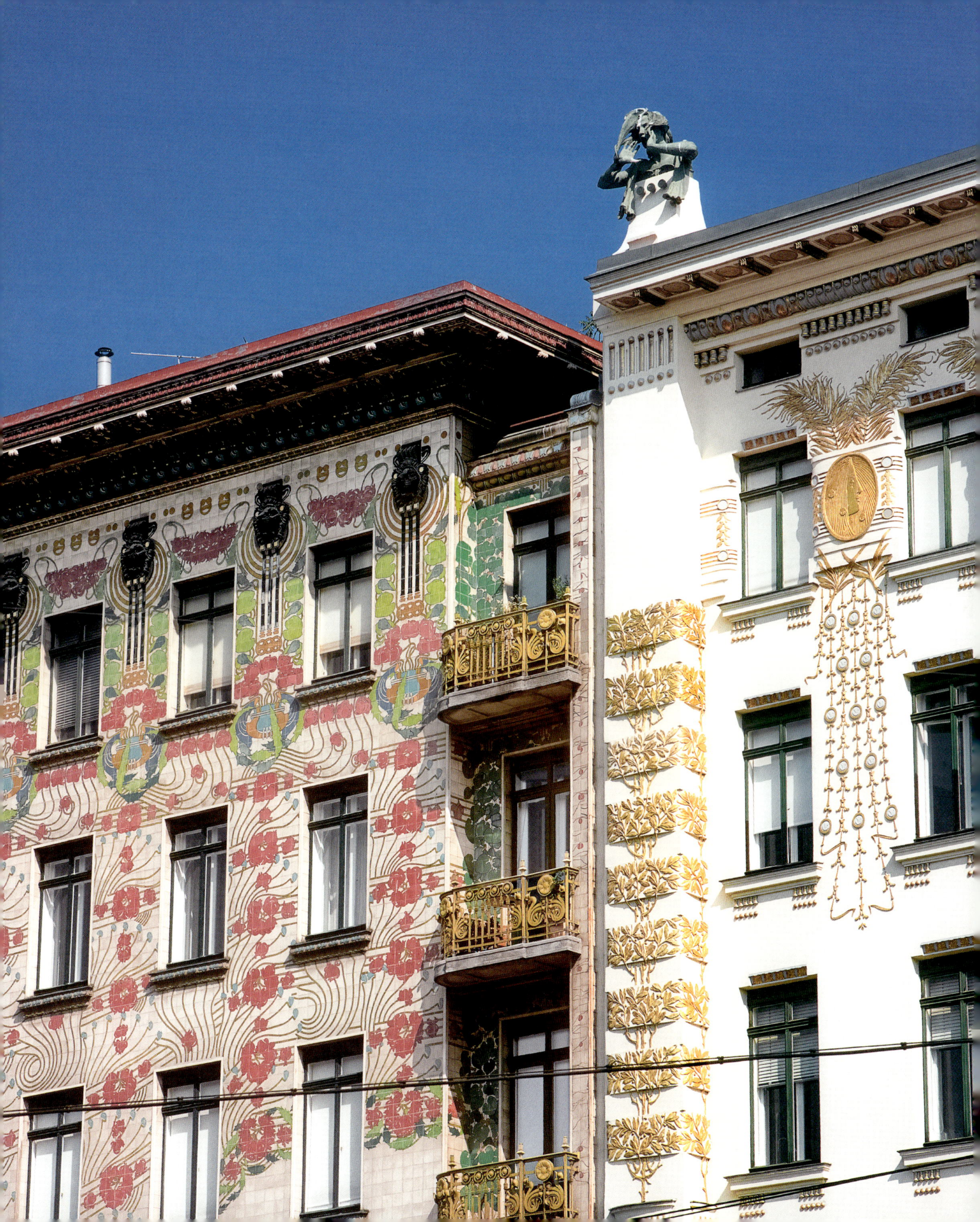

Karl Kraus (ed.)
Die Fackel, 1899

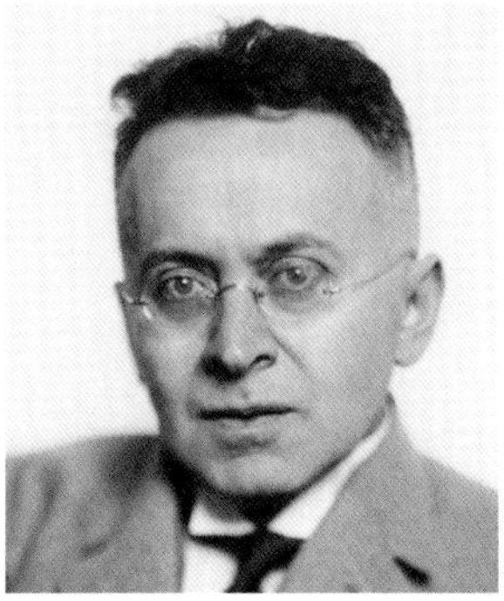

b. 1874 in Jičín
d. 1936 in Vienna

"Idiot" – that is the last word in the final issue of the magazine *Die Fackel*, which was published in November 1935. Karl Kraus, its founder and inventor, had filled 37 volumes and no fewer than 22,578 pages with his notorious notes. He had written more than three-quarters of the total himself. Kraus was proud of being a grumbler, proud of his lack of principles, and he cultivated an entire corpus of mortal enemies. He maintained these hostilities through his magazine and pursued them with headlines which he called "executions". The final word of his epilogue was perfectly suited to the very special educational tasks of *Die Fackel* (The Torch).

It had started in April 1899. Kraus, born in 1874 in Bohemia, had moved to Vienna at the age of two. On his 25th birthday he made himself a present of a newspaper. He had had a number of articles published in the monarchy's leading opinion-forming publication the *Neue Freie Presse*, and had taken his anger out on the city's writers by attributing to them a "demolished literature". His own paper would subsequently become highly successful with such insubordination. The first issues had to be reprinted and reached print runs of 30,000 copies.

Kraus initially saw himself as the spokesperson of the dissatisfied: "The political programme of this magazine", remarked the editorial in the first issue, "therefore seems wanting: not a resounding 'what we offer', but an honest 'what we shall demolish' is what we have chosen as the motto". An invitation to the dance: people could ask to see the publisher and present reports, conspiracies and outrages which *Die Fackel* would then investigate. When the whole thing deteriorated, predictably enough, into a succession of denunciations, Kraus abandoned this sounding out of a kind of herd intelligence in February 1904. From then on he worked with a fixed team of employees. But he was not content to let it go at that: from the end of 1911 all texts emerged from the workshop of the one and only, in all his fury and boldness, unbeatable authority of all by the name of Kraus.

Kraus's highly effective way of dealing with things and people consisted of a kind of reflexive repartee. His most famous comments, like his dismissal of Sigmund Freud – "Psychoanalysis is the mental illness of thinking it is its own therapy" – or of the Berlin gallerist and impresario Herwarth Walden (1879–1941) – "Among the many sacrifices he makes for art is art itself" – function according to the mechanism: an expression is used until the various meanings it carries, as is always the case in language, refute one another. The contradictions which emerge are then transferred to the people concerned.

Kraus's polemic *Die demolirte Literatur* (The Demolished Literature) had a cover picture created by the draughtsman, illustrator and caricaturist Hans Schliessmann (1852–1920). Kraus him-self often referred to it. No information is available about the cover page of the first issue of *Die Fackel*. Here, therefore, we can only surmise that Schliessmann was the author. In any case, it is impossible to overlook the instrument bringing light as it emerged from a cloudy sphere to penetrate the city whose silhouette loomed darkly. Its only purpose was to give the public a piece of its mind. The cover is red. Honest demolition was on the way. RM

Hans Schliessmann
Cover of the magazine
Die Fackel, 1899
First issue

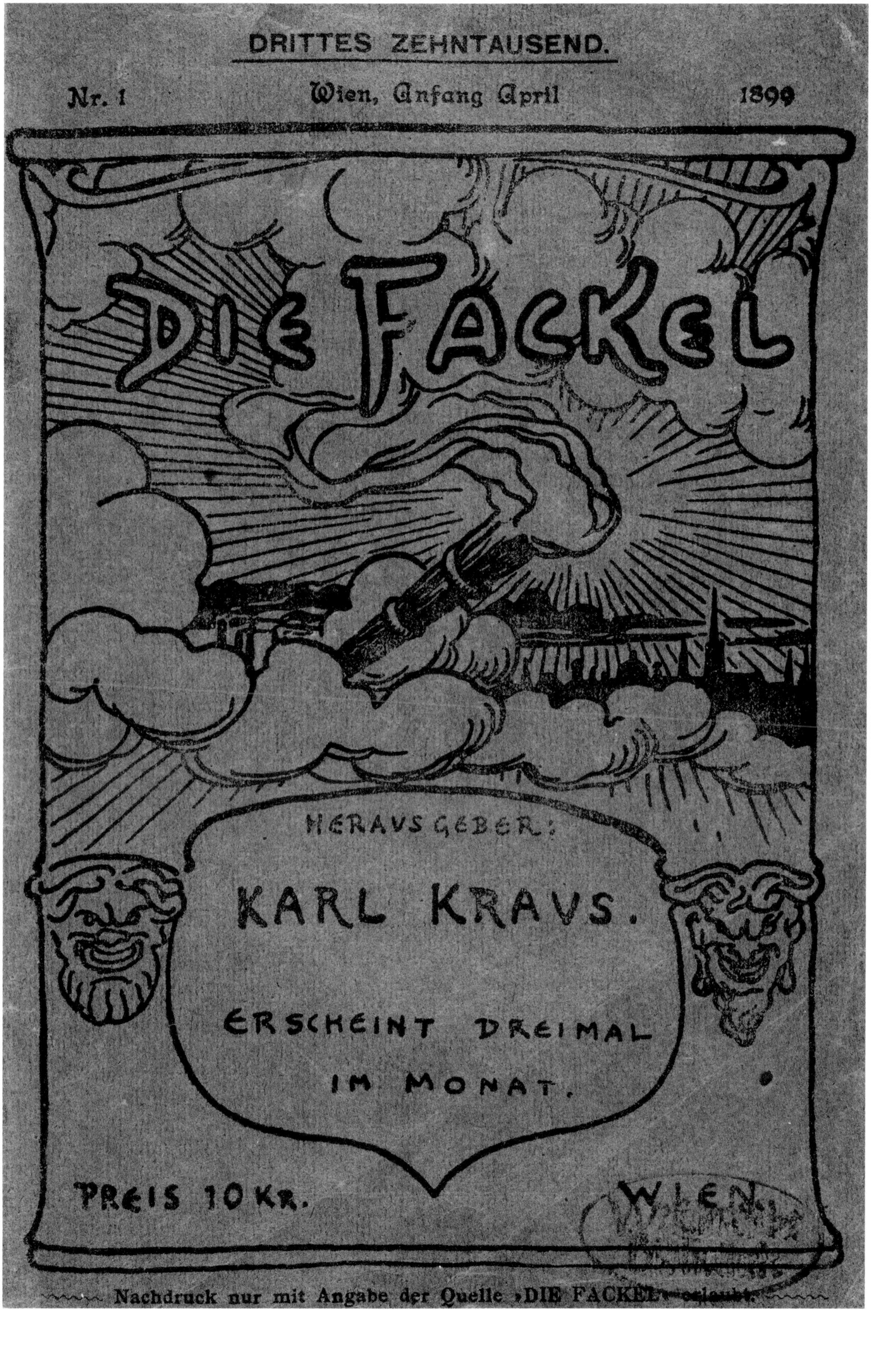
DRITTES ZEHNTAUSEND.
Nr. 1
Wien, Anfang April
1899
DIE FACKEL
HERAUSGEBER:
KARL KRAUS.
ERSCHEINT DREIMAL IM MONAT.
PREIS 10 KR.
WIEN.
Nachdruck nur mit Angabe der Quelle »DIE FACKEL« erlaubt.

Adolf Loos
Café Museum, 1899

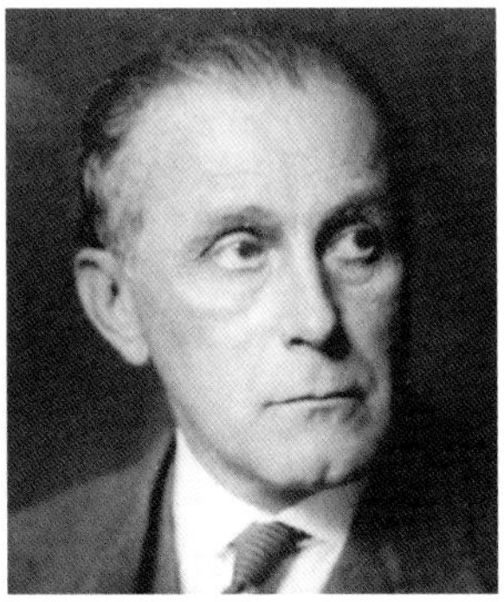

b. 1870 in Brno
d. 1933 in Vienna

"I have some shattering news for the aesthete: even Old Vienna was once new". Thus commented Karl Kraus in 1912 on his fellow citizens' attachment to the past. The illusion that everything had always been there and it would be best not to add anything to the present state had always been popular in Vienna. Even that Viennese institution, the coffee house, was not immune to this nostalgia. And yet the coffee house in the form in which it became an icon during the 20th century and is now regarded as a symbol of that institution can be traced back to a modern innovation. The Café Museum is the blueprint for this typology, the first Viennese café of this new type.

Its youthful architect Adolf Loos had recently returned from extensive travels through the United States and London, which had made a lasting impression on him. Loos thereupon remained at a deliberate distance from the Vienna Secessionists, who were just forming a group at this time. He realized at the outset that the fusion of art and architecture which they propagated was the wrong approach. Loos refused to be classified in any group, a position which remained unchanged, even though his almost obsessive preoccupation with interiors fits no place better than the Vienna of Sigmund Freud.

Loos was awarded the contract to design the interior decoration of the Café Museum in 1899 as a result of the altruistic intervention of his older colleague Max Fabiani. Coffee houses at that time were mostly cluttered, upholstered Biedermeier salons. Loos, with images from the metropolises he had recently visited still in his mind's eye, had a vision of a completely different type of cosiness, one that resulted not from "too much" but from "just the right amount". In Loos's view a well-made wooden chair adapted to a sitting posture was not only more attractive and effective, but also more comfortable than an upholstered armchair.

When it opened, the Café Museum astounded the Viennese public: it was an L-shaped room with smooth surfaces and without adornment and dividing walls. Standing free within the space as if on a stage was a basic stock of furniture: tables with marble tops, light bentwood chairs and billiard tables. It was a cosmopolitan place that was cosy at the same time in a specifically Austrian way. It was not long after before intellectuals and coffee house writers like Peter Altenberg and Karl Kraus decided on the Museum as their regular café. They were joined by artists like Gustav Klimt and Egon Schiele.

For Adolf Loos it marked the start of a remarkable career which made him one of the most influential Austrian architects of the early 20th century, and a pioneer of Modernism. His interior design for the café from 1899 was copied countless times. To this day it provides the basic formula for Viennese coffee houses and their culture. The café is now listed as part of the intangible cultural heritage by UNESCO. The subsequent fate of the Café Museum followed a curious path. In 1930/31 it was renovated by Josef Zotti (1882–1953), who replaced the bentwood chairs with imitation leather armchairs – a different, more fashionable form of cosmopolitan elegance. In 2003, during the course of reconstruction, this interior was exchanged for the original Loos furnishings once more, whose harsh sterility lacks any sense of comfort. When the café was reopened in 2010 they were replaced yet again by replicas of Josef Zotti's furnishings. Nostalgia is not so easy after all. Karl Kraus would have been amused. MN

Café Museum, 1899

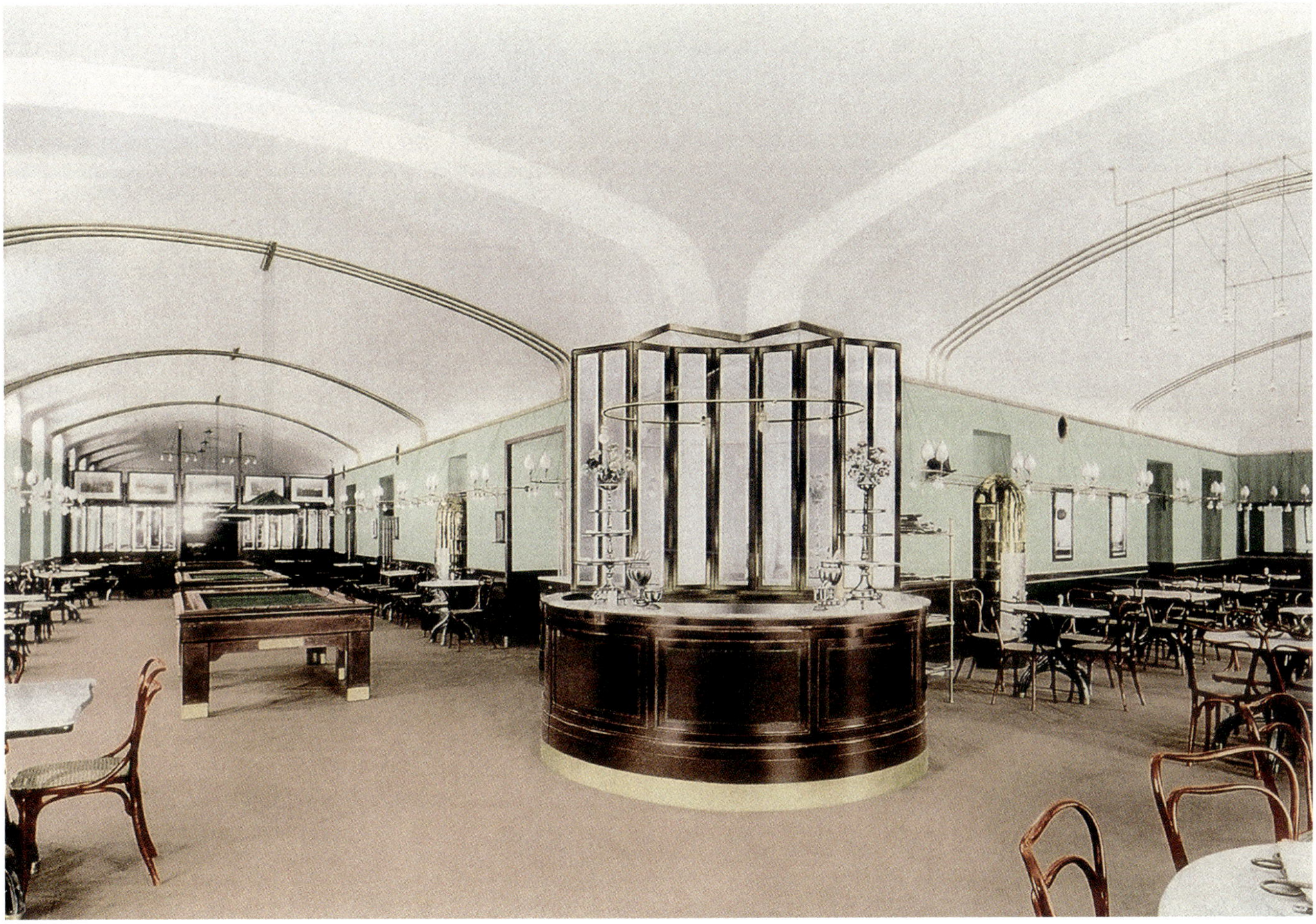

Wilhelm Gause
Court Ball, 1900

b. 1853 in Krefeld
d. 1916 in Krems

PAGE 45
Court Ball, 1900
Watercolour, 49.8 x 69.3 cm
(19½ x 27¼ in.)
Vienna, Wien Museum

Wilhelm List
Emperor Franz Joseph I, 1905
Oil on canvas, 50 x 69 cm (19¾ x 27¼ in.)
Painting from the conference room of the Postal Savings Bank built by Otto Wagner in Vienna

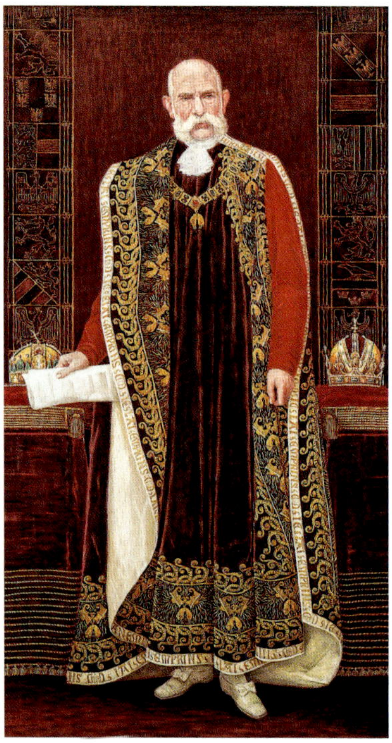

The *Hofball*, or "Court Ball", as etiquette demands, was the somewhat less exclusive of two celebrations His Majesty held at Carnival time. Only the high aristocracy was invited to the *Ball bei Hofe* – the "Ball at the Court". This was the society which jealously proclaimed its great love for the imperial house, in close proximity to the supreme person. The Court Ball took place at the beginning of the season, in other words in January and, in contrast, included sections of the diplomatic core, the army, ennobled members of the middle class and senior members of the civil service. Not only were guests invited to dance but also to a buffet of legendary opulence. The festive setting for this event were the so-called *Redoutensäle*, banqueting halls that extended between the library and the Spanish Riding School within the sprawling complex of the imperial residence known as the Hofburg.

This was the occasion for a sedate ceremonial encounter with the sovereign. Franz Joseph, born in 1830, had been on the throne for more than half a century. He was the head of state of the Danube monarchy, which extended across eastern Central Europe and the Balkans and included more than 50 million subjects – a multinational state whose centrifugal force was blocked solely by the venerability of the Emperor, his person and the length of time that the empire had existed. The empire, acquired and held together for aeons by the Habsburgs, Franz Joseph's dynasty was certainly liberal; censorship played a remarkably minor role. The monarch was much loved and so popular that no ambitious modernist campaigner had ever harboured thoughts of being a Republican.

Wilhelm Gause allows the general public to partake in an important act of state. Within a space of nearly 50 by 70 centimetres his watercolour accommodates the upper crust and with it the atmosphere, ambience and attraction of the top ten thousand. In particular, the ladies attract the eyewitness with their elaborate costumes, wasp waists, décolletés and liveliness of youth. Of course everyone only has eyes for the Emperor, while a group of gentlemen in their picturesque, vaguely operetta-like uniforms adorn the scene. In Gause's picture the Emperor looks as he did in public – and as he intended to look in public: ageless, obviously not young, but in full possession of his virility and drive.

The great jubilee had taken place in 1898. The occasion for celebration was the 50th anniversary of the reign of Emperor Franz Joseph, and the whole of Vienna, including the city's artists had turned out in their Sunday best. But then an event occurred which the Emperor described with the words, "I am to be spared nothing". Empress Elisabeth – "Sisi" – was assassinated by an anarchist. All festivities were put on hold. This event occurred more than a year before Gause recorded the Court Ball. There is no hint of grief in the glory and glamour of this glittering night.

Gause was born in 1853 in Krefeld and moved to Vienna in 1879. He died in the Wachau in 1916. He was an illustrator and chronicler of his time who frequently veered beyond the status quo. He was not a court reporter, and his detached somewhat dispassionate gaze acknowledged unemployment and all aspects of life for the other half of society. Gause supplied popular themes that were ignored by the exclusivity of Vienna around 1900, such as its artificiality and snobbishness. The Emperor and his prominent guests served Gause well in his exploration of the popular. RM

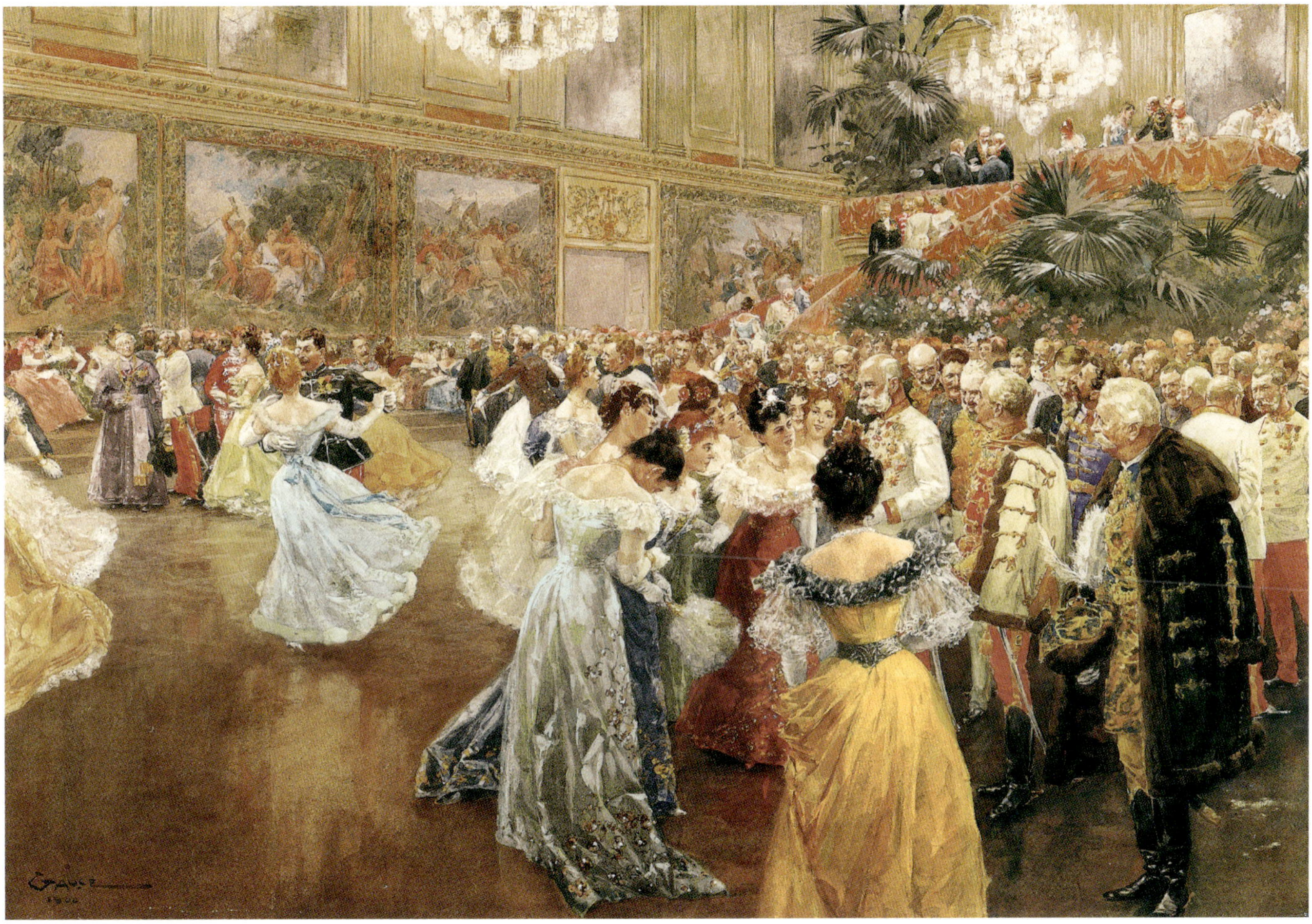

Max Fabiani

Artaria House, 1900–1902

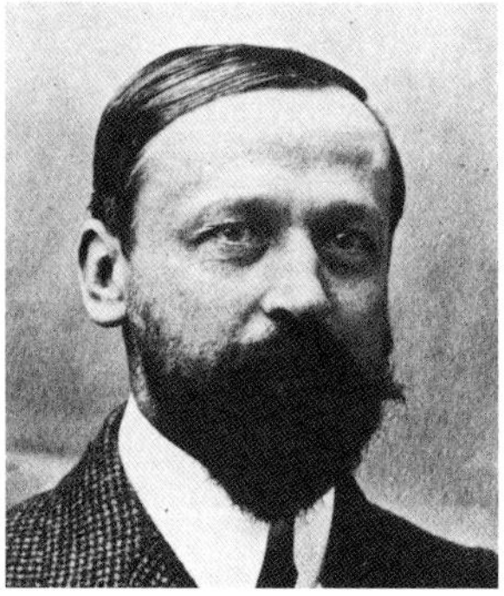

b. 1865 in Kobdilj
d. 1962 in Gorizia

Of all the architects who left their mark on Vienna at the turn of the century, there was none who embodied so perfectly the imperial and royal multinational state of Austria-Hungary as Max Fabiani. He was born in Slovenia near the Italian border and grew up speaking three languages. After moving to Vienna he worked from 1894 in the office of Otto Wagner, where he became the office manager in 1899. Fabiani made a lively contribution to the discussions about Wagner's epoch-making book *Moderne Architektur*, and continued to develop Wagner's ideas in a highly individual manner in his own buildings. Like Wagner, Fabiani was a member of the Secession, but later distanced himself from the movement. In 1902, he was the first architect in the monarchy to be awarded a doctorate. He was influential within the profession as a publicist and as Professor for Ornamentation and Interior Decoration at the Technical University, and was also extremely well-connected within Viennese society.

The offices for the long-established publishing house Artaria & Co., which had been founded in 1770, occupied a special position at the prestigious Kohlmarkt – not only because the building is set back from the line of neighbouring buildings in adherence with the development plan of the time, but also because of its appearance, which radiates Mediterranean brightness and lightness. The prominently protruding roof, a recurring element in the buildings of Fabiani's teacher Wagner, juts out into the street like a delicate screen. The façade facing the street shows a clear division between the shop area and the office floors. The ground floor and mezzanine are framed and joined together by four slender supports, of which the outer ones are each adorned with what look like male and female caryatids. The four floors above this are clad in smooth honey-coloured marble sheets and structured only by narrow horizontal bands – a decidedly sober design for the time. Only the bay windows protrude from the level of the façade. In the way it dispenses with any form of excessive decoration, the Artaria House is regarded as a model for Adolf Loos's radical house on Michaelerplatz (ill. p. 71), which only a few years later would stand diagonally opposite and would provoke a substantial scandal.

Artaria House, 1900–1902

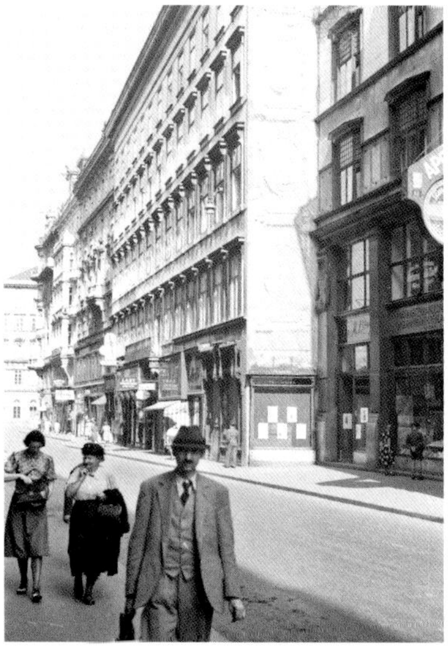

Fabiani pursued a similarly consistent and modern subdivision of the façade on the Portois & Fix office building on Ungargasse in the 3rd district, which was built at almost the same time. There as well, the decorative elements have been reduced to a minimum and the office storeys are clad with a smooth tiled façade which shimmers in various shades of green. Fabiani realized a considerably more flamboyant variation of the Artaria House in 1905/06: the Casa Bartoli in Trieste.

In the following years, Max Fabiani's affinity with the monarchy would be intensified further still through his friendship with the heir to the throne Archduke Franz Ferdinand, whose personal adviser he became in 1902. Just as the monarchy became more strongly nationalist during the years leading up to the First World War, so too were Fabiani's later designs, such as the Urania adult education centre (1909/10), which was more historicist and conservative. Fabiani returned to his native land of Slovenia after the war, where he had already designed the general zoning plan for the capital Ljubljana. It had been destroyed by an earthquake in 1895. The publishing house's bookshop on the ground floor of the Artaria House would remain in existence for more than a century, until it was replaced by a fashion boutique in 2014. MN

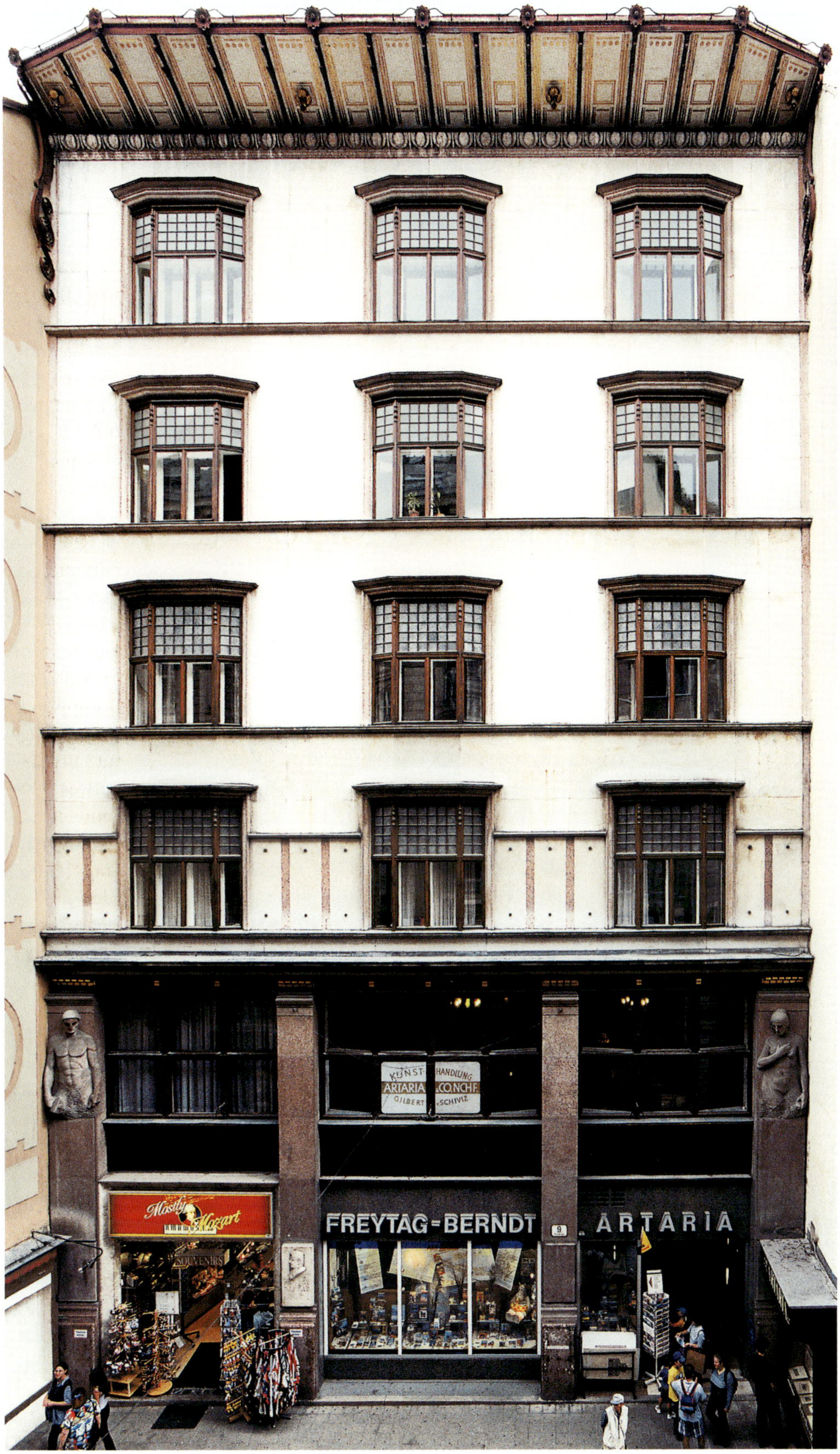
KUNST HANDLUNG
ARTARIA & CO. NCHF.
GILBERT & SCHIVIZ
Mostly Mozart
SOUVENIRS
FREYTAG-BERNDT
9
ARTARIA

Josef Hoffmann

Overdoors in the Beethoven exhibition of the Secession, 1902

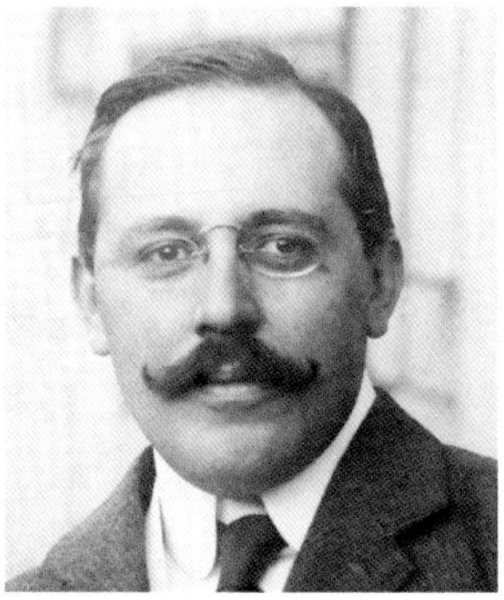

b. 1870 in Brtnice
d. 1956 in Vienna

A number of curious exhibits have been displayed in a variety of presentations since the enthusiasm for Vienna around 1900 gathered speed from the 1980s onward. Known as overdoors or supraporte, Josef Hoffmann is regarded as the artist who was responsible for them. These overdoors, as the name suggests, were once mounted above a door structure. In the Secession's famous Beethoven exhibition held in 1902 the overdoors marked the way through to the central tract, to where Max Klinger's (1857–1920) *Beethoven Statue* (ill. p. 21) stood. The central tract could be reached through two side rooms. Klimt had mounted his *Beethoven Frieze* (ill. pp. 20/21) in the one on the left. The overdoors were also part of a passage; they belonged to the diverse accessories and ornaments with which the Secessionists created the charm of the setting within the exhibition. Hoffmann had the overall responsibility for this *Gesamtkunstwerk*.

When the Beethoven exhibition came to an end in June 1902, the magnificent decorations disappeared. All that remains are photographs taken at the time by Moritz Nähr (1859–1945). In his documentation, Nähr's attention captured, above all, the entire exhibition's overwhelming effect. Josef Hoffmann worked in turn with a view of an overall concept described by the term *Raumkunst* – "spatial art". Franz Servaes (1862–1947), the art critic of the *Neue Freie Presse*, characterized this concept in 1900 as follows: "The spatial artist is interested in the artistic incorporation of the separately created works which are scattered across the space with a view to the organic arrangement of all units in a space which is experienced as a united whole and which fulfils the purpose for which it was intended".

Accordingly, the reliefs were "created separately". The material used was listed as carved mortar in the brochure that accompanied the exhibition. They were made of plaster applied to the section of wall above the doors which had been specially hollowed out. But in doing so they served an "organic arrangement". That, in turn, can still be seen if one studies them separately. Their framework of battens emphasizes the vertical; at the same time, the rectangular shape of what was almost a square, with sides nearly one metre long, introduces a centralizing counter-tendency. This surrounding square can be found again precisely in the middle; a miniature version occupies the central vertical, which occurs because one can look through to the base of the relief. This central vertical is the axis of symmetry since some of the battens are so positioned that they mirror each other. Beside them, plates swirl around in a colourful array, but here too a sort of link, a hint of repetition can also be detected. Symmetry, relationship, pattern and base: Hoffmann tried to spell out what we might call a language of ornamentation – a language of decoration, overall coherence, cohesion.

Since the 1980s, the overdoors have been seen as individual items. They hang separately on walls as if they are no more than reliefs. And they are presented as if they are purely abstract. They are treated as prime examples of autonomous art. Among all the starting points that occurred in Vienna, they should also be counted among the beginnings of Modernism – and immediately after 1900 at that. This, however, would be too much of a good thing. And in any case, the overdoors, as they are displayed today, are only replicas. RM

Side room of the Beethoven exhibition with ***Overdoor***, 1902
Plaster relief

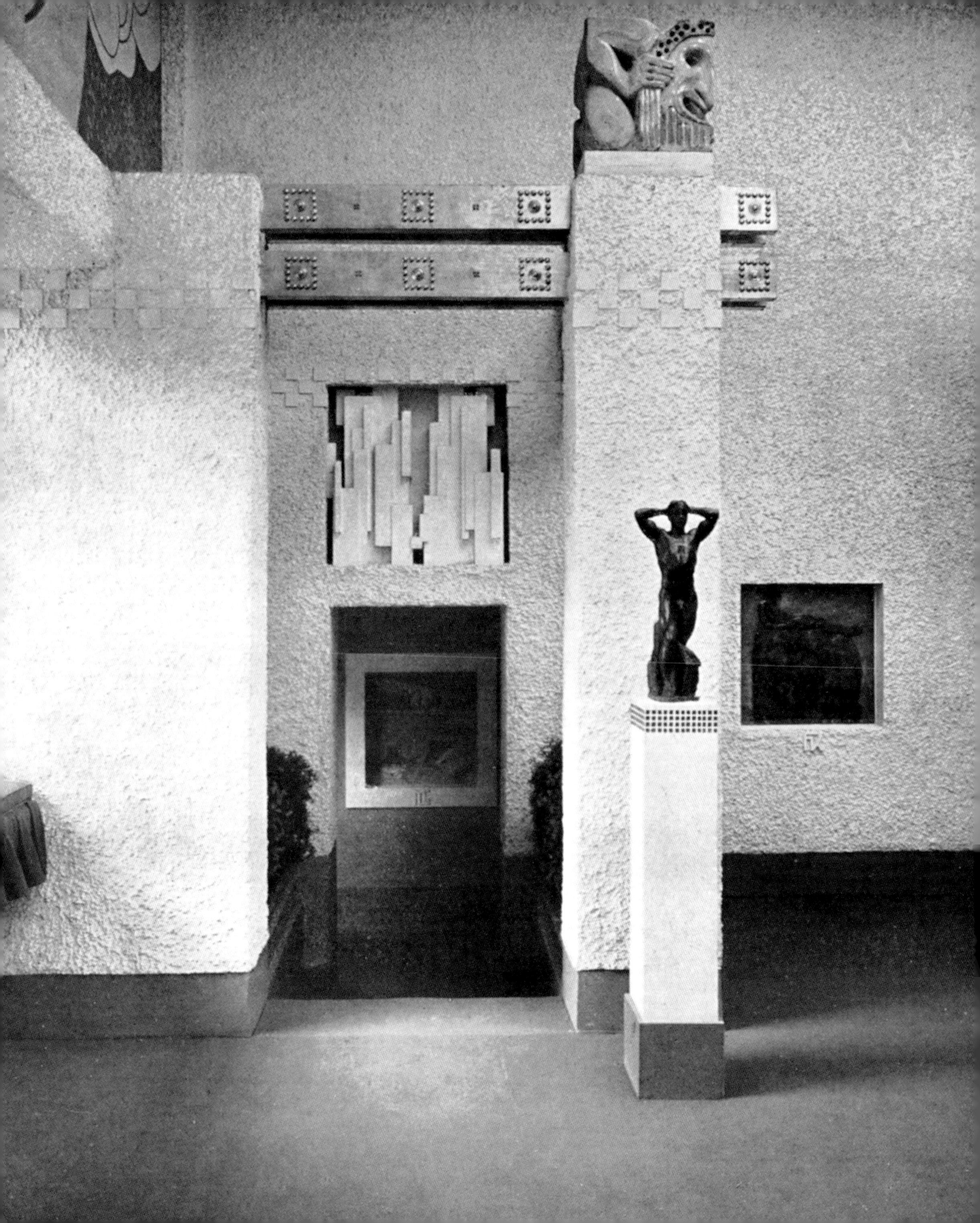

Jože Plečnik
Zacherlhaus, 1903–1905

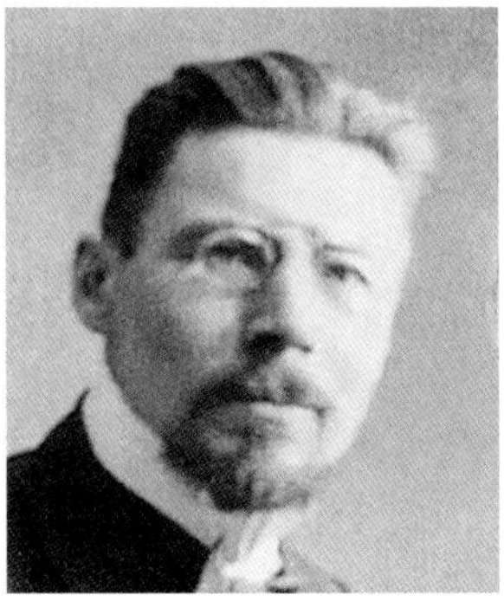

b. 1872 in Ljubljana
d. 1957 in Ljubljana

A narrow, irregularly shaped plot of land facing the street on three sides, 180 metres away from Saint Stephen's Cathedral in Vienna: not an easy task for an architect, especially if the brief was to create an impressive office building. The client Johann Evangelist Zacherl (1857–1936) was the son of the founder of a dynasty that had achieved prosperity with the manufacture of an insecticide. The architect Jože Plečnik accepted the challenge and created a building, in the Zacherlhaus, that was tailor-made for the plot. Born in Slovenia, Plečnik was one of Otto Wagner's most talented students, and the house at the heart of Vienna's 1st district became the synthesis of Wagner's principles, combined with Plečnik's own interpretation of façade, ornamentation and space.

Built on a grid of reinforced concrete beams, it is a building that does not deny the technology of its time. The façade, which runs around three street fronts, demonstrates – like the work of Otto Wagner in general – the influential *Bekleidungstheorie* which the architect Gottfried Semper had formulated half a century earlier. It states that the exterior shell and supporting structure of a building are fundamentally different. In Semper's view the former is like fabric which envelops the latter. The Zacherlhaus is a perfect example of the theory's application. The upper storeys are clad with grey granite panels which are fixed using vertical battens of the same material. Plečnik wraps this fabric, which appears light and heavy at the same time, around both corners like wallpaper. The more prominent one, which points towards the cathedral, is rounded and the other has a sharp edge. The windows are partly and gently curved outwards and are inserted accurately into this membrane. The precisely composed rhythm is contrasted and complemented by the almost black, three-dimensional Expressionist cornice at the upper end, which seems to consist of superimposed panels of slate. It is held by a row of powerful Atlases after the design of the sculptor Franz Metzner (1870–1919). Bright and dark, light and heavy, horizontal and vertical, static and dynamic thus form a precisely balanced equilibrium.

On the long side a bronze sculpture of the Archangel Michael has been positioned in front of the façade. It was created by the sculptor Ferdinand Andri in homage to Michael Zacherl, the client's son. Inside the building, precisely positioned sculptures also set a dramatic accent. The long, relatively narrow entrance on the narrow side is clad in dark marble and leads like a tunnel to the oval stairwell in the middle, whose banisters are surmounted by slender candelabras which evoke insects and hence, business success. For Plečnik the building was a promise of things to come. Further buildings in Vienna would follow, including the Heilig-Geist-Kirche in Ottakring, built between 1911 and 1913. Plečnik's masterly treatment of historical, formal vocabulary led to him being awarded the long-term commission to carry out the restoration of Prague Castle in the 1920s, before he returned to Ljubljana and created his impressive and diverse late works. The Zacherlhaus in Vienna is still in the possession of the owning family. It is one of the few buildings that have remained virtually unchanged. MN

PAGE 51
Stairwell of the ***Zacherlhaus***
Photograph by Keiichi Tahara

Zacherlhaus, 1903–05
Photograph from 1906

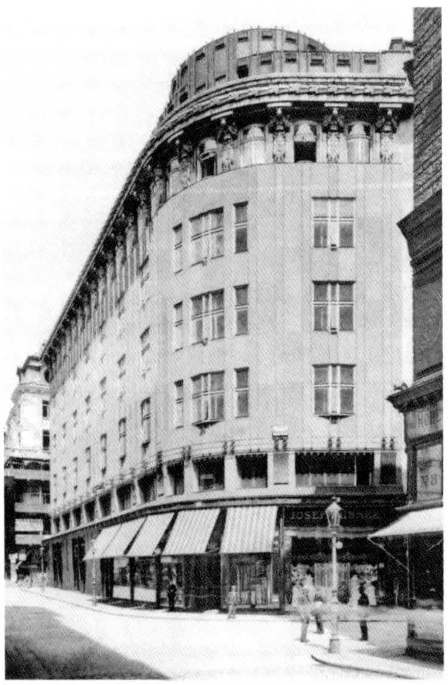

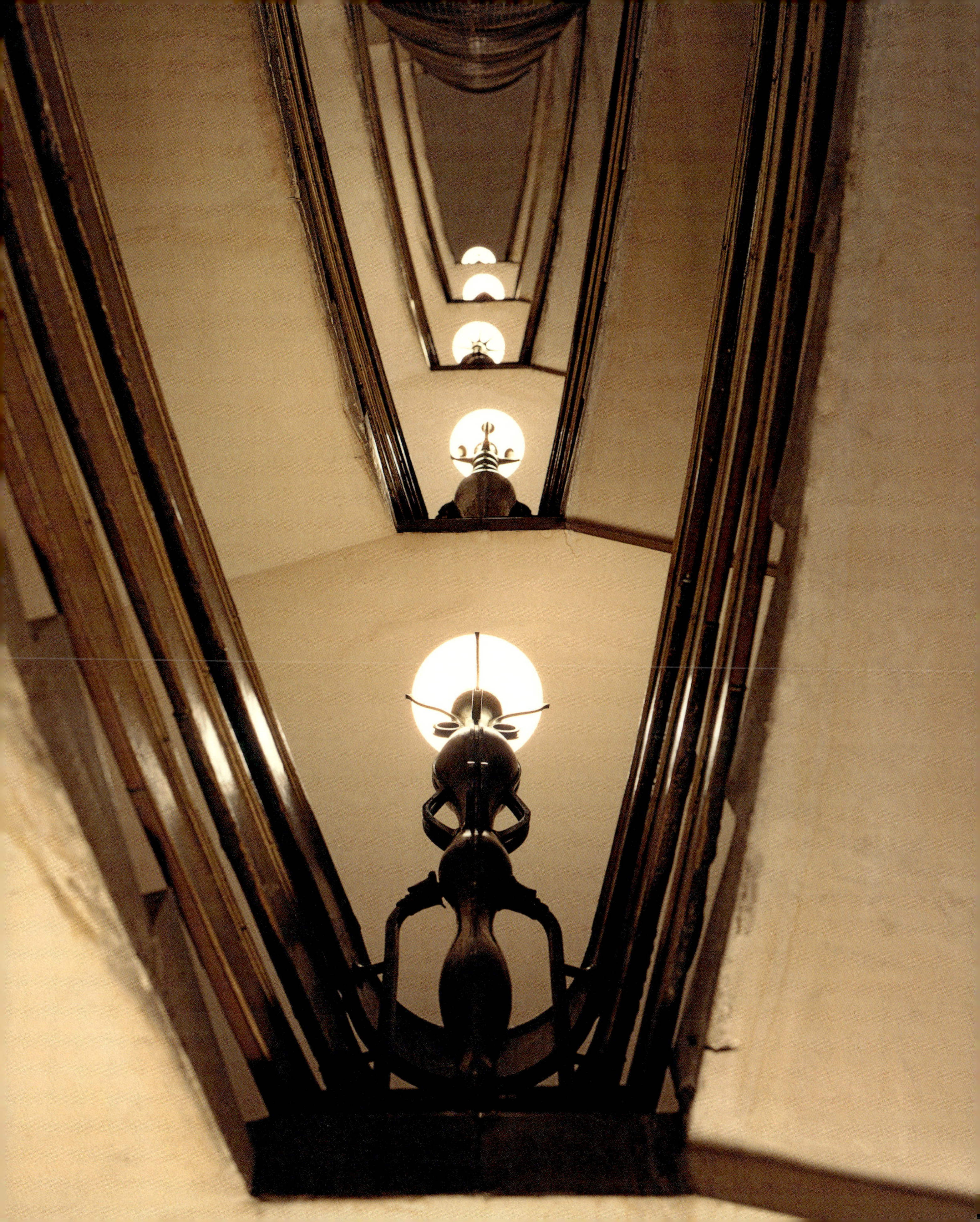

Koloman Moser
Armchair, 1903

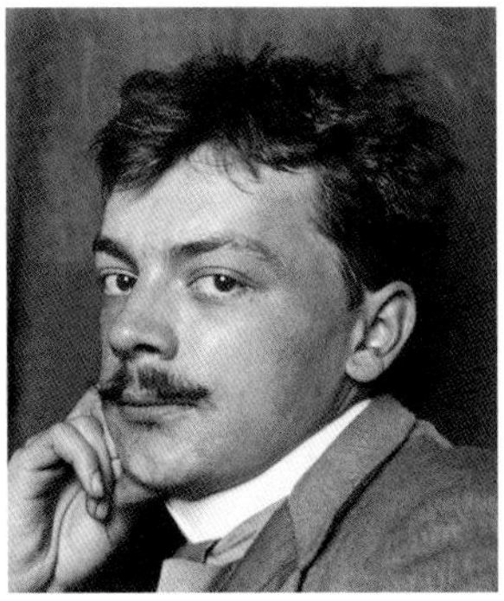

b. 1868 in Vienna
d. 1918 in Vienna

No other building in the Vienna of around 1900 is more representative of the rise and fall of the Jewish haute bourgeoisie and its receptive attitude towards Modernism than the sanatorium in Purkersdorf. In 1903, Victor Zuckerkandl (1851–1927), the Managing Director of the Silesian Ironworks in Gleiwitz (today Gliwice, Poland), acquired an extensive plot of land on the western edge of the city with the aim of building an institute for hydrotherapy, complete with spa gardens. His sister-in-law Berta Zuckerkandl (1864–1945) recommended Josef Hoffmann as the architect. The latter had just established the Wiener Werkstätte, together with the industrialist Fritz Waerndorfer (1868–1939) and Koloman Moser. In 1904, the sanatorium was the first major order for the production facility; it was to become something like the specialist for the *Gesamtkunstwerk*.

Construction work proceeded until 1906 on the elegant retreat in Purkersdorf. Its library, dining rooms, salons, and games and writing room were completely furnished by Hoffmann and Moser. Reinforced concrete was eminently suitable as a new building material for the geometric forms which Hoffmann favoured. The square was applied consistently as a leitmotif. The Wiener Werkstätte and their partner firms, including the bentwood furniture manufacturer Jacob & Josef Kohn and the wicker furniture specialist Prag-Rudniker, produced the entire interior furnishings. In the entrance hall a design by Kolo Moser was used which he had presented in 1903 within the framework of the first Klimt exhibition in the Secession: a rigorously geometric, cube-shaped armchair with a seat with a chessboard pattern.

The sanatorium was more of a luxury hotel than a therapeutic institution. It became the meeting place of Viennese society surrounding Berta Zuckerkandl: the guests included Arthur Schnitzler, Alma and Gustav Mahler, Egon Friedell, Arnold Schönberg and Hugo von Hofmannsthal. After the death of Victor Zuckerkandl in 1927, the sanatorium was taken over by his relatives, but the world economic crisis took its toll and the establishment had difficulty staying afloat. In March 1938, Adolf Hitler invaded Austria. A few days after the *Anschluss*, the sanatorium was placed under temporary administration and those of the Zuckerkandls who were able to do so fled the country. In August 1939, the sanatorium underwent Aryanization. Towards the end of the Second World War the building served as a military hospital; after liberation in the spring of 1945 it was requisitioned by the Red Army. In 1952, the plundered ruin was returned to the Zuckerkandls. They sold the property to the Protestant Church, which converted the sanatorium into a hospital. It was closed down in 1975 and the buildings and park went into decline.

But some of the furnishings survived the confusion. During the late 1960s, John Sailer (b. 1937), who was to become one of the most important gallerists in Vienna, rang in the renaissance of Thonet furnishings. He consequently became interested in the armchairs in the sanatorium: after he gave the porter a tip, the latter took him up to the attic, where the dilapidated furniture was being stored. This included a large number of the bentwood chairs which Hoffmann had designed for the dining room; they later fetched absurdly high prices on the art market. Art dealers also did excellent business with Koloman Moser's geometric armchair. In 2000, an original specimen was auctioned at Christie's in London for £388,750 (the equivalent of approximately €650,000 at the time). Only ten of these chairs had originally been manufactured. TT

Armchair, 1903
Painted beech frame with wickerwork seat, 72.5 x 65.8 x 66.5 cm (28½ x 26 x 26¼ in.)
Vienna, Leopold Museum

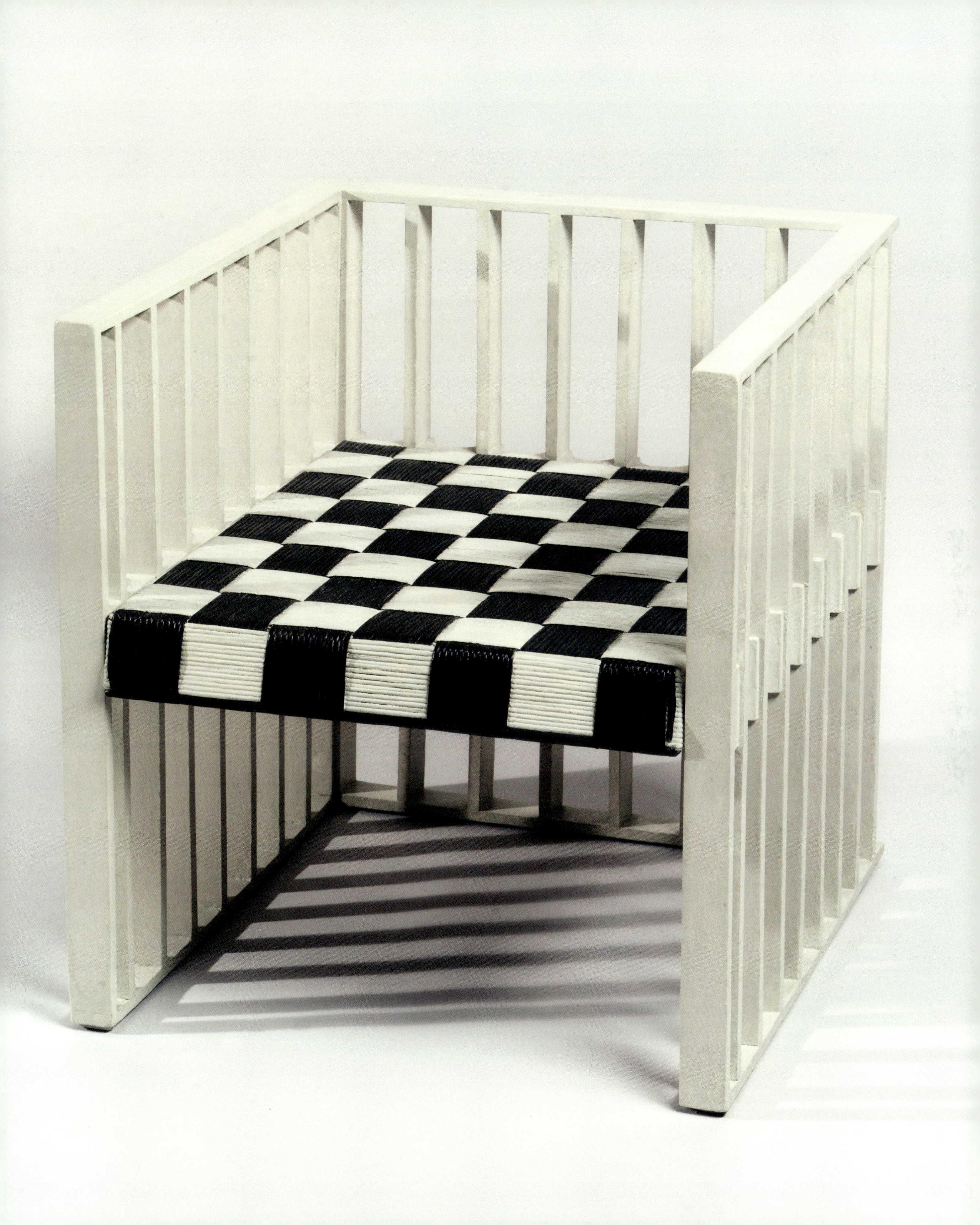

Otto Wagner

Postal Savings Bank, 1904–1906

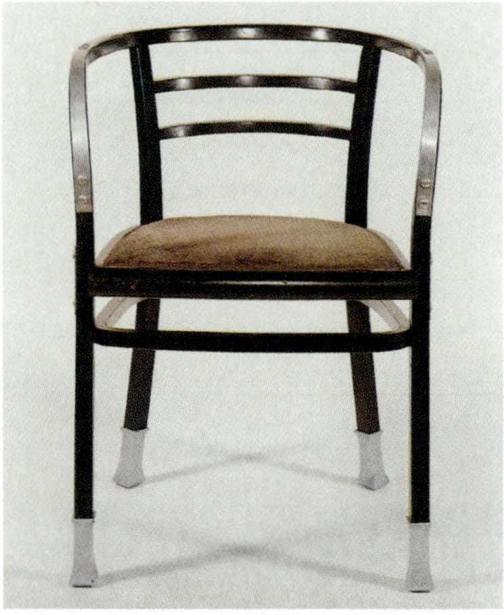

Otto Wagner
Armchair for the boardroom of the Postal Savings Bank, 1905/06
Bent solid beech and laminated wood frame with upholstered seat, aluminium fittings

Otto Wagner believed that "something impractical can never be beautiful". He considered it absurd to live modern life in rooms that were decorated in styles that imitated the past. Wagner regarded building and engineering as being one and the same thing. The beauty of practicality was implemented down to the last detail in the Postsparkassenamt (Postal Savings Bank) on the Ringstrasse. The competition for the Imperial and Royal Postal Savings Bank building had been announced in February 1903. The site was one of the last undeveloped plots on Ringstrasse (ill. p. 9) after the demolition of the Franz Joseph Barracks.

Wagner's winning design for the trapezoidal plot was strictly symmetrical. But that was the full extent of his references to classical typologies. The Postal Savings Bank is a thoroughly modern building. The façade is clad with square marble panels which are fixed using 17,000 metal bolts covered with aluminium, a new construction material at the time. This proved a practical solution in which the precisely positioned round bolts simultaneously structured the front facing the street. The function became an ornament: The role of the façade as a non-load-bearing cladding would recur throughout Wagner's entire later work.

The nucleus of the building is the banking hall, which lies exactly on the axis of symmetry. Compared with the solid appearance of the exterior, the hall, which is entirely covered with a glass roof, seems deliberately light and emphatically delicate. The use of the space, a place of encounter for customers and staff, was to be as pleasant as possible. Wagner fitted the hall with a floor of glass bricks that also allowed light to filter through to the rooms below. Here, too, he combined technology with aesthetics. Each detail is designed to make for easy use and to permit handling, cleaning and later repairs. The slender ventilation pipes are made of aluminium and located in front of the side walls; they look like sculptures and yet their technical function is still clearly recognizable.

The Postal Savings Bank was a high-tech building by the standards of the time, and Wagner made it into a *Gesamtkunstwerk* that left nothing to chance. Each detail has been perfected: the lifts, wall cladding, radiators, carpets, desks, seating and even safes were all designed by Wagner. The obviously sturdy permanence of the materials was due not only to Wagner's striving for the best possible craftsmanship; it was also intended to serve as an intentional signal to customers of the reliability of the bank. The uniform façade and its "armour" of stone panels can thus be interpreted as a visual symbol of a treasure chest for securely preserved values. Wagner's *Gesamtkunstwerk* thus involves not only the construction, façade, domestic engineering, furniture and accessories, but also the corporate identity of the public client.

The building, which occupies an entire block, was built in two phases, but was planned in detail by Wagner from the outset so that in the second phase, built between 1910 and 1912, no changes worth mentioning were necessary. Only a joint indicates the seam between the two parts. An equally telling example of the unity of aesthetics, usefulness and permanence is Wagner's church for the hospital am Steinhof – also his design and erected at the same time. MN

Postal Savings Bank, 1904–1906
View of the banking hall
Photograph by Keiichi Tahara

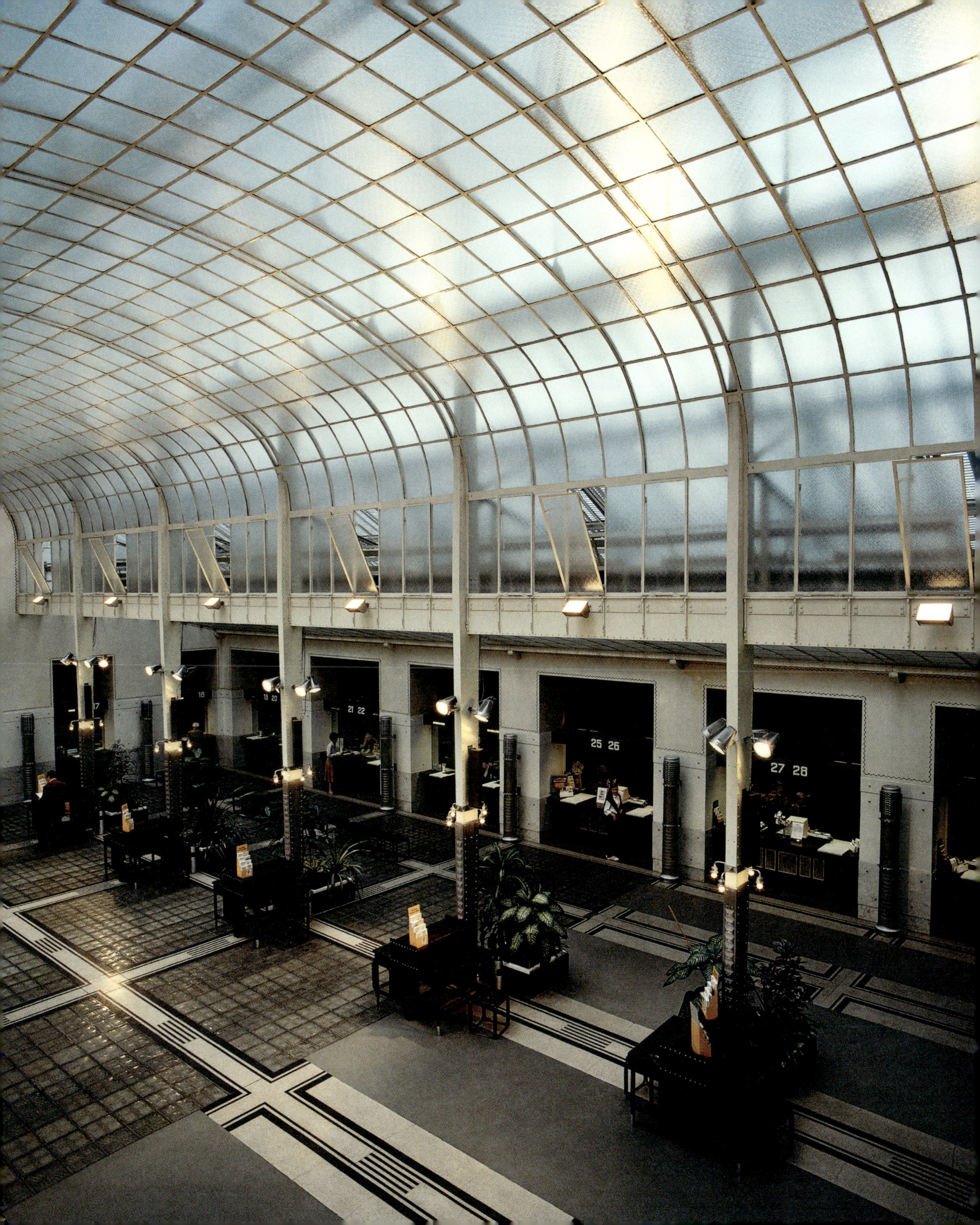
21 22
25 26
27 28

Josef Hoffmann

Palais Stoclet, Brussels, 1905–1911

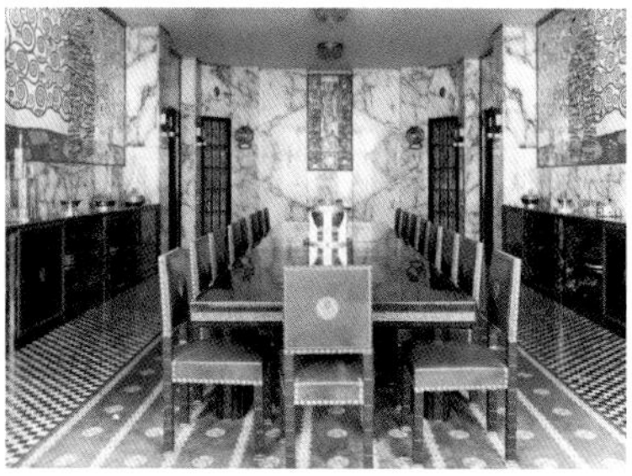

Dining room of the ***Palais Stoclet***

On the last pages of their *Arbeitsprogramm der Wiener Werkstätte*, published in 1905 as a brochure, the chair of the production cooperative summarized the entire range of services. He emphasized that they would also take over the "furnishing and building of entire houses". The board consisted of the two professors Josef Hoffmann and Koloman Moser and the industrialist, collector and patron of the arts Fritz Waerndorfer. The latter had been one of the initiators behind the founding of the Wiener Werkstätte after he had worked together with the talented duo on his own home in what had been a successful cooperation for all those involved.

They had already carried out prominent semi-public commissions when they furnished the salon of the Flöge sisters as well as the Purkersdorf Sanatorium. And they also had various ideas for flats. But what followed would put all past contracts in the shadows and would exceed all subsequent projects: the Palais Stoclet, designed in Vienna and realized in Brussels, would not only become the epitome of a Viennese *Gesamtkunstwerk*; it has also survived in its original form to this day.

Family and business affairs had made it necessary for the villa for Adolphe Stoclet (1871–1949) and his wife Suzanne (1874–1960), which had been planned for a site on the Hohe Warte in Vienna, to be built in Brussels instead, complete with its entire artistic interior design. Berta Zuckerkandl, who was always one of the first to be well informed in matters of this nature, immediately reported that the Wiener Werkstätte was to be expanded. In fact, eventually over a dozen artists were involved in the furnishing of the prestigious property. Gustav Klimt was one of those nominated; at the special request of the client he was to take over the artistic design of the dining room. He soon had a concrete idea which was nonetheless untypical of him. "Klimt has plans for a major work using silver- and gold-plated metal, enamel and semi-precious stones – in short, real materials instead of smearing oil paint", Waerndorfer explained to Stoclet.

Hoffmann may have been the architect and artistic mastermind behind the project, but Waerndorfer acted as the enthusiastic impresario. He liaised between the indecisive Klimt, who was often dissatisfied with the material samples, and a variety of craftsmen; he acted as the coordinator and drove the project forward. He corresponded with the client by post, reported on the progress of the project, issued demands for payment and chatted with Stoclet from one collector to another. And when finally Leopold Forstner (1878–1936) fitted the pieces of mosaic, the enamel tiles and the chased metal, ceramic, glass and mother-of-pearl pieces into the pre-cut marble panels, Waerndorfer jokingly observed, "I can only tell you honestly: you don't deserve the picture".

Later he was allotted the difficult task of explaining to Klimt that Stoclet wanted improvements to the face of the *Dancer* in his artwork. The master was only prepared to make the changes when the financier held back the final instalment. After that, everyone was satisfied. The vast total cost of the Palais Stoclet has never been made public, but the frieze alone, as Waerndorfer informed Stoclet, was priced at 117,000 crowns, of which 60,000 were for the fees of Klimt and Forstner. The frieze's *Expectation* crescendoes across nine marble panels via the vigilant *Knight* to reach *Fulfilment* – and remains Klimt's only mosaic. DG

Palais Stoclet, Brussels, 1905–1911
View of garden façade
Gelatin silver print, 1910

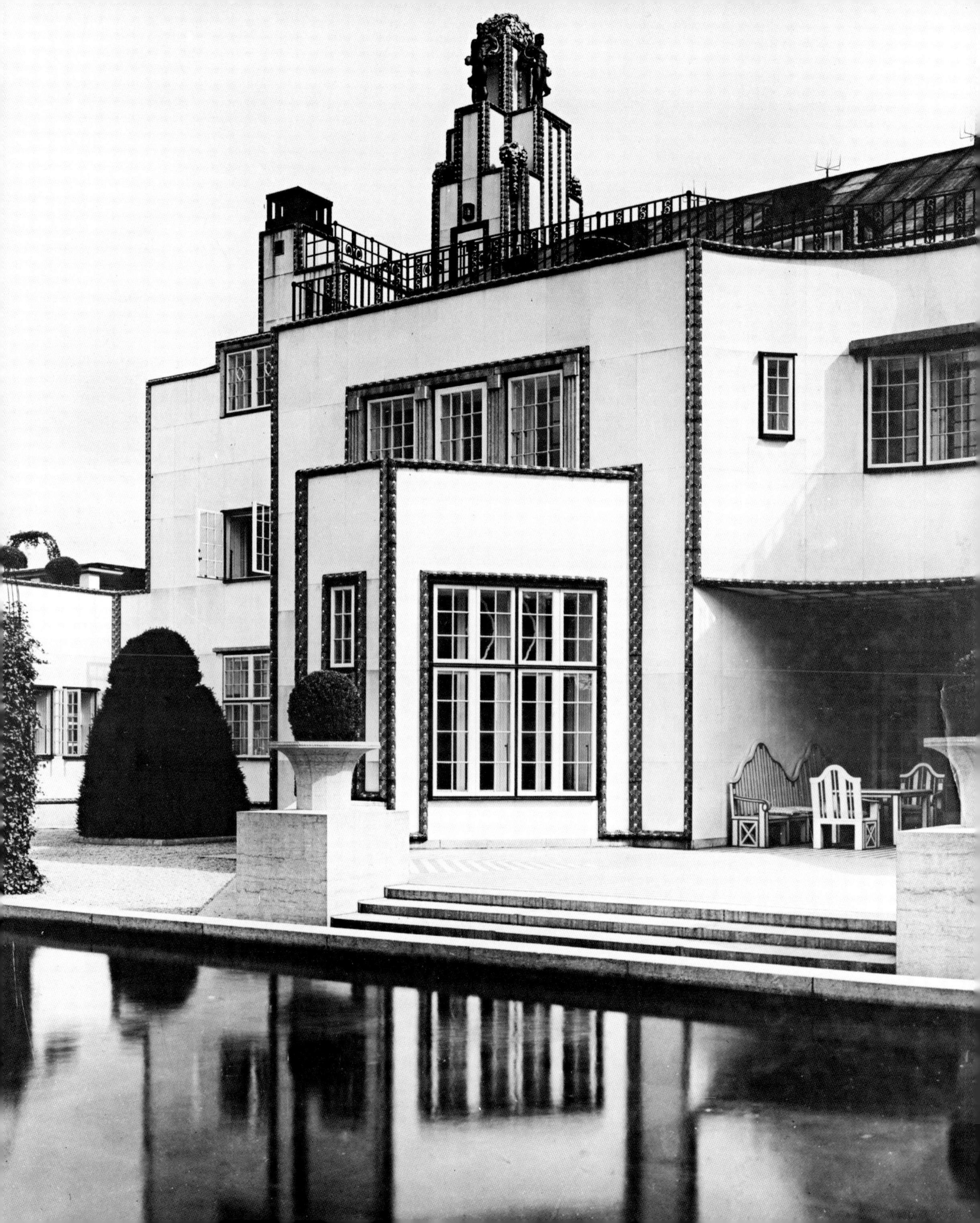

Moriz Jung
Nocturnal Conversation, 1907

b. 1885 in Mikulov
d. 1915 in Lubné

As we know, there are numerous ways of communicating – Moriz Jung invented some remarkable constellations for his series of postcards. On one of them the statesman is speaking to the editor at what appears to be epic length; on another, rivals resort to fisticuffs and communicate non-verbally. There is a vast empty space to be bridged by telephone. And between the interior of the coffee house and the street, gesticulating through the window is the only option. Unlike his many colleagues, whose sketches were often very static, stylized and caught up by the two-dimensional nature of the art, Moriz Jung shows himself to be witty and loquacious in his graphic works. As part of the more than 1,000 motifs that compose the Wiener Werkstätte postcards, he designed several, mostly six-part series. He also created cards with cartoon-like picture sequences which were published as larger-scale pictorial broadsheets. Each of the cards stands alone, although it is only when they are seen as a group that the ludicrous juxtaposition of situations is shown to be charming and even comic.

The fifth, and, in this case, exceptionally, final card in this series shows a *Nocturnal Conversation* on a street corner. With his collar turned up and his hat pulled down low over his face, the smoking man, whose black, two-dimensional silhouette contrasts with the white wall, is clearly going to some lengths to remain unrecognized. The feather on the lady's hat rises jauntily towards the man, followed by the tip of her nose, while further down, a small corner of her otherwise undefined cloak overlaps the dividing line of the edge of the house. Her appearance is concentrated entirely on the pale face as well as the headgear and the fur muff into which her hands have disappeared. It is not clear which of the two started the conversation, but where it is leading is beyond any doubt.

Who would not think of Josefine Mutzenbacher (1852–1904) in such scenes? She was virtually the very epitome of venal love in turn-of-the-century Vienna. In the fictional novel *The Life Story of a Viennese Whore, as Told by Herself* the protagonist tells with relish of her sexual development, which began at the age of five and ended at fourteen when she embarked on a paid professional career. Thereafter Pepi pursued her activities in the city centre. Ladies whose origins did not lie in fiction were able to earn almost as much as a privy councillor as "Graben nymphs".

Sex education, we learn from *Josefine Mutzenbacher*, took place unavoidably within the crowded living space of the proletariat. In the case of the sons of the *haute bourgeoisie* the tasks of this nature were undertaken by the chambermaid or other household staff, and the aristocracy had recourse to so-called *initiatrices*, who were usually actresses. Only the daughters from good families went into a marriage – which was seldom happy – as virgins and without "enlightenment".

People thought Felix Salten (1869–1945) was the author behind *Josefine Mutzenbacher*, which was published anonymously in 1906. Arthur Schnitzler (1862–1936), on the other hand, faced up to the scandal caused on all levels of society by his amorous, merry-go-round play *Reigen (La Ronde*; ill. p. 58), written in 1896/97 but first published privately in 1900, and premiered in Berlin in 1920. Thirty years later, Egon Friedell summarized it accurately as follows: while the theory was still in the process of being developed, Schnitzler "dramatized psychoanalysis". DG

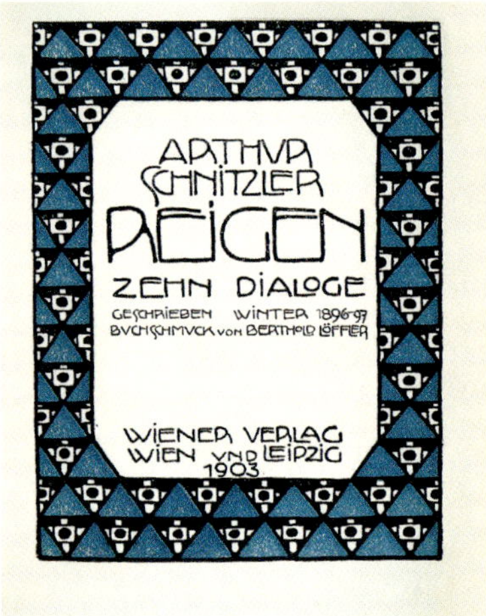

Bertold Löffler
Cover of the first edition of
Arthur Schnitzler's ***Reigen***, 1903
Wiener Verlag, Vienna/Leipzig

Nocturnal Conversation, 1907
Colour lithograph
Wiener Werkstätte postcard no. 66

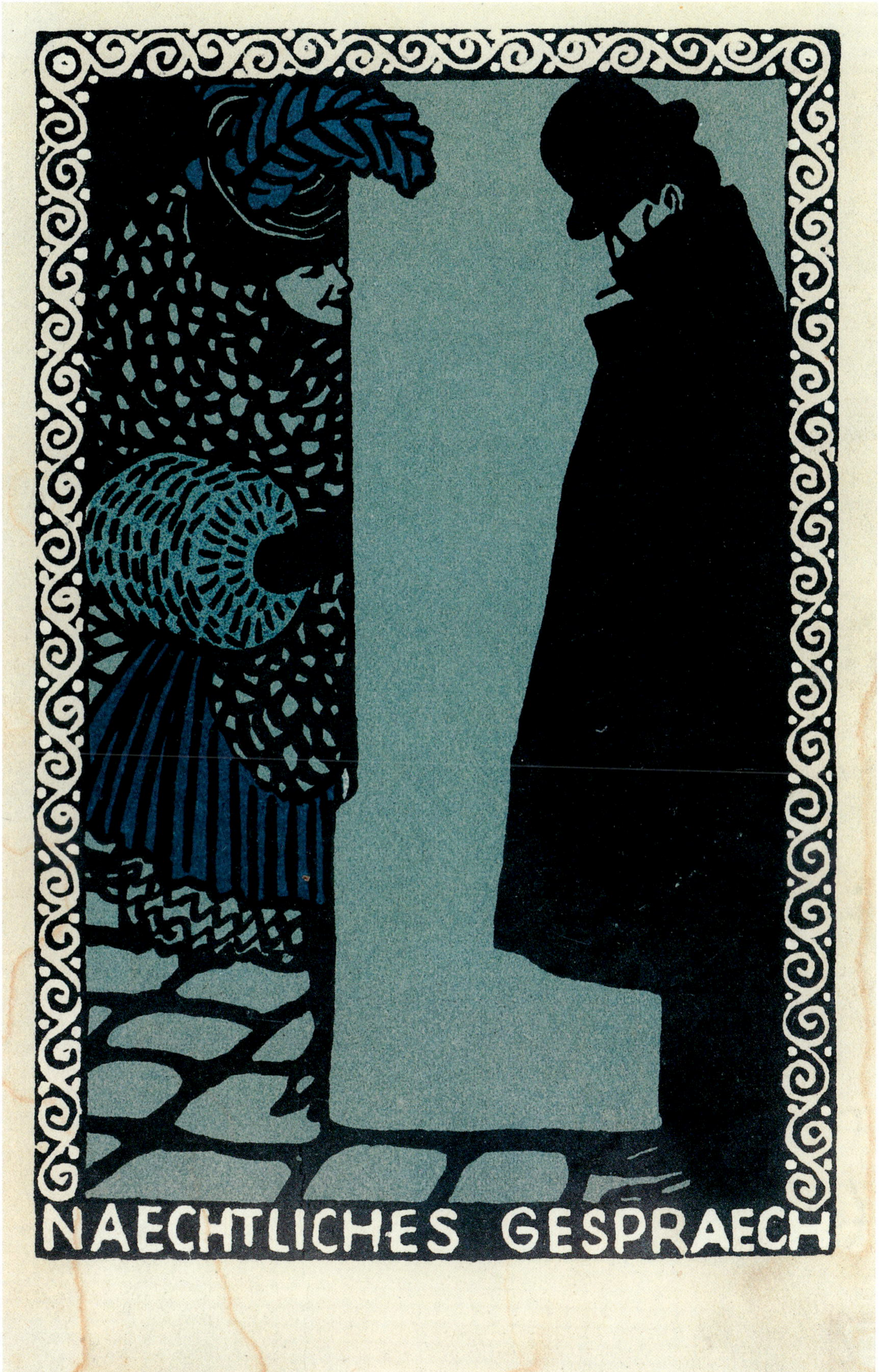
NAECHTLICHES GESPRAECH

Bertold Löffler

Poster for the Cabaret Fledermaus, 1907

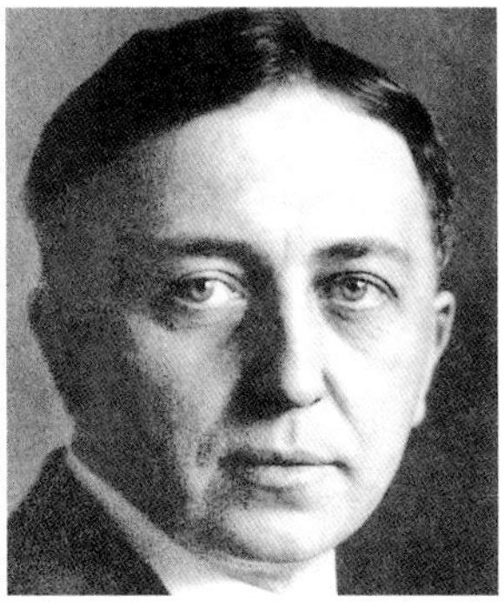

b. 1874 in Liberec
d. 1960 in Vienna

What did it take to produce a successful poster in the period around 1900? The forms had to be drawn clearly, the colours had to contrast each other and be applied to sizeable areas; and under no circumstances was the artist to get carried away by superfluous details. Berthold Löffler's *Poster for the Cabaret Fledermaus* is a classic example of these precepts. The people at the Wiener Werkstätte seem to have been aware of its signature character because the subject was also produced in a smaller format (40 x 30 cm), and as a postcard (no. 71). This was not the only card produced to draw attention to the project. It marked the only occasion in which the Wiener Werkstätte not only executed the commission, but also gave the order. Moriz Jung, for example, portrayed no fewer than a dozen quirky varieté numbers in his grandiose, graphic narrative style, and three cards (nos. 67, 74, 75). They give us insight finally into the interior of the *Gesamtkunstwerk* Josef Hoffmann had taken over for the master plan. It is otherwise documented by only a handful of photographs that have not survived.

The premises of the Cabaret Fledermaus were located in the basement and could be reached via the bar and cloakroom (ill. p. 60), the walls of which were covered up to head height with about 7,000 varied majolica tiles by Löffler and Michael Powolny (1871–1954). The colourful conglomeration of the entrance area contrasted with an elegant space for the audience. Apart from the delicate blue elements in the carpet pattern on the floor, everything was designed in contrasting black and white. Hoffmann cooperated with the company of Jacob & Josef Kohn for seating within this setting and made use of a construction principle he had already employed for Speisezimmermodell 322 (Dining room model 322) at the Purkersdorf Sanatorium and the legendary *Sitzmaschine (Modell 670)* (Seating machine model 670). The joints of the furniture were stabilized with balls screwed into the corners, which rendered the supporting elements that had previously been used obsolete. The balls were in contrasting colours and fitted in playfully into the concept of the Cabaret Fledermaus, which henceforth lent its name to an entire series of furnishings.

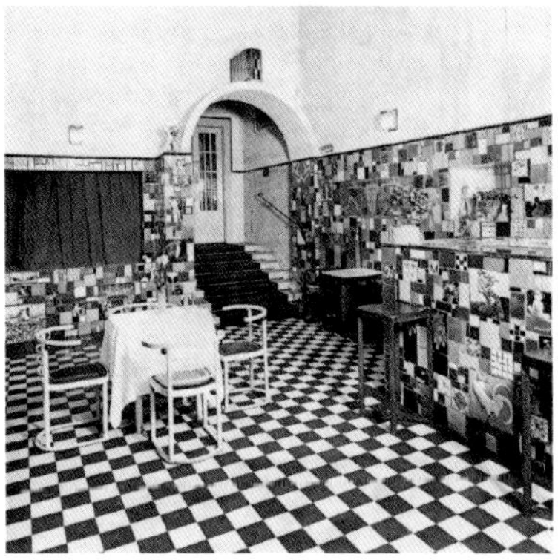

Entrance to the bar of the
Cabaret Fledermaus, 1907
Vienna I., Kärntnerstrasse 33

The programme and programmatics of the Wiener Werkstätte extended to the smallest details. The forms of the silverware recalled the age of Biedermeier and captivated in their simplicity; the cutlery left nothing to be required, even providing tiny forks for the consumption of corn on the cob; the red-leather drinks menu with paper marbling on the interior showed the same logo of the establishment in gold embossing which the usherettes wore on a badge on their lapel. The programmes were artistically designed as were the backdrops, costumes and props. Once again, the demands of the Wiener Werkstätte made them overreach their financial resources, so that after two seasons the project came to a halt.

On the occasion of the 25th anniversary of the Wiener Werkstätte Egon Friedell, who was not only author and actor of the Cabaret Fledermaus from February 1908 but also its artistic director (until May 1909) remembered the establishment as "a delightful combination of intimacy and elegance". Josef Hoffmann, on the other hand, recalled another positive aspect. As he recorded in his unpublished memoirs, in the Cabaret Fledermaus he had been able to realize the idea of the *Gesamtkunstwerk* "undisturbed by pruning on the part of the client". DG

Poster for the Cabaret Fledermaus, 1907
Colour lithograph, 63 x 43.5 cm
(24¾ x 17¼ in.)

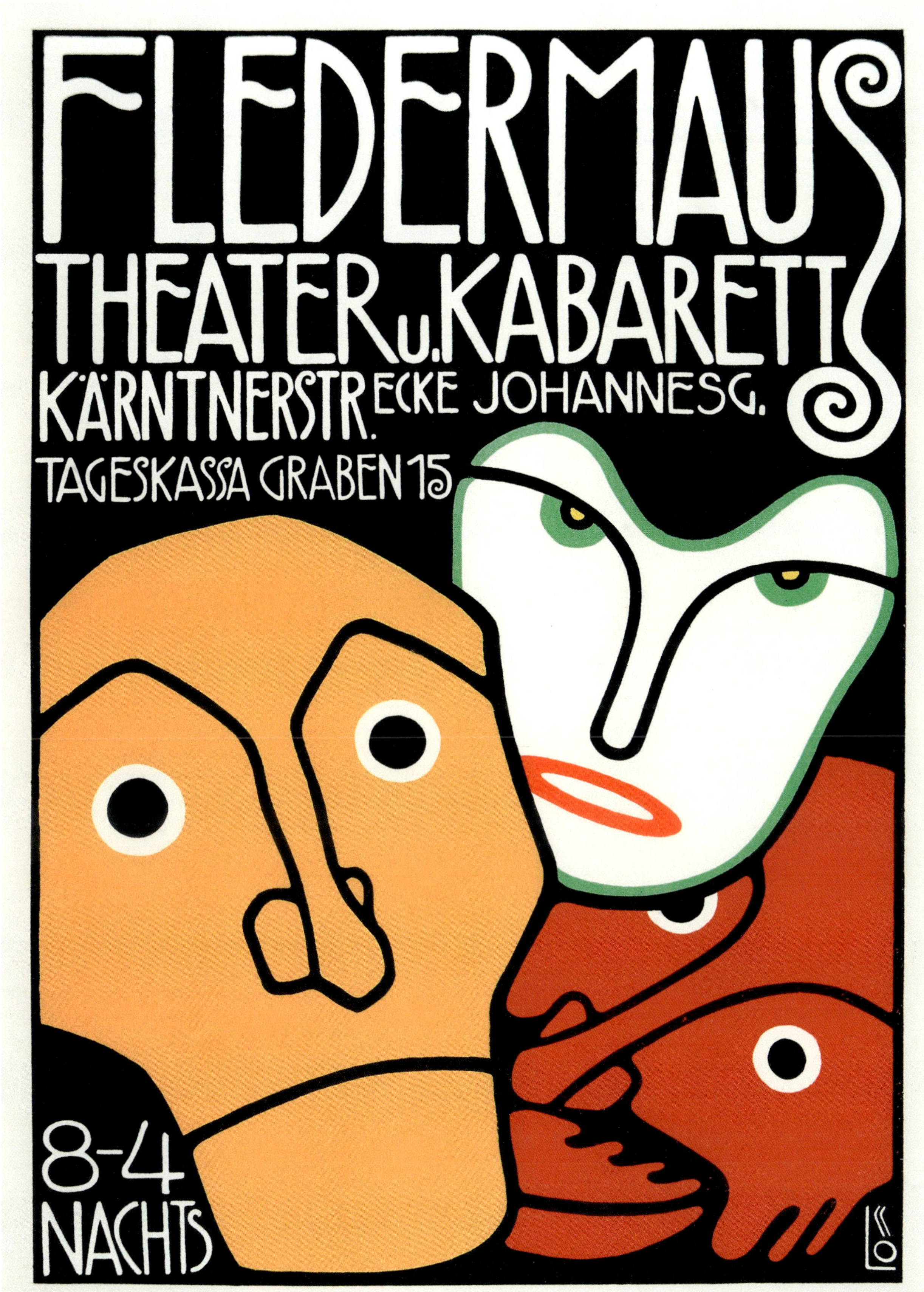
FLEDERMAUS
THEATER u. KABARETT
KÄRNTNERSTR. ECKE JOHANNESG.
TAGESKASSA GRABEN 15
8-4
NACHTS

Carl Otto Czeschka
Wittgenstein Vitrine, 1908

b. 1878 in Vienna
d. 1960 in Hamburg

PAGE 63
Wittgenstein Vitrine (detail), 1908
Silver, moonstone, opal, lapis lazuli, mother-of-pearl, baroque pearls, onyx, ivory, enamel, glass, pine and ebony veneers (replaced),
168.28 x 60.96 x 32.07 cm
(66¼ x 24 x 12½ in.)
Dallas Museum of Art, The Eugene and Margaret McDermott Art Fund, Inc. 2013.31.A

Wittgenstein Vitrine, 1908
Full side view

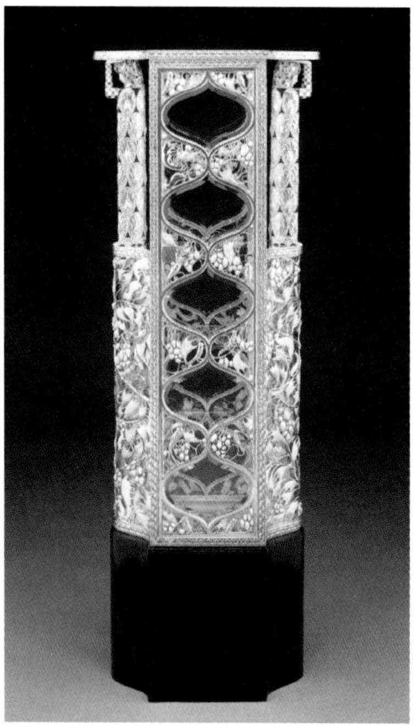

"It is the most important decorative artwork that has been created for the modern age in Vienna", asserted the critic Ludwig Hevesi with regard to this object in his review of the Kunstschau exhibition of 1908. It had also attracted a great deal of attention from his colleagues in the media. "An artwork of the first order", was how Joseph August Lux (1871–1947) described it. Richard Muther (1860–1909) went into raptures over the exhibit, describing the object as such: "In its indescribable elegance, its discrete combination of white, gold, silver and black, [it is] a superb example of good taste". A few lines earlier he had conceded, concerning the price of works of the Wiener Werkstätte, "admittedly, these things are not cheap".

Indeed, not only was the magnificent glass cabinet by Carl Otto Czeschka the central object in the room containing the presentation by the Wiener Werkstätte, but as an individual exhibit we could also certainly describe it as the star of the exhibition. The exquisite silver specimen on a pinewood plinth had taken two and a half years to produce; the model book of the Wiener Werkstätte names nine craftsmen who were involved. The book of samples also reveals that the cabinet was finished on 1 June 1908 – the day the Kunstschau opened – and notes the material costs at 10,855 crowns and the sales price at 25,000 crowns. During the first days of the exhibition Karl Wittgenstein, who was already a friend and supporter of the Wiener Werkstätte, generously purchased the cabinet for the Red Drawing Room of his property in Alleegasse (today's Argentinierstrasse). However, contemporary sources list the purchase price as 30,000 crowns, and 50,000 crowns are mentioned elsewhere. By comparison, the Ministry of Education purchased Klimt's *The Kiss* for 25,000 crowns from the exhibition.

The cabinet can be seen as a statement. Czeschka, who had worked for the Wiener Werkstätte since the autumn of 1905, aimed to counter "squaring", as the design principle of Hoffmann and Moser was mockingly summarized, with a different approach. He reintroduced something of the repertoire of forms derived from nature, and the cabinet is his masterpiece in this respect. Creatures of all kinds – mice, squirrels, weasels and a variety of bird species frolic between the stylized foliage and the fruits of oval-cut semi-precious stones, pearls and mother-of-pearl. Two caryatids standing at the sides support the top. Ivory, ebony and enamel are also used. The individual forms were not cut with a saw but were stamped out of metal and then embossed to produce a softer line. This opulent decorative unit is a masterpiece of craftsmanship, and this is not only because the various materials were perfectly and seamlessly combined.

Czeschka could have filled the gap left by Koloman Moser as the creative counterpart to Josef Hoffmann when Moser left the Wiener Werkstätte. However, by the time the cabinet was presented, its creator had been appointed to a post at the Kunstgewerbeschule (College of Applied Arts) in Hamburg. Wittgenstein's heirs, in turn, shipped the cabinet to the United States and it was only seldomly displayed in exhibitions. It has changed owners at least three times. Since 2014 it has formed part of a museum collection for the first time, in Dallas, Texas, having been purchased for an unknown amount in the millions of dollars. It has been extensively restored and is now on view in its original splendour. DG

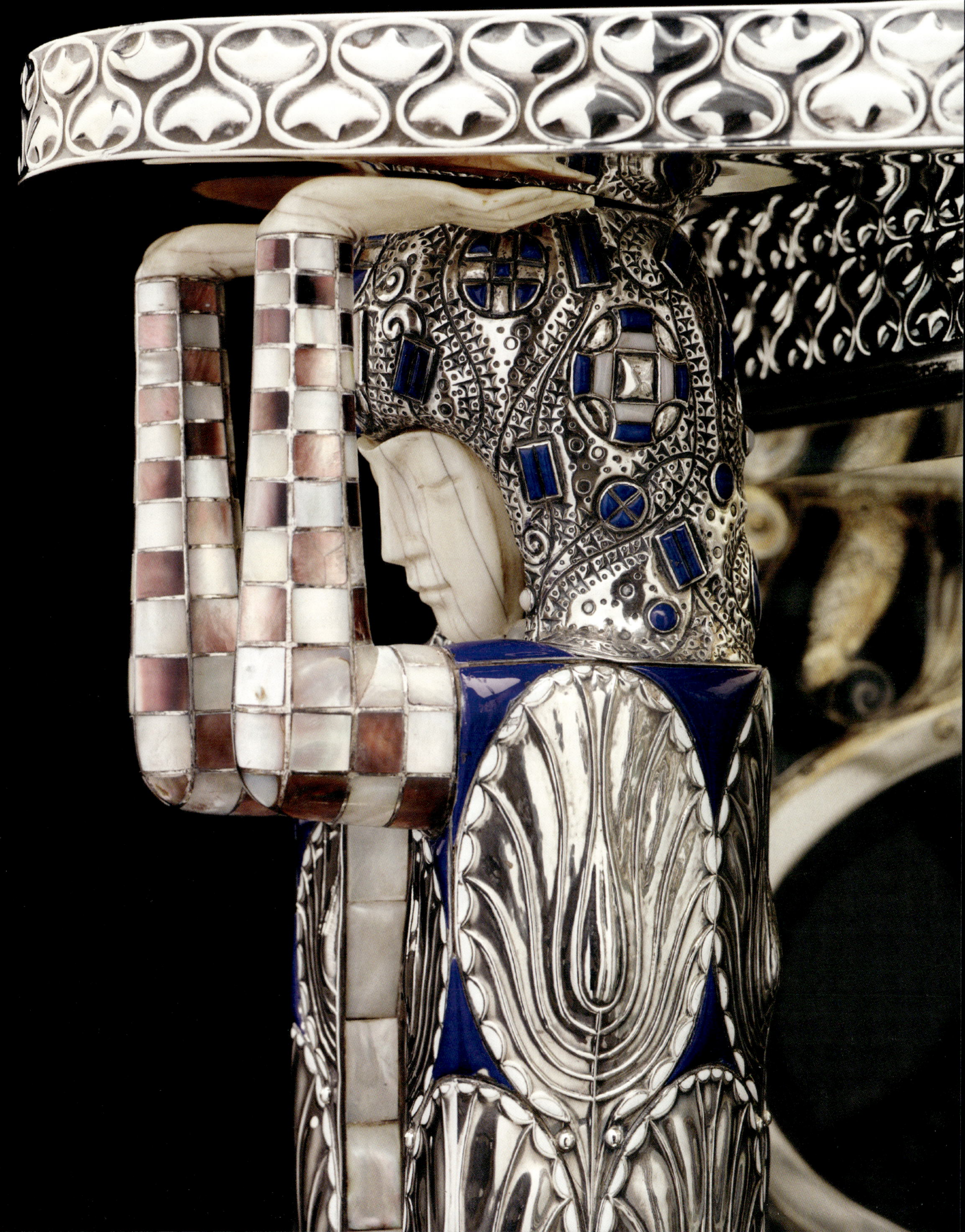

Richard Gerstl

Nude Self-Portrait, 1908

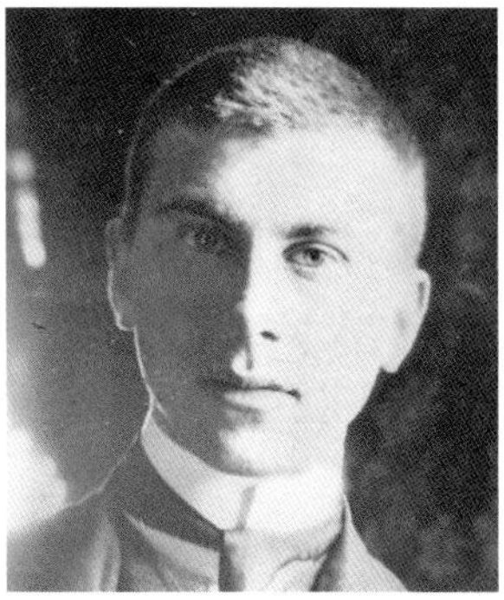

b. 1883 in Vienna
d. 1908 in Vienna

It lies in the nature of things that artists who achieve maturity at an early age should leave the stage at the summit of their creative achievement. Richard Gerstl did so of his own free will before he was able to take his place in the spotlight of public awareness. When he committed suicide at the age of only 25, he left an oeuvre of some 80 authenticated works, of which 60 have survived. None of them was exhibited during his lifetime. On one occasion, when he was offered a cooperation, he refused on the grounds that he did not wish to be represented in an exhibition which would also be showing the works of Gustav Klimt.

In general, this widely read, sensitive young man seems to have shown little enthusiasm for the art academy, where he had been admitted in the first instance to the class of Christian Griepenkerl (1839–1916), and later to that of Heinrich Lefler (1863–1919); nor did he demonstrate any interest in the Viennese art scene. International attitudes and trends were another matter: as a student he focused on Vincent van Gogh (1853–1890), gained inspiration from Edvard Munch (1863–1944), and his elaborate costumes recall at times the outfits of Édouard Manet (1832–1883) and sometimes also spanned the entire width of the canvas. Nonetheless, Gerstl cast a sly glance at the production of the Secessionists. He compared his own work with that of Carl Moll. He tried to counter Klimt's paintings with something that was almost identical conceptually, but that was the exact opposite in terms of brushwork. Only the Viennese master artist he was criticizing would have been incapable of registering the fact.

Gerstl's social contacts were limited to the circle surrounding the composer Arnold Schönberg, whom he had met in 1906. The younger man taught painting to Schönberg and his wife Mathilde, and at their invitation he spent the summer holidays among their circle of musical friends at Traunsee. There, in the open air, he first produced a series of landscape paintings in a very free, open artistic style. In view of the wealth of opulent shades of green, they were referred to, even in those days, as "spinach pictures".

What was portrayed during that summer in lush shades of green was translated during the next year to the artist's environment and its main characters. The terms, however, had changed: the youthful artist had become involved in an affair with the lady of the house. With rapid brushstrokes and strong colours Gerstl painted the Schönberg Family and Madame Schönberg alone as well as her brother, the composer Alexander von Zemlinsky (1871–1942), and the entire group of holidaymakers. Soon, however, the amorous adventure was discovered and the young lover was ejected from the circle of friends. Gerstl's *Nude Self-Portrait* came near the very end, and was completed on 12 September 1908. On 4 November the artist finally destroyed all his letters and documents and took his own life.

His pictures were put into storage. Only in 1931 did Gerstl's brother approach the gallerist Otto Nirenstein (later Kallir, 1894–1978), who took over the works and sent a small monographic exhibition through Germany. Some of the paintings were exhibited after the Second World War at the Venice Biennale in 1956. It was not until 1983, to mark the 100th anniversary of Gerstl's birth, that the Wien Museum staged the first comprehensive exhibition. Nowadays, the modern perception of Vienna around 1900 includes Richard Gerstl more or less as the fourth man, immediately after the eternal triangle of Klimt, Schiele and Kokoschka. DG

Nude Self-Portrait, 1908
Oil on canvas, 139.3 x 100 cm
(55 x 39¼ in.)
Vienna, Leopold Museum

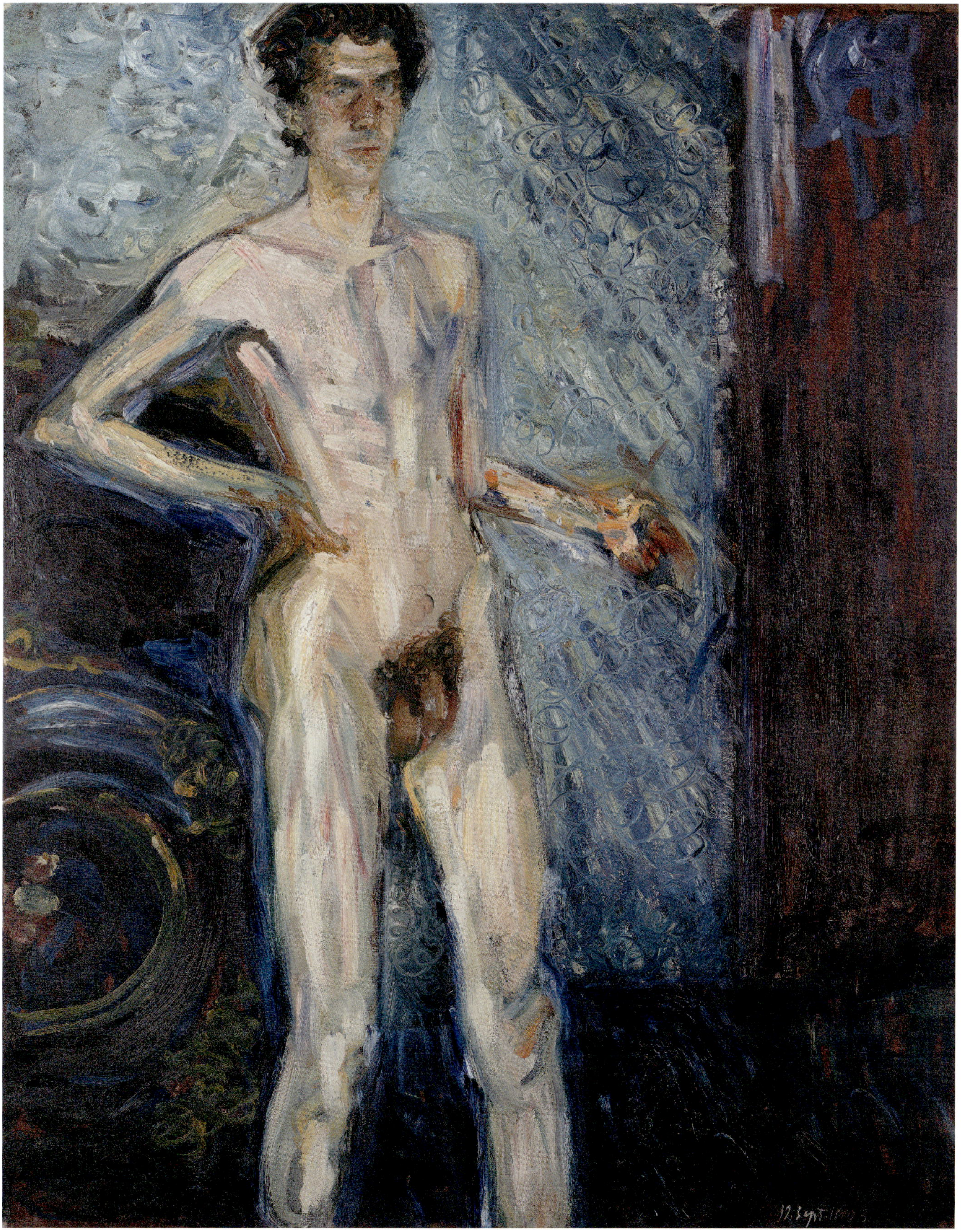

Oskar Kokoschka

Pietà, 1909

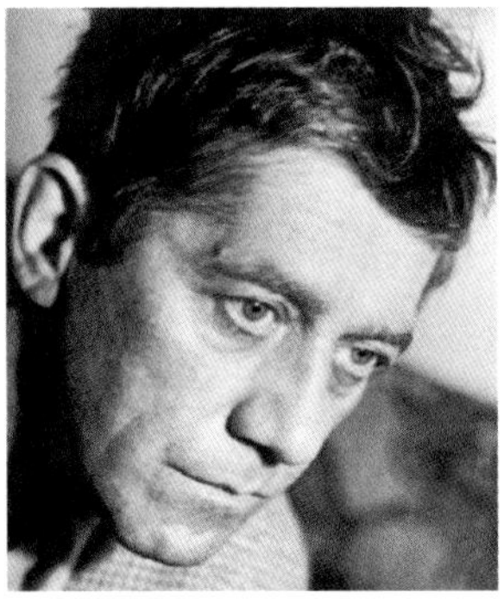

b. 1886 in Pöchlarn
d. 1980 in Montreux

"Children are amoral", declared Adolf Loos, writing in fashionable lower-case letters in his essay from 1908 which became famous for its title alone, *Ornament und Verbrechen* (Ornament and Crime): "and so, for us, are Papuans. If a Papuan slaughters his enemies and eats them, that doesn't make him a criminal. But if a modern man kills someone and eats him, he is either a criminal or a degenerate. The Papuan tattoos his skin, his boat, his oars… He is not a criminal. But a modern man who tattoos himself is either a criminal or a degenerate". It seems that this somewhat simplified worldview which Adolf Loos volunteers inspired Oskar Kokoschka in particular.

For Kokoschka, tattooing becomes a sort of catalytic procedure for special exposure. What can be seen on the surface of the skin is not a signature of ill will. It is the physiology of the body itself. Loos was aware that tattooing has something primitive about it. Kokoschka makes it into an agency of his Primitivism. What is perhaps the most famous picture from Kokoschka's early years in Vienna offers for its part the interweaving of lines and strands. It is the poster that announces a "drama" and a "comedy" to be performed at the Kunstschau of 1909, a rendezvous of the artists surrounding Klimt. Extremely contrasting are the depictions of a woman and a man: he is a mass of raw red flesh and looks as though he has been skinned while she is greyish-white, her neck bearing the tattooing of nerves, muscles and sinews, with a head as bony as a skull.

Opposite numbers are on top of each other: The woman is supporting the man, who has degenerated into a corpse, in front of her breast. A pietà asserts itself, the Christian image formula of Mary, the mother of Christ, grief-stricken as she holds her son Jesus Christ in her lap. And Vienna around 1900 asserts itself in the radical adoption of motifs from Gustav Klimt, namely the *Lovers* from the *Beethoven Frieze* and the sentimental *The Kiss*, the supreme icon of fin-de-siècle enthusiasm. Egon Schiele, four years younger than Kokoschka and not yet in his line of sight at that time, would, in turn, make sense of Klimt's cliché work of 1912, lending it a blasphemous bias and distilling from it the lovers *Cardinal and Nun*.

Then there was also the event for which Kokoschka's lithograph would serve as a poster. On 4 July 1909 at the Cabaret Fledermaus, the drama *Mörder, Hoffnung der Frauen* (Murderer, Hope of Women) had its premiere as part of the Kunstschau – the drama alone, because the comedy entitled *Sphinx und Strohmann* (Sphinx and Stooge) which had also been announced, had already been performed as part of a Kokoschka matinee on 29 March of that year. *Mörder, Hoffnung der Frauen* relied no less on the battle of the sexes and violence: "Who is she who proudly grazes among them like an animal", asks the protagonist, simply described as "Man", in the Old-Testament jargon of the Song of Songs. And they chant: "You men, burn my sign into her flesh with a hot iron". Here the Expressionist predilection for the elevated and the hysterical, for the declamatory and for becoming involved in the circumstances, comes very much into its own. Ludwig Hevesi (1843–1910), the critic and loyal accompanist of the Secession, is said to have coined his description of Kokoschka as the "head savage" on the occasion of the premiere of the work. Kokoschka would go on to live up to it. RM

Pietà, 1909
Poster for the Kunstschau
Colour lithograph, 118.1 x 76.2 cm
(46½ x 30 in.)

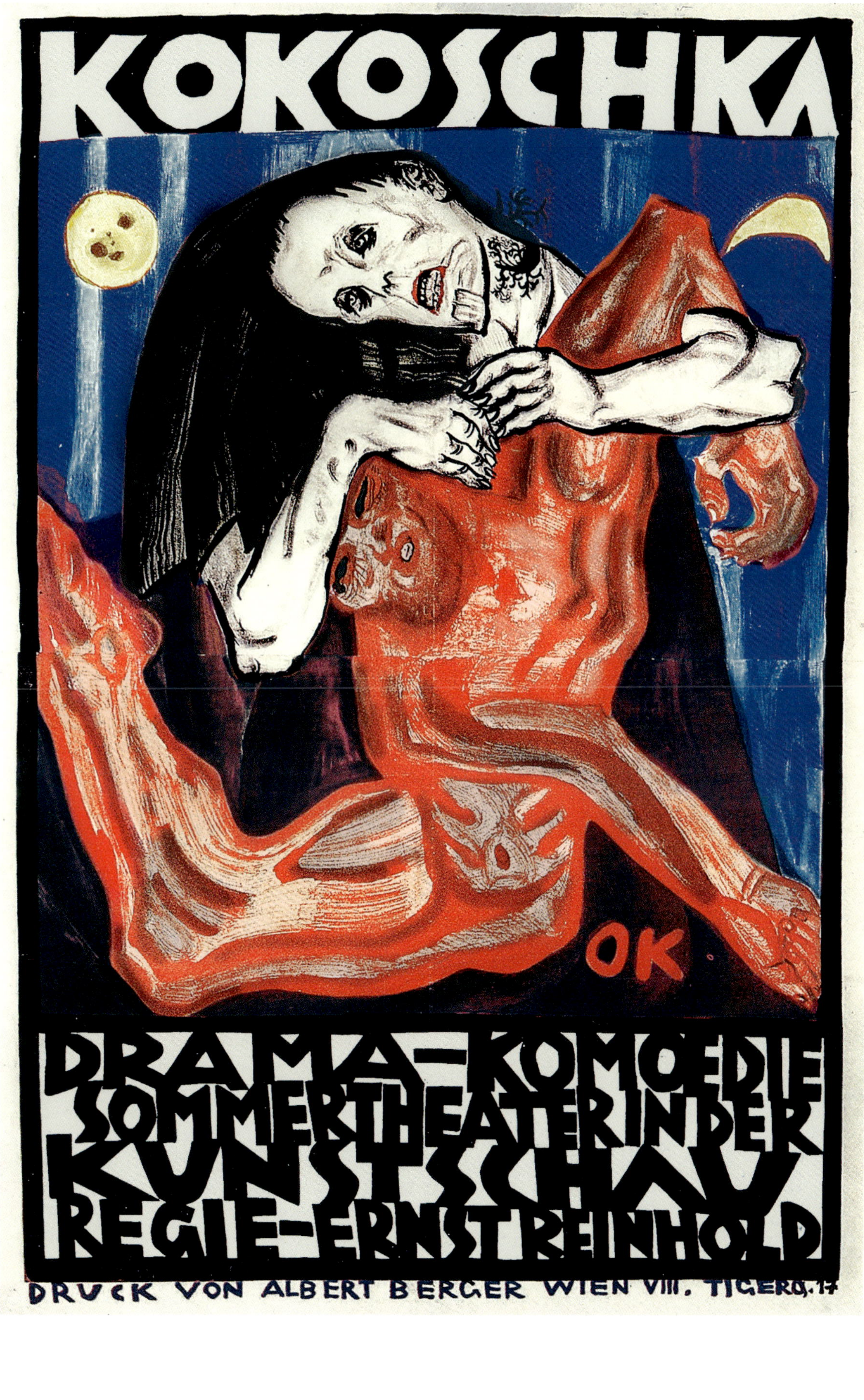
KOKOSCHKA
OK
DRAMA-KOMOEDIE
SOMMERTHEATER IN DER
KUNSTSCHAU
REGIE-ERNST REINHOLD
DRUCK VON ALBERT BERGER WIEN VIII. TIGERG.17

Ditha Moser

Calendar for the year 1910

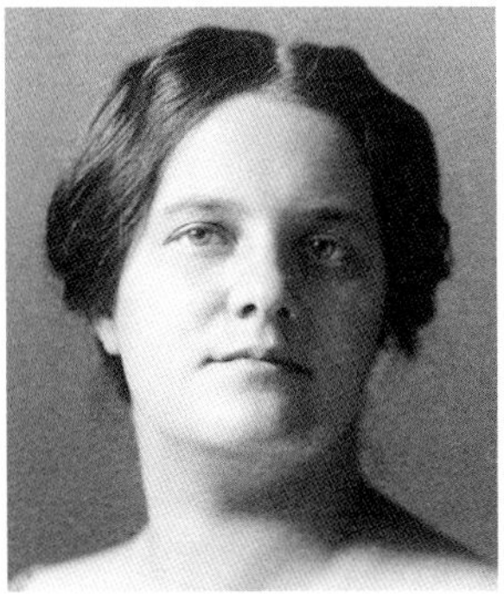

b. 1883 in Vienna
d. 1969 in Mödling

We can confidently describe Ditha Moser as a daughter from a wealthy family. Born as Editha von Mautner Markhof into a family that had achieved considerable wealth with one of the biggest breweries in Europe and the production of compressed yeast and spirits, she enjoyed a carefree childhood until her father committed suicide in 1896. Even after that she was financially secure.

She was musically and artistically talented and began to study architecture with Josef Hoffmann at the Kunstgewerbeschule in 1902; until 1905, she continued to do courses in figurative drawing, writing and heraldry under Carl Otto Czeschka and Rudolf von Larisch (1856–1934) as well as weaving and enamelwork under Leopoldine Guttmann (1856–1939) and Adele von Stark (1859–1923).

Ditha Moser was a member of that first generation of women for whom many paths in education were open. From 1892 on, it had been possible for girls to attend a private grammar school, and from 1897, the university increasingly began to be open for them, starting with the Faculty of Philosophy. Before that, women scientists had had to go to Zurich to complete their studies. There the university had admitted women since the 1860s. Although the Vienna Academy of Fine Arts did not admit women until after the First World War, the Kunstgewerbeschule allowed access to women from the start, albeit with various restrictions. The Graphische Lehr- und Versuchsanstalt (Institute of Graphics) trained women in certain subjects. Otherwise, there were also private art schools or external studies under professors from the Academy, who saw the teaching of private students as a lucrative source of additional income.

The young artist married Koloman Moser, 15 years her senior, in the summer of 1905 and they had two sons. She focused on graphic design and is famous today for two card games and three calendars which were printed between 1906 and 1911 in small print runs, no doubt as gifts for family and friends. In 1906, her tarot card game was produced; in it she made use of places in her immediate vicinity for the subjects. The art critic Ludwig Hevesi charmingly observed that no one would want to play the Queen of Hearts because she was far too pretty to be given away. Ditha Moser's figures are often stylized into geometrical forms and are always shown with a rigorous front view or an equally rigorous profile.

The square calendar for 1910, reduced to black and gold on cream-coloured paper, is folded as a fanfold. It is divided not according to the months, but day by day, and is illustrated with the corresponding deities of ancient cosmology. Moser has designed an appropriate background pattern for each day and has developed all the figures from a rectangle, out of which the upper half of the body, with its individual characteristics, appears to grow. The script was specially designed and so the entire harmonious ensemble looks in succession like a perfect example of commercial artwork of the time. Although Ditha Moser's card games have been reprinted for some years, we must note that the works for which she is famous today were reserved in those days for a small circle. Despite her considerable talent the graphic artist soon abandoned her artistic activities. The daughter from a wealthy family became a wife. DG

Calendar for the year 1910
Calendar pages for Sunday and Monday
Woodcut, each page: 16 x 16 cm
(6¼ x 6¼ in.)
Vienna, Österreichisches Museum
für angewandte Kunst

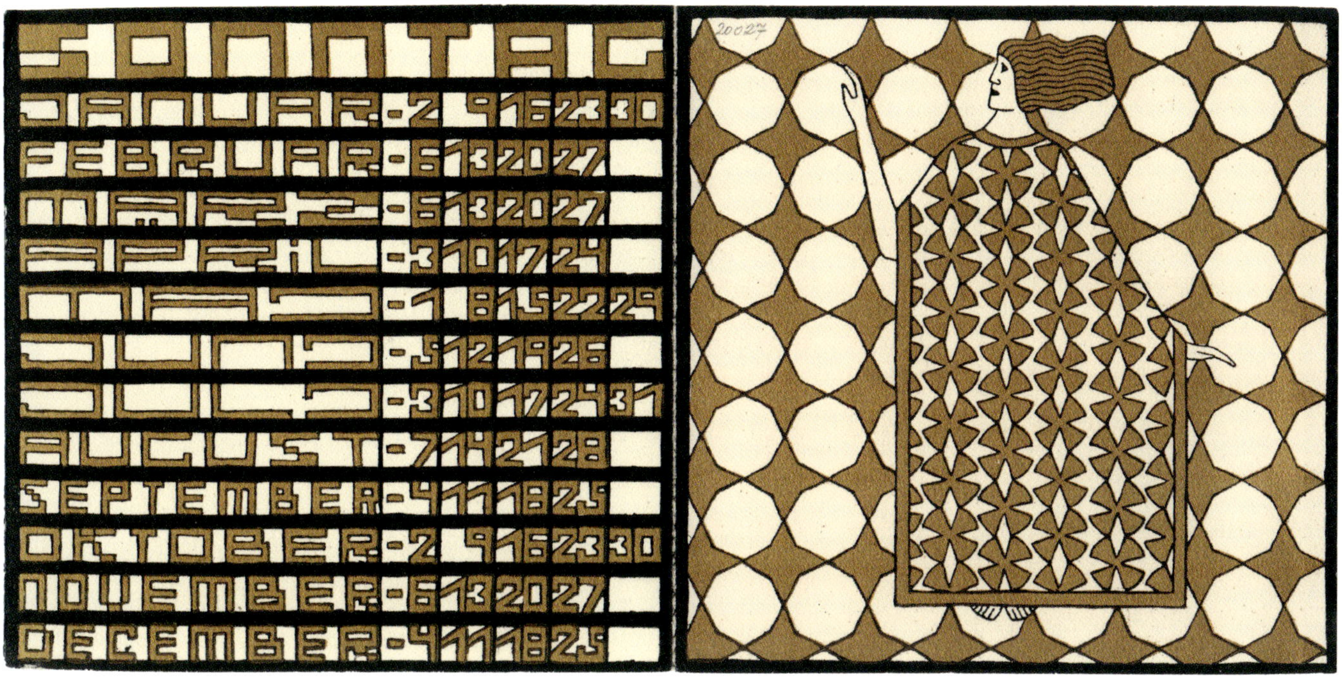

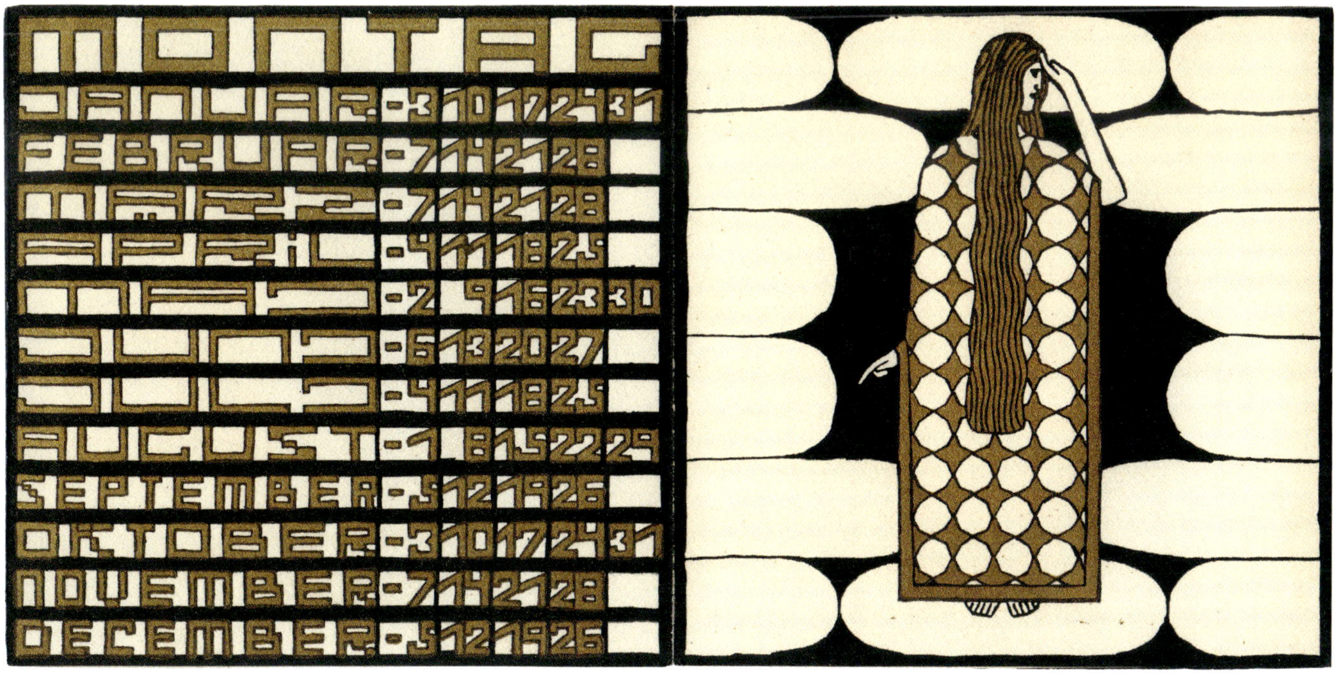

Adolf Loos
Haus am Michaelerplatz, 1910/11

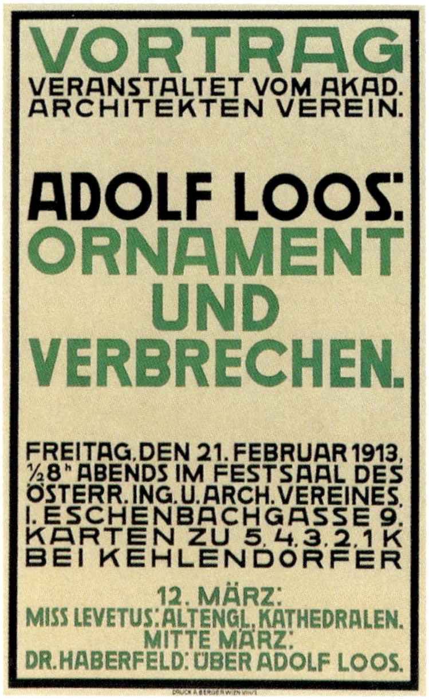

Poster for the lecture ***Ornament and Crime*** by Adolf Loos, 21 February 1913

PAGE 71
Poster for the lecture ***A Monster of a House*** by Adolf Loos, 11 December 1911

Haus am Michaelerplatz, 1910/11
Photograph from 1913

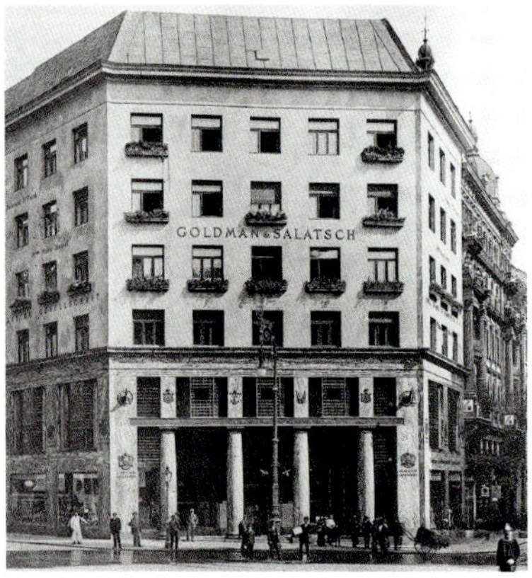

"I have made the following observation and announced it to the world: the evolution of culture is synonymous with the removal of ornamentation from objects in everyday use. I had thought to introduce a new joy into the world: but it did not thank me for it". Looking back in his epochal essay *Ornament und Verbrechen* (Ornament and Crime), Adolf Loos came to this melancholy conclusion. It does not take a great deal of detective work to discover to which of his buildings he was referring. The Haus am Michaelerplatz presents his radical approach to architecture in concentrated form, and the reaction "it did not thank me" is a mild understatement.

Loos's aversion to ornamentation had concrete grounds. At the turn of the century, the Ringstrasse, the Hofburg and the houses of the Gründerzeit were a parade of historicism. Set pieces from the past, often hackneyed, were used indiscriminately and excessively; the façades were covered in exaggerated decoration. Loos, who had broadened his horizons on journeys to London and the United States, found this disparity anathematic. He thus viewed the opportunity to build an office building on Michaelerplatz, one of the most prominent intersections in the city centre in Vienna, directly opposite the Hofburg, as more than just a challenge. The opportunity had arisen because the owners of the fashion shop Goldman & Salatsch were dissatisfied with the results of a competition for a new building which had been put to tender in 1909 and subsequently commissioned the architect directly.

The façade was completed in September 1910. The Viennese public was horrified. All the upper floors were clad with unadorned rendering, and in the case of the windows there was no framework at all. "A house without eyebrows", wrote the press scornfully. Emperor Franz Joseph supposedly avoided looking out across Michaelerplatz from this point onwards. With the support of his fellow architects, however, Loos asserted himself. In fact, he was by no means keen to incite the citizens – nor was he determined to avoid all ornamentation at any price. He saw the office floors, however, as being subordinate to the sales rooms, and felt that an office window did not require any decoration. The structural construction of reinforced concrete, in contrast, was simply in line with the latest technology at that time. And finally, the street front on the ground floor was anything but sparse, and the same applied to the sales rooms inside. The architect chose to finish them with exclusive materials like marble and mahogany and had display cases delivered from England.

Loos thought in room sequences, not in stacked floors. Each room was allotted an appropriate height. In this way Loos signalled the start of the modern age with his building and distanced himself determinedly from the mixture of fine art and architecture as it had been propagated by the Secessionists. "The artwork aims to drag people out of their complacency. A house must be comfortable. Only a very small part of architecture belongs to art: the tomb and the memorial. Everything else which serves a purpose is to be excluded from the realm of art", was his credo. Unlike the later architects of the Bauhaus, the unity of form and function did not mean a clinical industrial product for Loos. He was only concerned that things should be appropriate. Viennese citizens did eventually thank him for the Haus am Michaelerplatz. They named it after him. And it has been listed as a protected building since 1947. MN

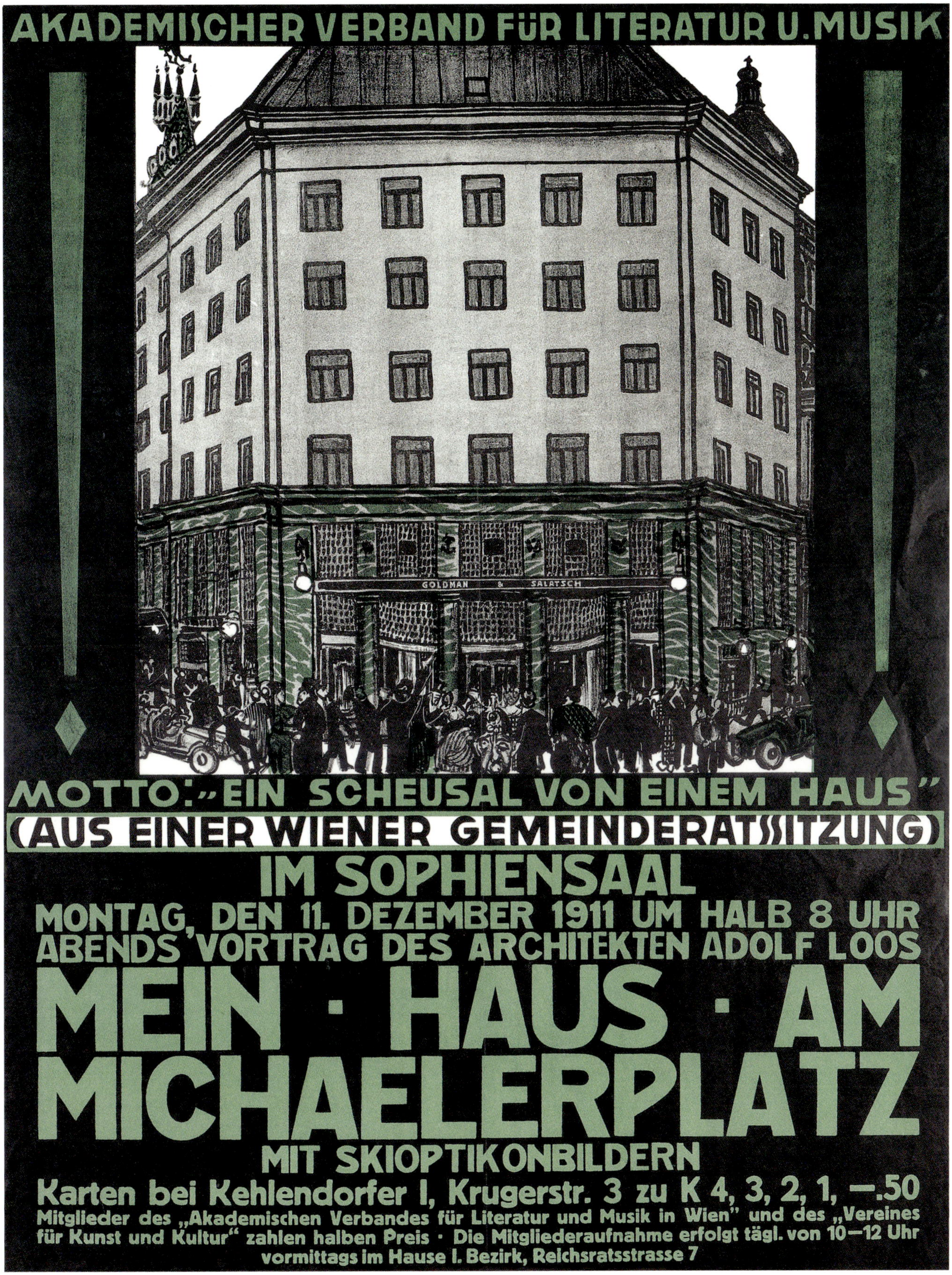
AKADEMISCHER VERBAND FÜR LITERATUR U. MUSIK
GOLDMAN & SALATSCH
MOTTO: „EIN SCHEUSAL VON EINEM HAUS"
(AUS EINER WIENER GEMEINDERATSSITZUNG)
IM SOPHIENSAAL
MONTAG, DEN 11. DEZEMBER 1911 UM HALB 8 UHR
ABENDS VORTRAG DES ARCHITEKTEN ADOLF LOOS
MEIN · HAUS · AM
MICHAELERPLATZ
MIT SKIOPTIKONBILDERN
Karten bei Kehlendorfer I, Krugerstr. 3 zu K 4, 3, 2, 1, –.50
Mitglieder des „Akademischen Verbandes für Literatur und Musik in Wien" und des „Vereines
für Kunst und Kultur" zahlen halben Preis · Die Mitgliederaufnahme erfolgt tägl. von 10–12 Uhr
vormittags im Hause I. Bezirk, Reichsratsstrasse 7

Arnold Schönberg

Gaze, 1910

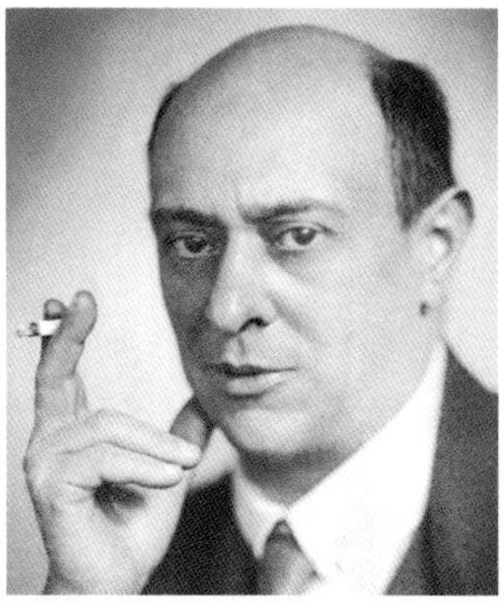

b. 1874 in Vienna
d. 1951 in Los Angeles

One might think that in the city based on the principle of the *Gesamtkunstwerk*, a large number of all-round talents must have appeared on the scene. That was not the case. The masters dutifully remained faithful to their chosen trade. If architects turned their attention to design or painters to interior decoration it was not a departure into another profession. But then there was Arnold Schönberg. The musician and composer, whose dodecaphonic system would spark one of the most profound revolutions in the modern age during the 1920s, was also active as a painter.

When we notice that an artwork bears the signature Schönberg, we, of course, observe it more carefully. We stare back, so to speak, because at least a dozen of Schönberg's paintings include the act of looking in their title: including, for example, *Gaze*, dated May 1910. The small-format picture presents a close-up face in a spectacular manner. This face is dominated by the act of staring, because the eyes, the mirror of the soul, seek intensive contact. It is hard to say whether the eyes are fearful or trying to stare at someone or something. They have something captivating about them, emphasized by their red outlines. The shape of the head reveals the form of the skull. The mouth and nose look hollow, as if they had been mummified. There are no ears. This remarkable reduction, in which an individual with notable acoustic skills is clearly practising a form of demonstrative restraint, can be found in all of Schönberg's *Gaze* pictures.

Schönberg's spectacles have literally turned out to be very radical on the whole. We may feel that he has exaggerated somewhat with the appeal we read in these faces. In any case, he made art history with them. Among the heroes of the Vienna art scene, he was the only one who made it into a foundational charter of the international avant-garde – the almanac *Der Blaue Reiter*, published in Munich in early 1912. The almanac was preceded by an exhibition in which Schönberg did not participate. But he did appear in the accompanying brochure. He was represented with two illustrations and an essay contribution entitled "The Relationship to the Text". In it the musician, who had presented himself as a painter, also revealed his skills as a writer. He called this multiple use of artistic possibilities "parallel walking". The fact that he also tried his hand as a stage designer fits perfectly into this colourful image.

During this time Schönberg had already hidden his artistic vein again, because his period as a visual artist covers precisely the years from 1908 until 1911. His musical compositions had brought him too little income and he simply wanted to earn money. In 1910, he did, indeed, have a first solo art exhibition in the Kunstsalon Heller in Vienna. He had imagined that he might realize a price of between 200 and 400 crowns per picture – a handsome sum. His reasoning is enlightening: Schönberg thought that a purchaser would be able to own a painting by someone who would eventually also occupy a central position in the history or music; and thus the public would, in turn, be able to share in his multiple talents. We do not know whether this argument caught on. We do know, however, that Gustav Mahler, Schönberg's former role model and epitome of the musician in Vienna around 1900, purchased a number of his artworks anonymously – not to offend the maestro. RM

Gaze, 1910
Oil on cardboard, 32.2 x 24.6 cm
(12¾ x 9¾ in.)
Vienna, Arnold Schönberg Center

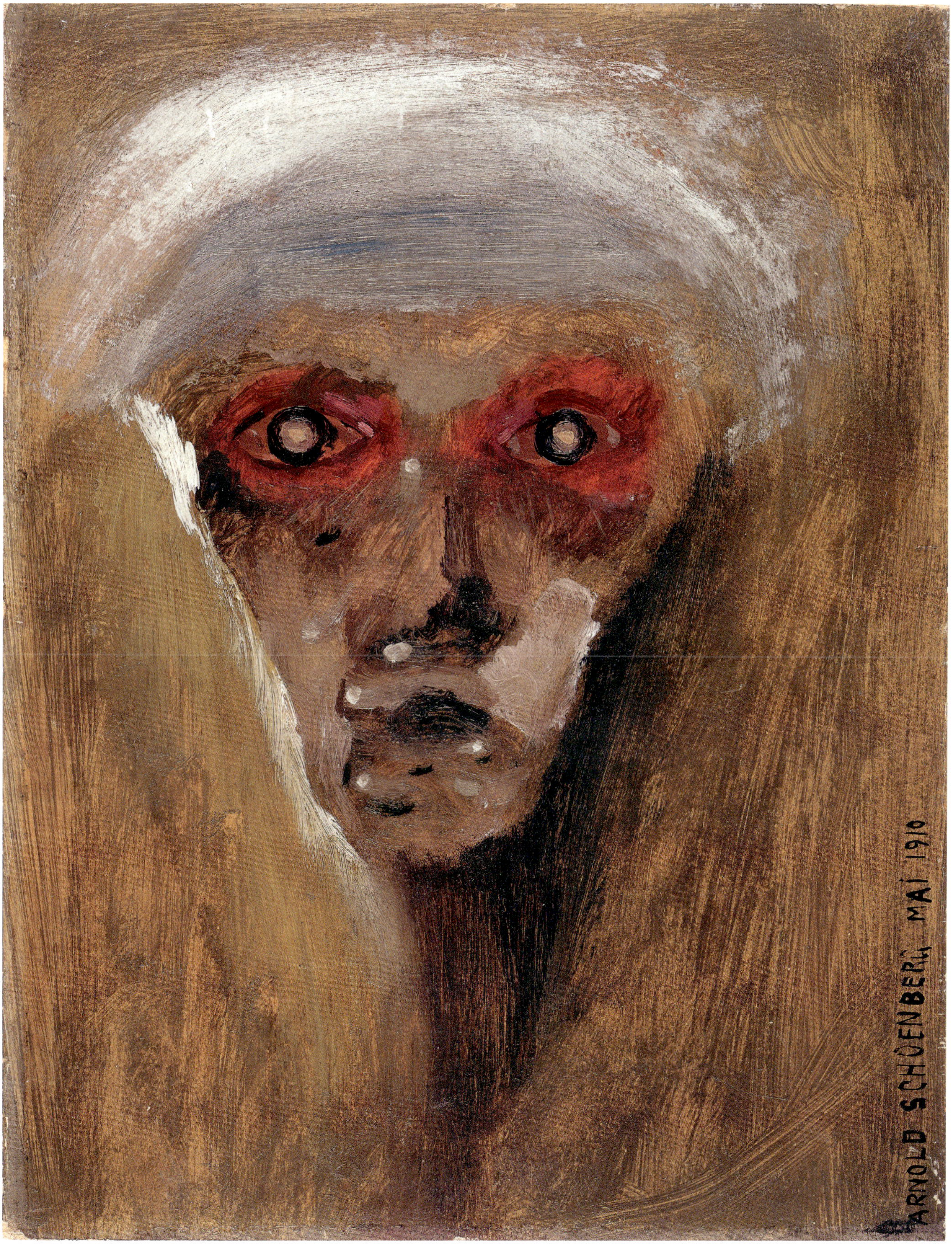
ARNOLD SCHOENBERG MAI 1910

Egon Schiele

Seated Male Nude (Self-Portrait), 1910

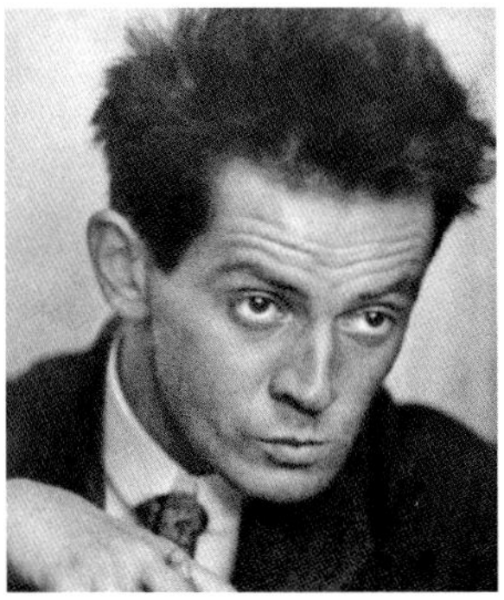

b. 1890 in Tulln
d. 1918 in Vienna

Egon Schiele was ahead of his time. As early as 1908, after two years at the Academy of Fine Arts in Vienna, he developed his inimitable angular style, which at that time was still embedded in the ornamentalism of Jugendstil: *Nude Boy Lying on a Patterned Blanket* and *Stylized Flowers against a Decorative Background* show this interim step very clearly.

The following year he then dispensed with all ornamentation: *Autumn Tree with Fuchsias* and *Sunflower* look as if they have been cropped given the neutral background in shades of white. And in 1910, at the age of only 20, Schiele broke free from all his role models. "With impressive force", observes Schiele expert Tobias G. Natter, he found his way "to a repertoire of expression that would redefine the art of the modern age".

Schiele anticipated the egocentric "selfie" culture of the present day with unprecedented radicalism: he posed as an anorexic model in front of the mirror, adopting unconventional poses, pulling faces, questioning himself, and his body in his own image. According to Natter, it is a question of "self-renunciation, often even deformation, created out of pleasure and delight in play-acting, marked by authenticity and the courage of affirmation". Much of what Schiele had previously tested on a small scale he now presented on his canvas in 1910 in a large format and with vehemence. The *Seated Male Nude* shows a torso; the format is almost square and the length of one side measures 1.5 metres. The self-portrait possesses expressive drama and colourfulness which Schiele possibly never surpassed.

It was in that year that Schiele met the wealthy collector Carl Reininghaus (1857–1929). The eldest son of a brewery owner purchased several drawings from him as well as the *Nude Male* – for a sum which lay considerably above what the 20-year-old artist could expect to command. According to Natter, Reininghaus shared Schiele's interest in the erotic, and he supported him in 1912 in the Neulengbach affair, when the artist was arrested and taken into investigative custody because of the alleged abduction and rape of a girl. The accusation was proved to be unfounded, but the court nonetheless sentenced him for the dissemination of immoral drawings.

A year later, the friendship cooled. Schiele died in 1918 and Reininghaus in 1929. His collection became subject of inheritance lawsuits and the subsequent fate of the *Nude Male* is obscure. A certain Friedl Aigner is thought to have owned the work after that. During the National Socialist era, a local group leader is said to have made derogatory remarks about the "degenerate picture", whereupon the old lady had the nude picture put in the coal cellar.

This was the story told by the ophthalmologist Rudolf Leopold (1925–2010), who acquired the painting in 1954 at an auction in the Dorotheum in Vienna. The chair of the auction house did not even dare show the picture. Art dealers had commented in "Nazi language" that the painting was "foreign to the species", and even a "disgrace to Austria"; that it should really be burned. The collector added that people thought he was "a complete idiot" because he purchased the painting for 3,000 schillings – a grotesquely low amount. Leopold's eyes always used to light up when he spoke about Schiele. The outstanding importance of the artist for the collector was demonstrated by the logo he chose for the Leopold Museum: one of the three matchstick men with his legs spread out that Schiele had painted with Indian ink on a small sheet of paper in 1910. TT

Seated Male Nude (Self-Portrait), 1910
Oil, opaque colour on canvas,
152.5 x 150 cm (60 x 59 in.)
Vienna, Leopold Museum

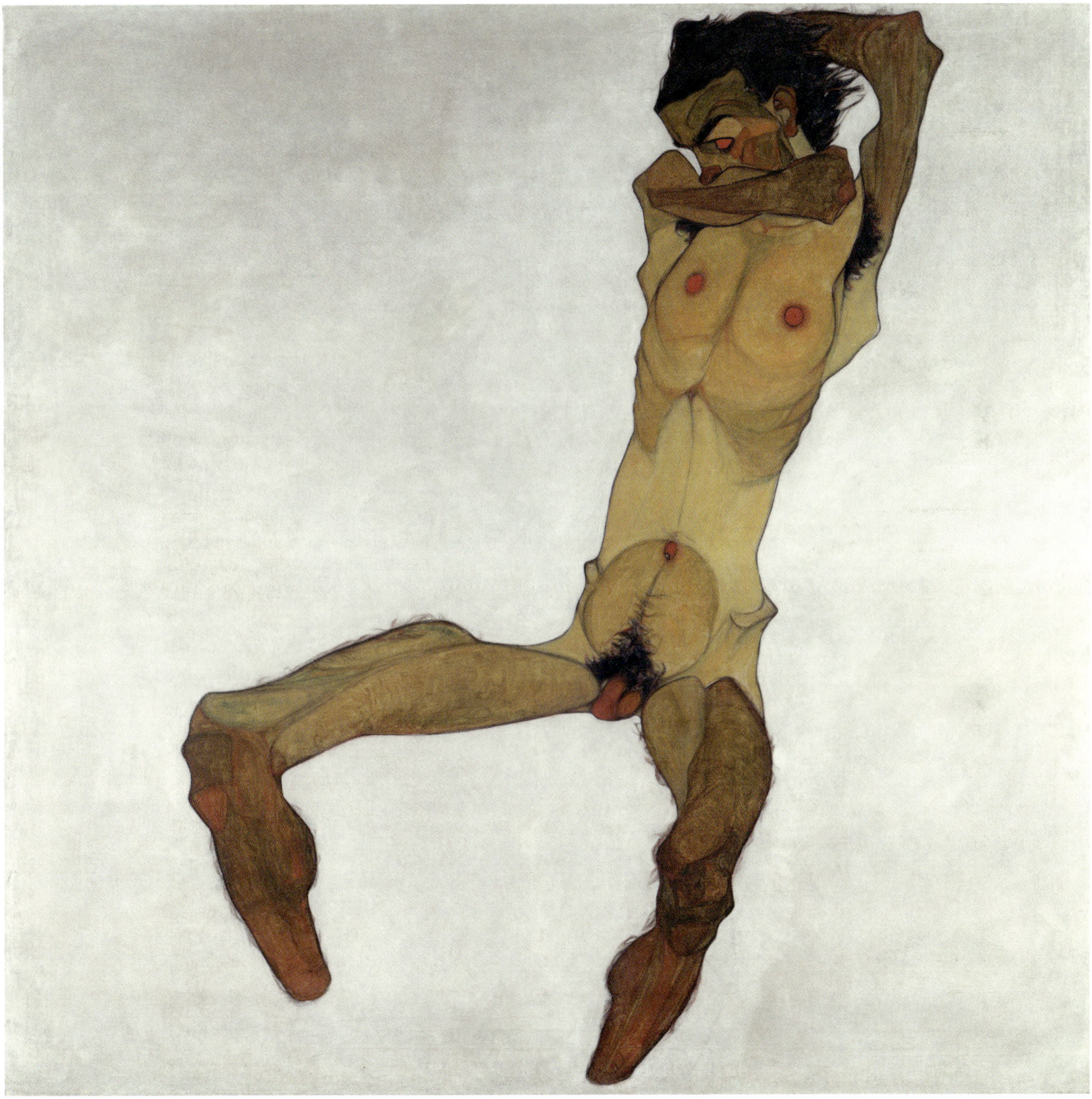

Emil Mayer

Onlookers at the Prater, c. 1910

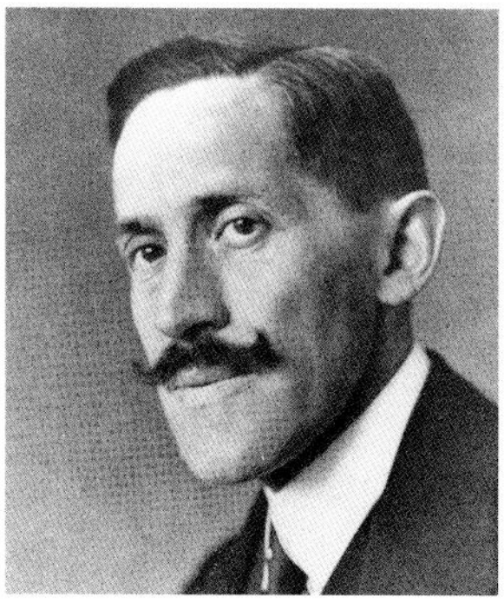

b. 1871 in Nový Bydžov
d. 1938 in Vienna

Whether in front of or behind the picket fence, it is all a question of perspective. "Here, in front of the picket fence stands an eager, indiscriminating crowd of onlookers. Schoolboys, apprentices, schoolgirls, youth of all kinds, unnoticed and in a leisurely mood. Admittedly: this public cannot pay. Nor do they want to. But they bring admiration, respect and zeal. These lads and lasses are only what is known in the theatre as the enthusiastic youth in the gallery." Felix Salten (1869–1945), who was thought to be the author of *Josefine Mutzenbacher* and who had achieved global success with *Bambi – A Life in the Woods*, spent a good deal of time researching the Wurstelprater in Vienna. He did not describe what he witnessed mercilessly, but with a certain conceit. He observed the attractions, the rides and the gourmet pleasures but, above all, the protagonists of this demi-monde and the ultimate destination of many an artist's career which had begun in the city centre: barkers, jugglers, showmen presenting human curiosities and skills, the women's band, hawkers of food of all kinds, and also the consumers of what was on offer. And then there was also the petty criminals known locally as spivs, crooks or proles.

Printed in 1911 by the Rosenbaum brothers' publishing house, *Wurstelprater* was illustrated with a series of existing photographs by the lawyer and amateur photographer Emil Mayer. He had already been successful with these images in a hand-coloured version at lectures in the Urania adult education centre. Some years previously, Max Winter (1870–1937), who is regarded today as a pioneer of social reporting in the German-speaking region, had mingled, in the interests of his work, with homeless people and vagabonds who searched for items of saleable value among the refuse and the sewers of Vienna. The journalist Emil Kläger (1880–1936) had also set out to document this subculture with the judge and amateur photographer Hermann Drawe (1867–1925): published in 1908, they entitled their work *Durch die Wiener Quartiere des Elends und Verbrechens* (Through Vienna's Districts of Destitution and Crime), with a subtitle *Ein Wanderbuch aus dem Jenseits* (A Stroll from the Other Side). Between 1904 and 1906, the accompanying slide lecture at the Urania was attended by 60,000 visitors.

Emil Mayer was, however, uninterested in presenting a grim social report. It was the settings rather than the people that he documented in his direct, terse style, a life in Vienna that was facing extinction as a result of major urban restructuring. Viennese types were very popular in a variety of media-based forms; Mayer's images even appeared as a series of postcards. It is notable that in this recording of the "old days" in the publication about the Wurstelprater, new, modern achievements such as the Big Wheel, the cinema, and high-speed photography are all missing.

If anyone – not only in Vienna – contributed during this time to the progress of the relatively new medium's artistic aspects, it came from the species represented by the enthusiastic amateur photographer Mayer. Apart from the snapshot-like nature of the moment he also staged surface textures and linearity which do not necessarily lead to depth in space. Thus onlookers look like extras in a slat relief. Even now, more than a century later, one may feel as if one is in the middle of the event. DG

Onlookers at the Prater, c. 1910
Hand-coloured lantern slide
Vienna, Österreichisches Volkshochschularchiv

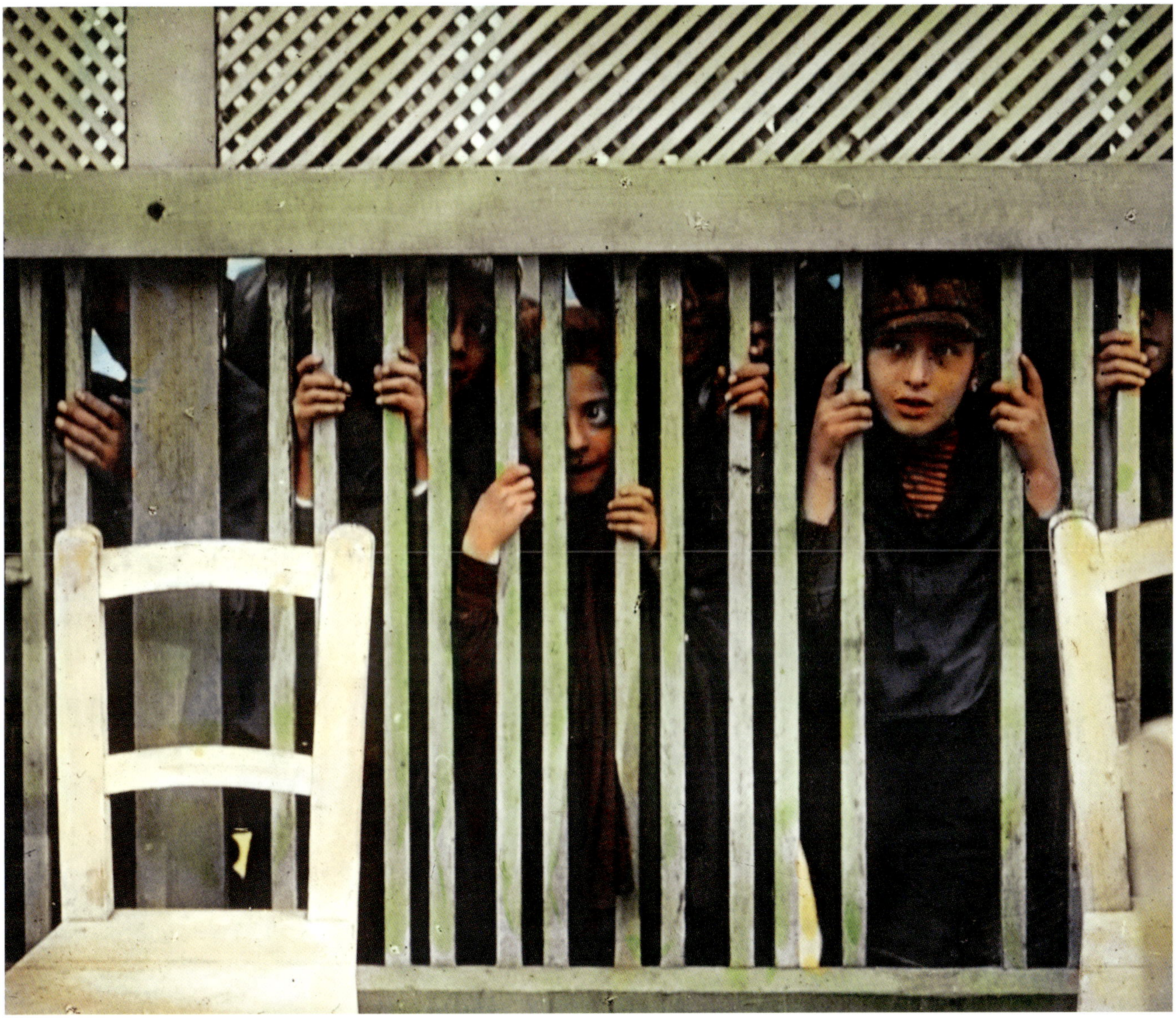

Josef Hoffmann
Glass Collection Bronzite Series B, Lobmeyr, 1912

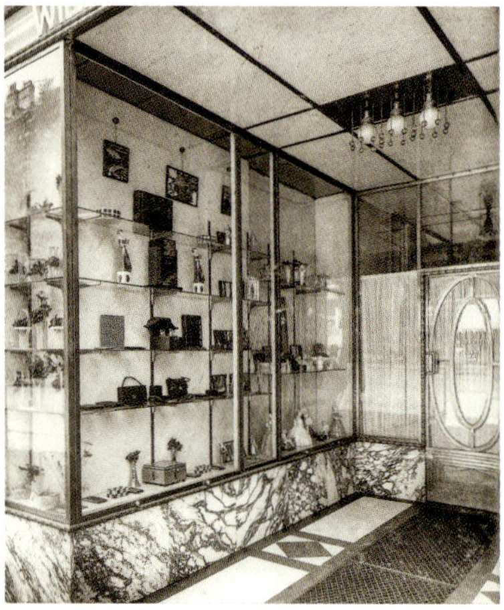

Josef Hoffmann
Entrance to the salesroom
of the Wiener Werkstätte, 1907
Vienna I, Am Graben 15

One of the defining new ideas characterizing Vienna around 1900 was the unification of art, architecture and craftsmanship – or, indeed, the whole of life – to form a *Gesamtkunstwerk*. It was the worldview of the Secession, from which a number of further movements would soon develop. One of them, the Wiener Werkstätte, was founded in 1903 by two members of the Secession: the architect Josef Hoffmann and artist Koloman Moser. Hoffmann, in particular, like many important architects of that time, a former employee of Otto Wagner, had been impressed by the 19th-century British Arts and Crafts movement. Like the latter, the Wiener Werkstätte aimed to unite art, architecture and craftsmanship.

Craftsman-like quality was the first commandment. The range of the Werkstätte was almost unlimited; its products included furniture, lights, leather, enamel, ceramics, graphics, jewellery, fashion and fabrics and it even had its own hat department. The first years were successful. By 1905, the Wiener Werkstätte employed a workforce of about 100. The working conditions were as progressive as the products, with appropriate pay and a relatively high ratio of women.

Josef Hoffmann, who had been Professor of Architecture at the Kunstgewerbeschule in Vienna since 1899, extended spatial art, which was the aim of the Secessionists, to include items of everyday use and especially the design of interior spaces. Life gained its dignity not through pomposity, but through "simplicity, honesty and uprightness", observed Hoffmann in 1901. Hoffmann was, nonetheless, strongly criticized by Adolf Loos for his connection between art objects and everyday items; he considered the products of the Wiener Werkstätte to be too pretentious.

The Palais Stoclet in Brussels (ill. pp. 56, 57), planned and designed by Hoffmann, was definitively one of the most important Art Nouveau buildings. However, his principles as an interior designer were considerably less sumptuous and floral than those of his Belgian or French colleagues. After all, he had adopted a preference for the square from role models like the Scottish architect Charles Rennie Mackintosh (1868–1928). The nickname his colleagues gave him was "Quadratl-Hoffmann", "Square Hoffmann".

His designs for the Wiener Werkstätte also demonstrated restraint and straightforwardness. The *Glass Collection Bronzite Series B* that he designed in 1912 for Lobmeyr, the traditional Viennese glass manufacturers, traced simple geometric lines in black enamel on matt glass. The clear lines of the multi-piece set demonstrated Hoffmann's architectural aspirations, which extended to all everyday objects. Lobmeyr had begun to cooperate with the Wiener Werkstätte in 1910; they valued their principle that "it is better to work on one object for ten days that to produce ten objects in one day".

The *Glass Collection Bronzite Series B* was presented at the exhibition of the Deutsche Werkbund (German Association of Craftsmen) in 1914. The latter pursued similar aims to those of the Wiener Werkstätte and also counted Hoffmann as a member. During the 1920s, when the influence of the Wiener Werkstätte declined, Hoffmann remained loyal to his predilection for interior spaces and their furnishings. His last notable artistic statement was the Austrian Pavilion for the Biennale site in Venice in 1934. MN

Glass Collection Bronzite Series B, Lobmeyr, 1912
First released in 1914
Glass enameled with black
bronzite decoration

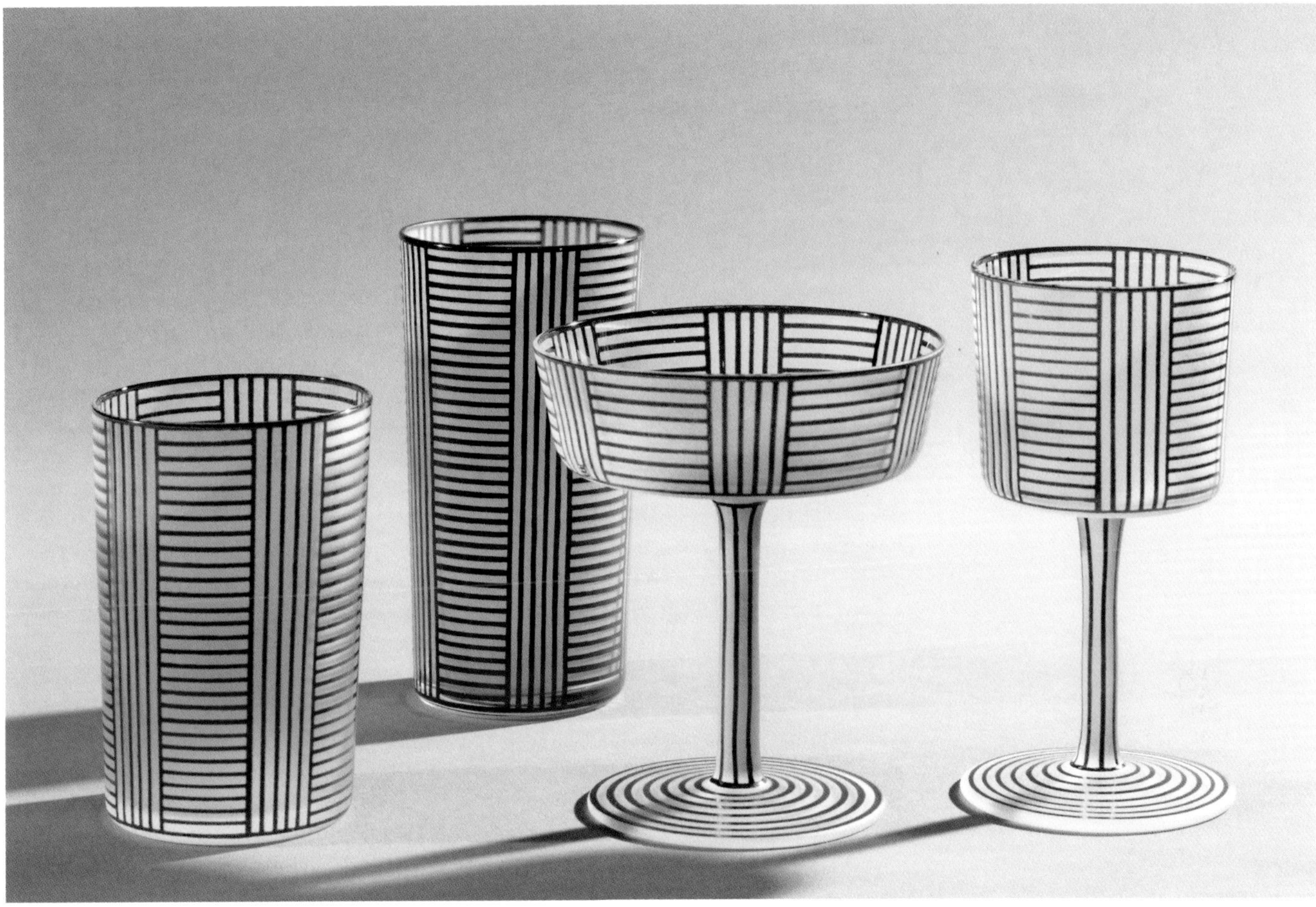

Max Oppenheimer
Portrait of Tilla Durieux, 1912

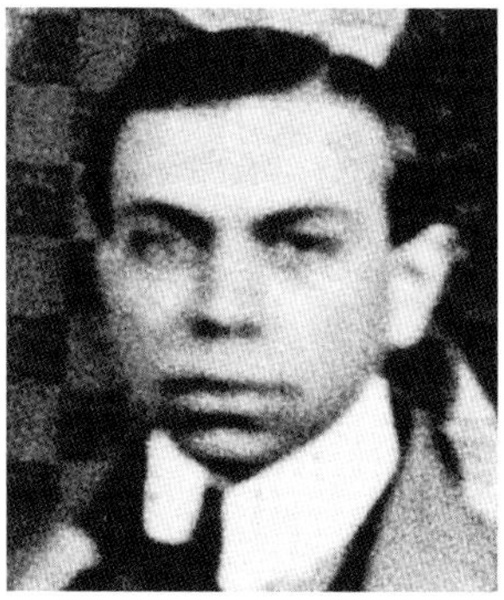

b. 1885 in Vienna
d. 1954 in New York

Tilla Durieux (1880–1971) was born in Vienna but became a celebrated actress – even a star – in Berlin. Her real name was Ottilie Godeffroy, but since her parents had vetoed her choice of career she adopted an artist's name derived from "du Rieux", the name of her paternal grandmother. She made her debut in 1902 in Olomouc in what is now the Czech Republic. From 1903 until 1911 she was engaged at the Deutsche Theater in Berlin; this was followed by the Königliche Schauspielhaus and, from 1919, the Staatstheater. From 1907 she performed at matinees for workers in the suburbs of Berlin on Sundays when there were no rehearsals. She left Germany in 1933 because her husband was a Jew.

Durieux had already been married twice previously: to the painter Eugen Spiro (1874–1972), from whom she was divorced in 1906. She had then married Paul Cassirer (1871–1926) in 1910; he committed suicide in 1926 when she threatened him with divorce. Paul Cassirer had founded an art dealership in 1898 together with his cousin Bruno Cassirer (1872–1941); it had become a leading gallery for French Impressionism. The Cassirers subsequently also supported German Modernism, especially Max Liebermann (1847–1935) and Lovis Corinth (1858–1925). In addition, Cassirer published the works of men of letters, including Hermann Bahr.

Cassirer was not only Durieux's husband, he was also her manager. According to the publicist Wilhelm Herzog (1884–1960), he took care of her, and treated and trained her like "a promising, elegant racehorse"; he was her "head of advertising, businessman, agent and director at the same time". Thus it was so that many of the artists whom Cassirer protected would end up painting the diva. No fewer than 21 portraitists of Durieux were exhibited between 1898 and 1933 in the Kunstsalon Cassirer. Five of them had painted commissioned portraits of the actress.

One of these was Max Oppenheimer, who was known as Mopp. He too came from Vienna. He had initially studied at the Academy of Fine Arts and thereafter in Prague. Influenced most significantly by Kokoschka, he belonged to the circle of Viennese Expressionism. Oppenheimer lived in Berlin from 1911 to 1915.

Oppenheimer tells of the origin of the painting in his autobiography *Menschen finden ihren Maler* (People Find Their Painter), which was published in 1938, when he fled to New York. Initially he could find no suitable pose: "Nothing which expressed the dramatic aspect of this remarkable woman, who was like a big cat. I turned this way and that, walked closer and away again. One minute the shadows on her face were too heavy, and the next there was rigidity in her body and expression, and a mocking twitch around her mouth that seemed to say: Don't torture yourself; it won't work out! Resigned, she sat down at the piano; the light streamed fully onto her face and the severity smoothed out the velvet folds of her dress, which left her arms free. – I barely managed to say: 'Please, stay for a couple – –' and in haste, with a few lines, I had sketched out the pose. Colours: pinkish, greyish-green – grey and black danced on the canvas before my eyes. Brushes rolled onto the ground; I painted and rampaged for three hours which seemed to me like minutes, fascinated, stimulated by the feeling of success".

The result is a sensitive likeness with sparing Expressionist gestures. It must have found favour because the oil painting was exhibited in Cassirer's salon. TT

Portrait of Tilla Durieux, 1912
Oil on canvas, 95.5 x 78.9 cm
(37½ x 31 in.)
Vienna, Leopold Museum

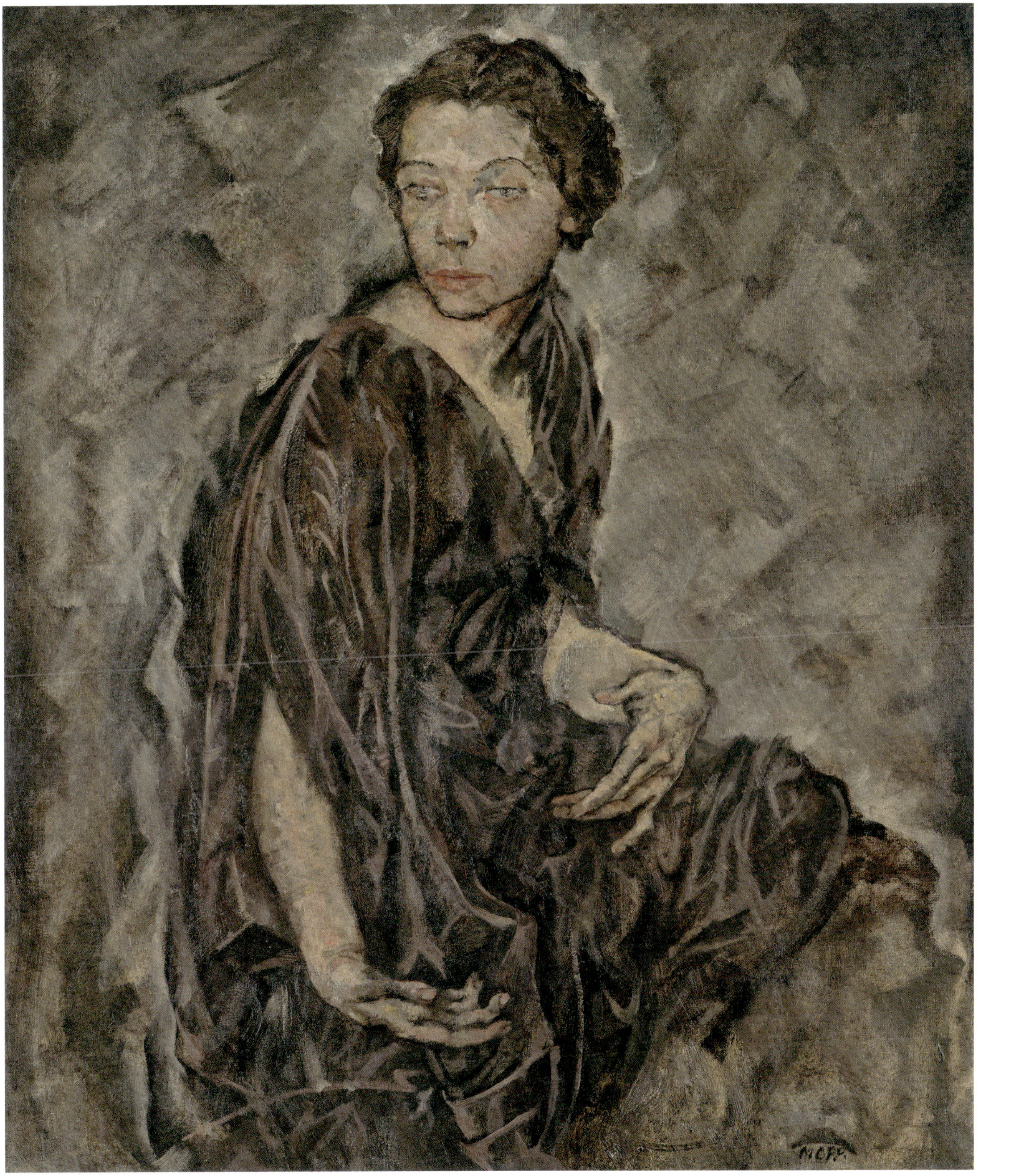
MOPP

Egon Schiele
Cover of the magazine Der Ruf, 1912

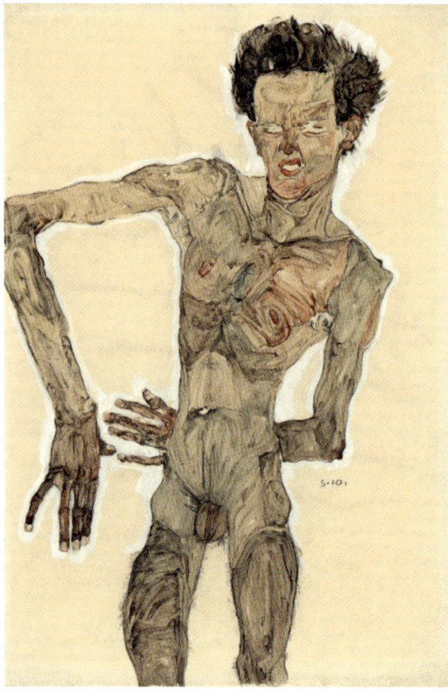

Egon Schiele
Nude Self-Portrait, Grimacing, 1910
Pencil, watercolour and gouache, heightened with white,
55.8 x 36.9 cm (22 x 14½ in.)
Vienna, Albertina

Egon Schiele was the son of a railway worker, and one of the specialities in his art was derailing trains. The body is the medium of his artworks – that of models and especially his own. The body is then manoeuvred into exaggerated, eccentric, passionate and expressive poses. Thus the gestures become contorted and the facial expressions become grimaces. Schiele's exploration of expression, his absolute trademark, is devoid of significance here. When Schiele studies a body we do not have to be able to make out a pathognomic quality which records a fleeting passion like anger, grief or joy, nor a physiognomic one which attempts to determine the character of an individual. In the pure presentation of exemplary processes of movement, he remains committed to the unique characteristic of Viennese culture around 1900: ornamentation.

In 1910, Schiele, who was just 20 years old, presented himself in what was his preferred manner at the time, namely nude, in a drawing (ill. p. 82). The arms are bent to the extreme into a pose as if the act of recording himself must have been linked with violent distaste. This work stands at the beginning of a series of templates which would be used in 1912 for posters and publications in the public space. Here the head was extracted from Schiele's drawing and presented separately as if it had never been part of a larger unit, including a body. Isolated in this way, it was used in three contexts. Egon Friedell, the cabarettist, satirist and later author of a magnificent and extensive cultural history used it in April of that year as a motif for an announcement about a lecture on irony. In June, it served as the subject for a poster advertising two concerts by living Austrian composers. And in November, it landed on the cover of the magazine *Der Ruf*, whose third issue was devoted to the subject of war.

Der Ruf was one of numerous short-lived publications in which Expressionism raised its voice in Vienna. In the first issue's (February 1912) editorial, the publisher Robert Müller (1887–1924) wrote optimistically and confidently of the future: "It will be the most emphatic era; it will be Gothic, bizarre and fantastic, modern-prehistoric". Indeed, the third issue extolled this enthusiasm, which was linked with human experience. Müller presented an apologia for war, and granted that proceeds from the extremely low sales be donated to an association for the creation of an Austrian air force. The sensitivity towards the problems to come, one and a half years before this insight became topical during the First World War, and which we would like to attribute to this issue, was still somewhat nebulous.

Schiele himself supplied an eye-catching image of sorts. He frequented the publishers' circle: in 1918, he would dedicate a pencil drawing to Robert Müller. Moreover, he had a gaudy motif ready and waiting. His grimaces were attention-seeking enough; the red with which the face was underlaid added to the effect in the interest of mass communication. As a subject, the head was suitable for irony, for contemporary music, and also for war. It was open enough for all kinds of interpretations. That was, not least, the secret of Schiele's art. RM

Cover of the magazine Der Ruf
Issue no. 3 on the subject of war, November 1912
Colour lithograph, 22.9 x 14.8 cm
(9 x 6 in.)

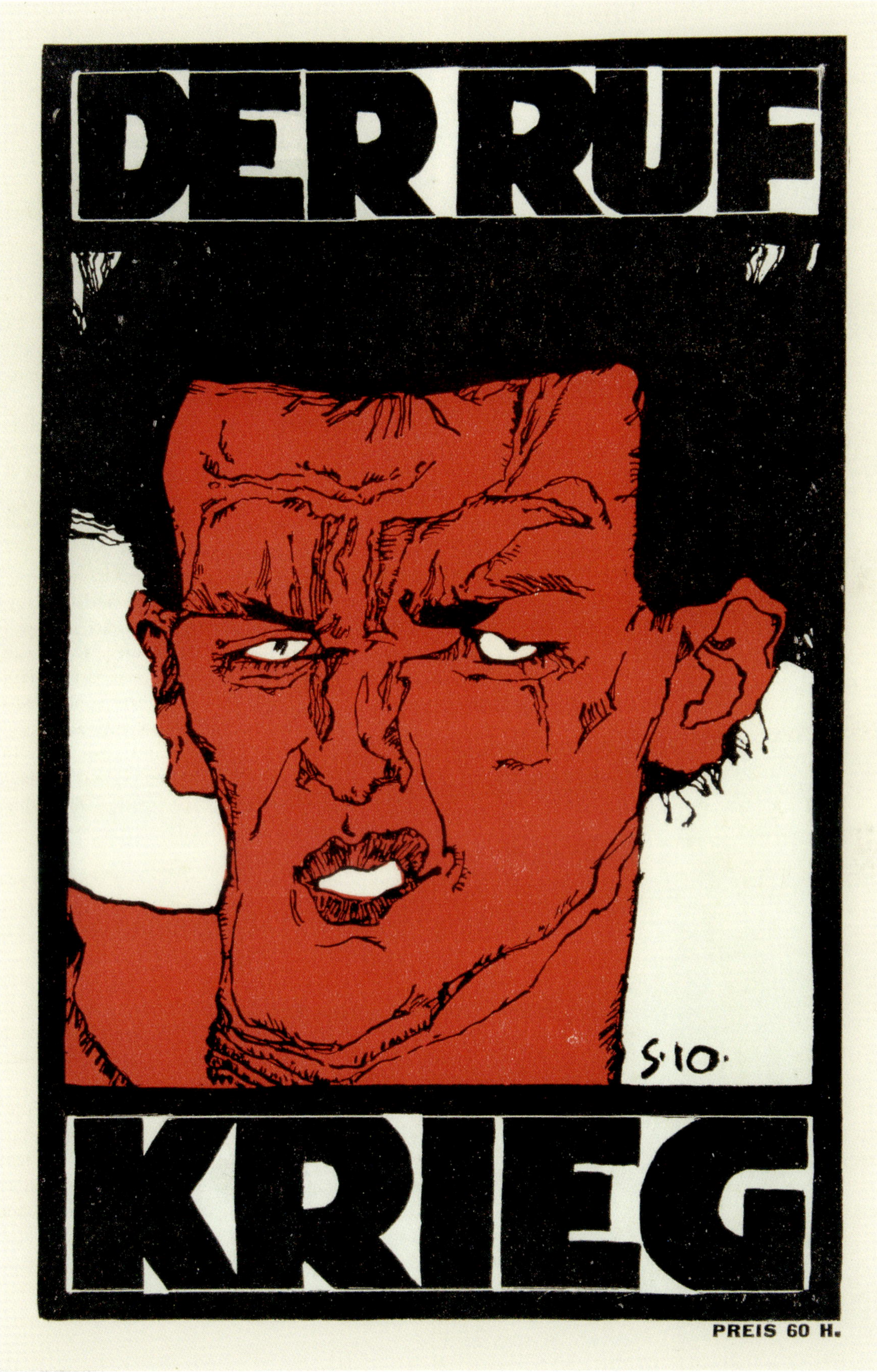
DER RUF
S.10.
KRIEG
PREIS 60 H.

Mauritz Stiller
Das fremde Mädchen [The Strange Girl], 1913

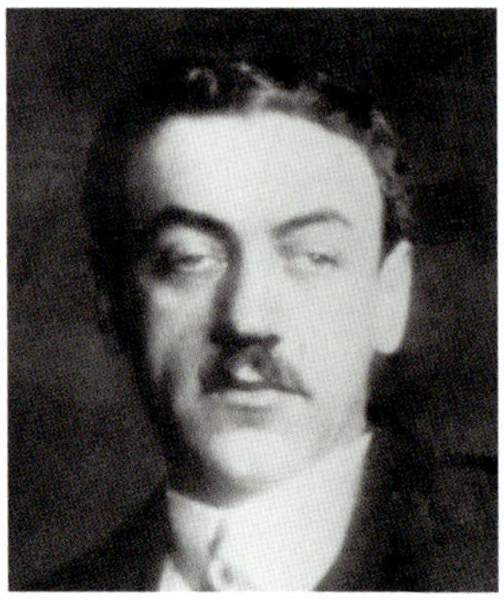

b. 1883 in Helsinki
d. 1928 in Stockholm

PAGE 85
Das fremde Mädchen
[The Strange Girl], 1913
Film stills

Das fremde Mädchen
[The Strange Girl], 1913
Film poster

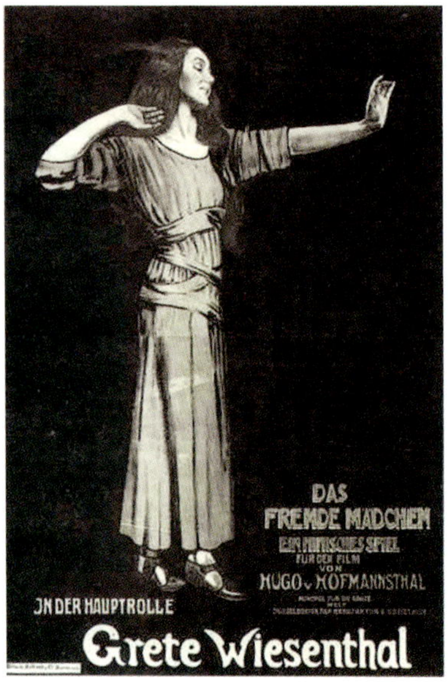

"Anyone who cannot inform his audience that he will be bringing them *Das fremde Mädchen* [The Strange Girl], four acts, by Hugo von Hofmannsthal – with Grete Wiesenthal in the principal role and with specially composed music by Hannes Ruch – has simply missed the biggest source of income and the biggest box-office draw". In 1913, the film distribution company Anna Christensen, Vienna VI, Mariahilferstrasse 53, attempted to drum together various cinematographic establishments to commit themselves to a particularly artificial example of cinema with these powerful words. Vienna was one of the capitals of this new medium, which was soon to be certain of victory. Initially, moving pictures were a matter for variété and for what was seen as cheap pleasure. In particular, Saturn-Film, founded in 1906, had distinguished itself with lascivious films that were shot through keyholes, which inevitably attracted an audience.

But then the art film appeared on the scene. We would not be treading on the toes of *Das fremde Mädchen's* production team if we were to observe that, contrary to the distributor's vociferous announcements, it failed to achieve sensational success. The plot in its 54 minutes was far too out of touch with reality. Hugo von Hofmannsthal had developed the script; he was one of the most obstinate inhabitants of the ivory tower, the author of precious-pretentious scenarios to which his script for *Das fremde Mädchen* belonged. Intended to be played in mime, it presents the encounter between a wealthy man and an enchanting, elf-like figure. The girl, however, is a sort of decoy for the underworld; she drags the man into the gutter, eventually rescues him from the rabble and then dies a sudden but ultimately expected death. In the end, in Hofmannsthal's own words: "… the dead girl lies quite still and beautiful in the middle on the stones, unaware of everything else".

Eventually, the film came from Sweden as did its director Mauritz Stiller. Stiller is regarded as the man who discovered that country's greatest export success, Greta Garbo (1905–1990). But before that, Grete Wiesenthal was also a special attraction. She was born in Vienna and joined the ballet company of the opera whilst still a child. She was a solo dancer at the age of 17 and was successful, above all, in pantomimes. She was a highly regarded member of the circle of Viennese intellectuals, moved in the groups around Altenberg, Loos and Kokoschka, and married the latter's student companion and closest friend Erwin Lang. Hofmannsthal, an elegant figure on the fringes of the aesthetic activities, was sufficiently involved to write *Das fremde Mädchen* with her in mind.

The work had its premiere as a pantomime in 1911 in the theatre on Königgrätzer Strasse. There was a test screening of the film on 21 August 1913 in the Beethoven Room in the city centre, Strauchgasse 4, a location where Karl Kraus, for example, also presented his lectures. And so the group of insiders was almost complete. The only person missing was the composer, who was specially mentioned in the distributor's advertisement. Hannes Ruch, whose real name was Hans Richard Weinhöppel (1867–1928), was a native of Munich. He had attracted attention in particular as the producer of couplets and was, for a short while, the musical director of the short-lived Cabaret Fledermaus. He too belonged to the, of course Viennese, circle of the initiated – popularly known as the Adabeis, the in-crowd. RM

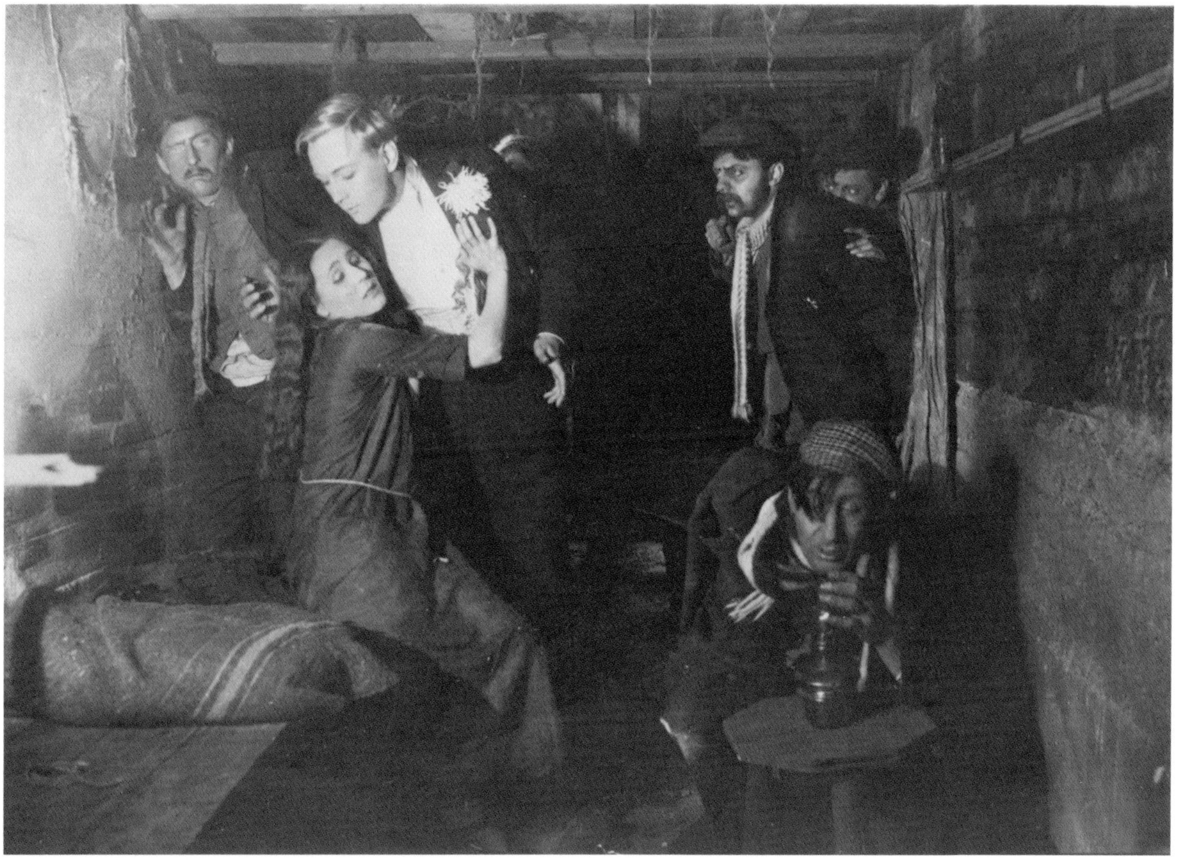

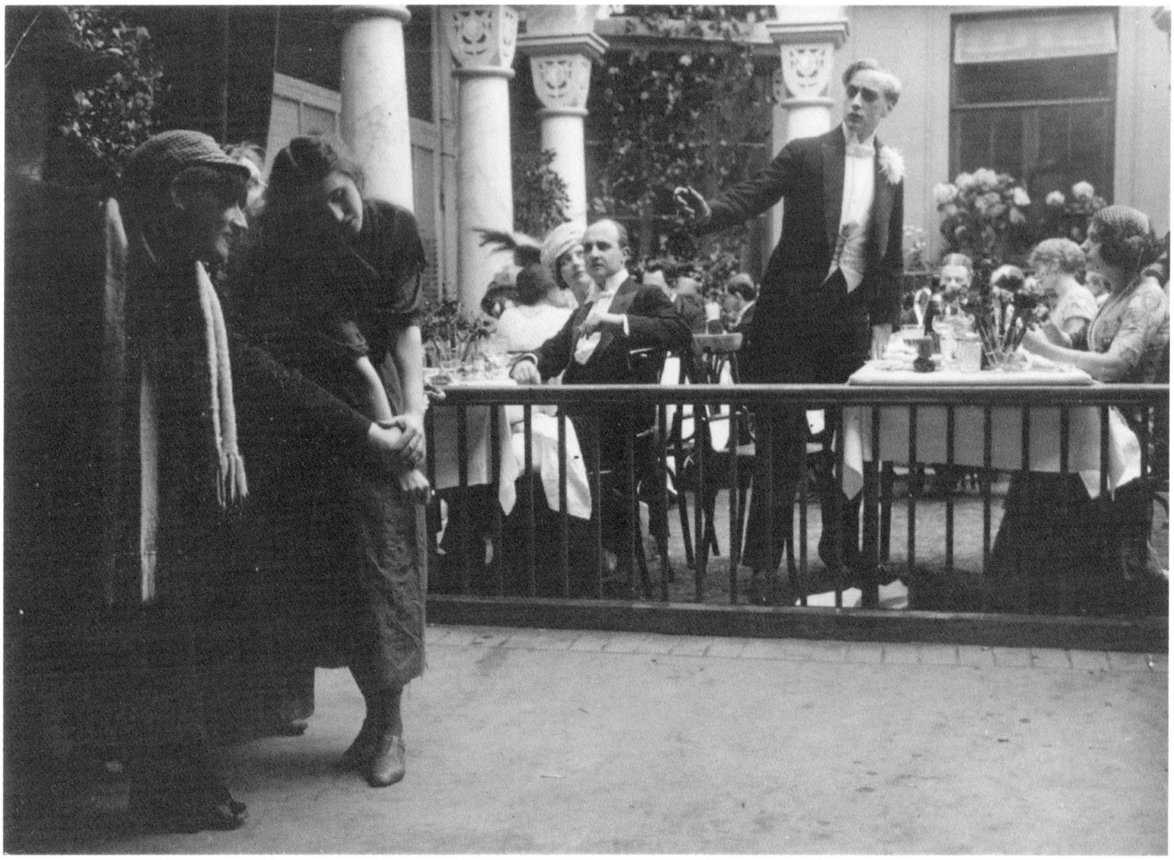

Emilie Flöge
Reform dress, 1913

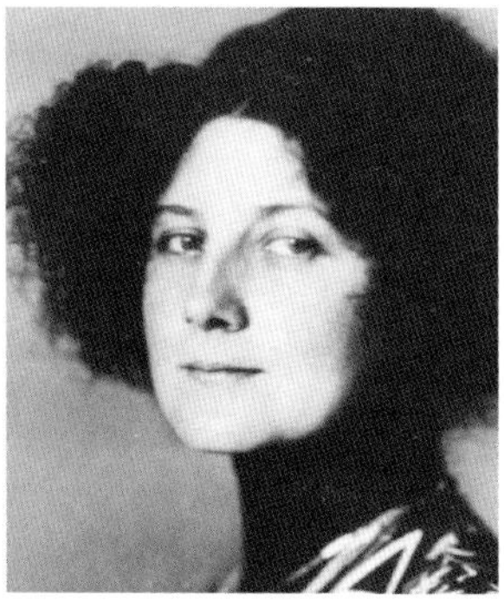

b. 1874 in Vienna
d. 1952 in Vienna

Berta Zuckerkandl may have been very influential through her salon and her journalistic activities, but if we think of the image of women in Vienna around 1900, Emilie Flöge would be the first to come to mind. As the lifelong companion of Gustav Klimt she was his model and muse, was the recipient of numerous items of jewellery from the Wiener Werkstätte, and was also the his estate trustee. She was also part of the salon of the Flöge sisters – a businesswoman, fashion designer and client for one of the first room designs by the Wiener Werkstätte. The reception, fitting room and office occupied the rooms on the first floor of the Casa Piccola on Mariahilferstrasse; the dressmaker's studio and the living quarters were also on this floor. In addition to the design of the business premises Josef Hoffmann and Koloman Moser also developed the entire corporate identity, from the company nameplate to all the printed papers for the business and the invoices and writing paper, and even the labels in the clothing.

The Flöge sisters' establishment was considered one of the leading fashion houses in Vienna. The other sisters were Pauline (1867–1917), who like Emilie was not married, and Helene (1871–1936), the widow of Klimt's brother Ernst (1864–1892). While Pauline and Helene, and later, also the latter's daughter ran the reception and did the bookkeeping, Emilie was the creative partner in the business. The corset-less Reform fashion which was already propagated, for example, in Germany, initially found little favour in conservative Vienna; Berta Zuckerkandl considered the expression "formless Reform sacks" to be a fitting description. Instead, they followed the fashion of Paris, which Emilie visited at least twice a year. She also found inspiration in her collection of folkloric embroidery, especially from what is now Slovakia and the Czech Republic as well as Romania. She presented the evidence for her passion in display cases in the studio, and some of the pieces would become part of her creations.

It was in artist circles that people were willing to concede more freedom of movement for the female body. We know that Alfred Roller and Koloman Moser designed dresses of this kind for their wives, and Emilie Flöge also made herself costumes for which laced bodices were not needed. Her designs ranged from a tunic-like gown to the elegantly elaborate summer outfits which, photographed by Klimt, were presented in 1906/07 as a long series of photographs in the magazine *Deutsche Kunst und Dekoration*.

The summer dress in which she can be seen in private colour photographs taken during the summer holidays in the Salzkammergut in 1913 (complete with jewellery by Koloman Moser from the Wiener Werkstätte) shows a less elaborate but no less sophisticated cut. The silhouette of the striped cotton dress follows the contours of her body and seems to have been designed around one of the finds from her collection. In the centre, reaching from the neckline to the upper thighs, a strip of satin-stitch embroidery from Rybany in Western Slovakia has been inserted; the fabric underneath has been gathered and permits sufficient freedom of movement for the legs.

Painter's smocks with embroidered inserts have been documented as being among the ones Klimt wore in his Viennese studio and also during the summer on the Attersee. It seems possible to surmise therefore that these too may have come from his companion. In that case, the master artist would also have become the model of his muse. DG

Emilie Flöge in a Reform dress of her own design, 1913
Lumière autochrome
by Friedrich Walker

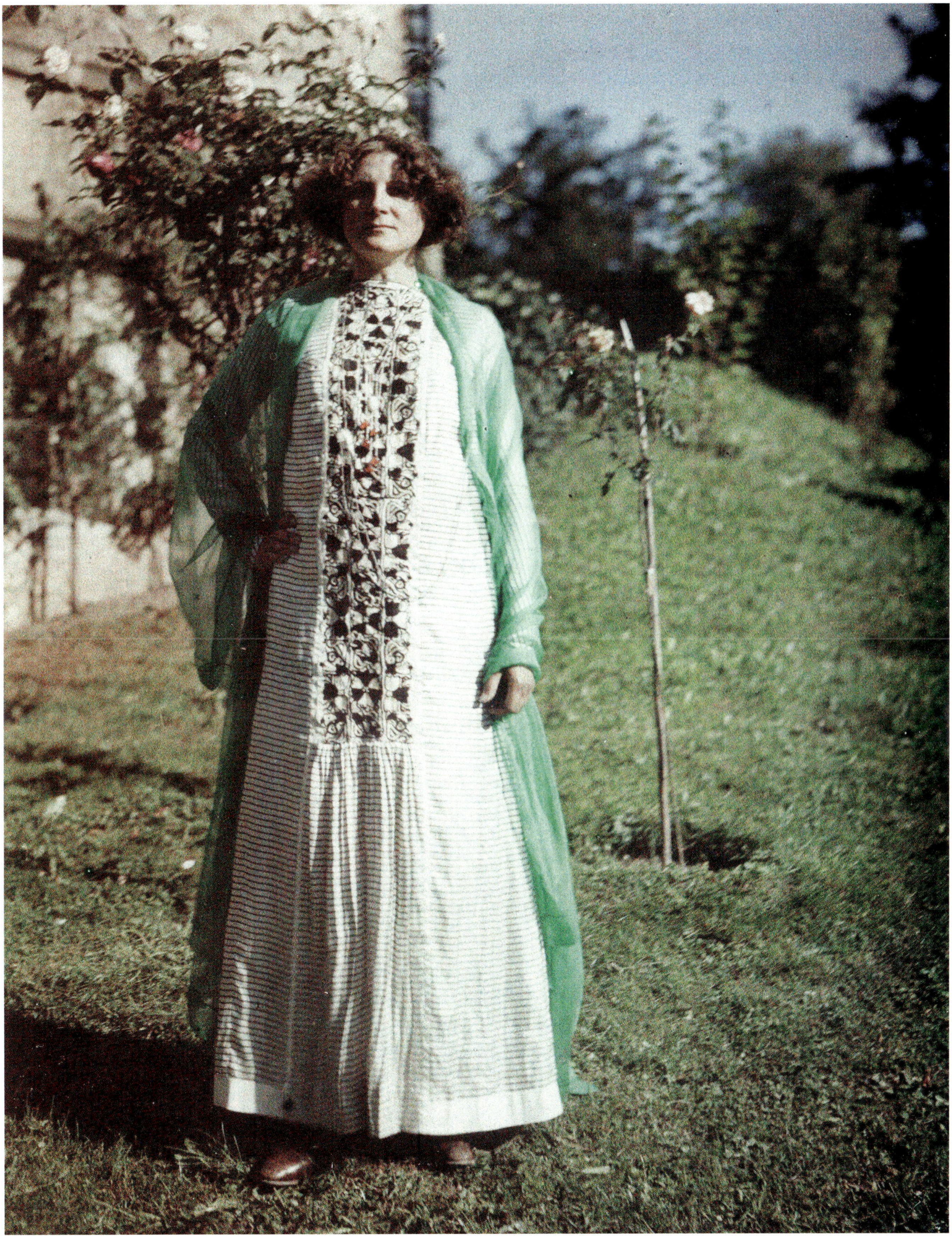

Oskar Kokoschka
The Bride of the Wind, 1913/14

PAGE 89
The Bride of the Wind, 1913/14
Oil on canvas, 181 x 221 cm (71¼ x 87 in.)
Basel, Kunstmuseum Basel

Franz Löwy
Portrait of Alma Maria Mahler-Werfel, 1910

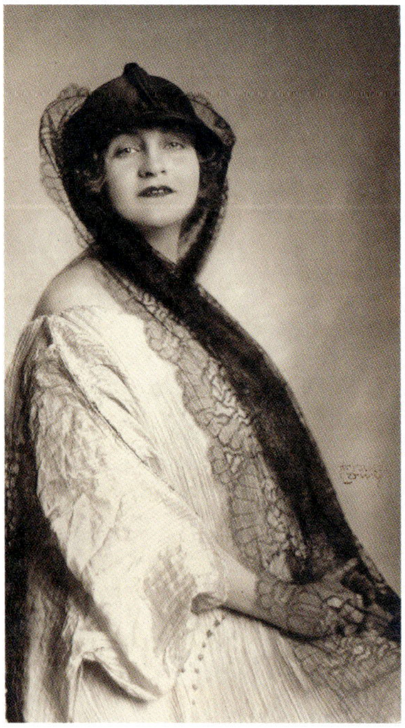

One of the strangest, quirkiest, most notorious love affairs in the history of art took place in Vienna around 1900. To be more precise: in April 1912, the widow of the world-famous composer Gustav Mahler (ill. p. 88) entered the life of the artist Oskar Kokoschka. This resulted in the most gruelling years of his life – and some of his loveliest artworks.

Alma Schindler was born in 1879, married Mahler in 1901 and was widowed in 1911. In 1915, she married Walter Gropius (1883–1969) and was divorced in 1920; in 1929 she married Franz Werfel (1890–1945) and was widowed in 1945. She is not exactly one of the most popular characters in cultural history. Until her death in 1964, she was described in general as having an insatiable appetite as regards not only for the consumption of food and drink, but also men, money and reputation. On the one hand she was deeply anti-Semitic; on the other, many of the men in her life were Jews, and she shared their fate, in other words, emigration and the loss of those riches on which she placed so much value.

Her amour fou with Kokoschka lasted for three years. Soon after they met she became pregnant and had an abortion, to Kokoschka's intense dismay. Not long after meeting her, Kokoschka suffered from severe manifestations of jealousy, which he then expressed in the following manner in one of the 400-odd letters he wrote to her: "And if I had to scratch out of your brain every single one of the alien ideas which go entirely against the grain as far as I am concerned, I would do it, before sharing the redeeming joy with you – I would rather die of hunger – and you. I will suffer no alien gods beside me". *Allos Makar* was the title of a series of texts and illustrations from 1914 in which he rearranged the syllables of their first names to create a Greek title that could be translated as: "Happiness is different". It was no less than the truth. In July 1915 he wrote his last letter to her: "Now I have abandoned all claims to your heart".

Within a short period of time Kokoschka created a number of double portraits. The poses are designed to show intimacy, but the faces refuse to follow suit completely, the big eyes concede there is a world which lies elsewhere than in mutual love; they gaze past each other, look shadowy and withdrawn. Kokoschka does not tend towards the melancholy; his figures are impetuous or nervous but not consumed with grief; nor do the faces of the double portraits show a mentality of sadness, but rather the special foresight related to the situation, that this togetherness will not last. We should credit the painter with the fact that throughout his career there was a quality of apprehension and foresight which he transferred to his portraits: here he felt them first-hand.

The Bride of the Wind marks without doubt the high point of the pictorial sequence. It was completed in 1914. The title is derived from Georg Trakl (1887–1914), the lyricist, who saw the work in Kokoschka's studio. The application of the paint became more pastose during the course of its completion; the colour scheme became more clearly focused on contrasts; it does not quite suit the dreaminess in an indeterminate elsewhere. A completely conventional difference between the sexes creeps in: the woman, Alma, utterly passive, is asleep in safety so to speak while the man, Oskar, eyes wide open and somewhat stiff, is ready to leap out of bed into the world, into reality. In this painting, something prevents him from succumbing to the intimacy. It is his sense of that reality. RM

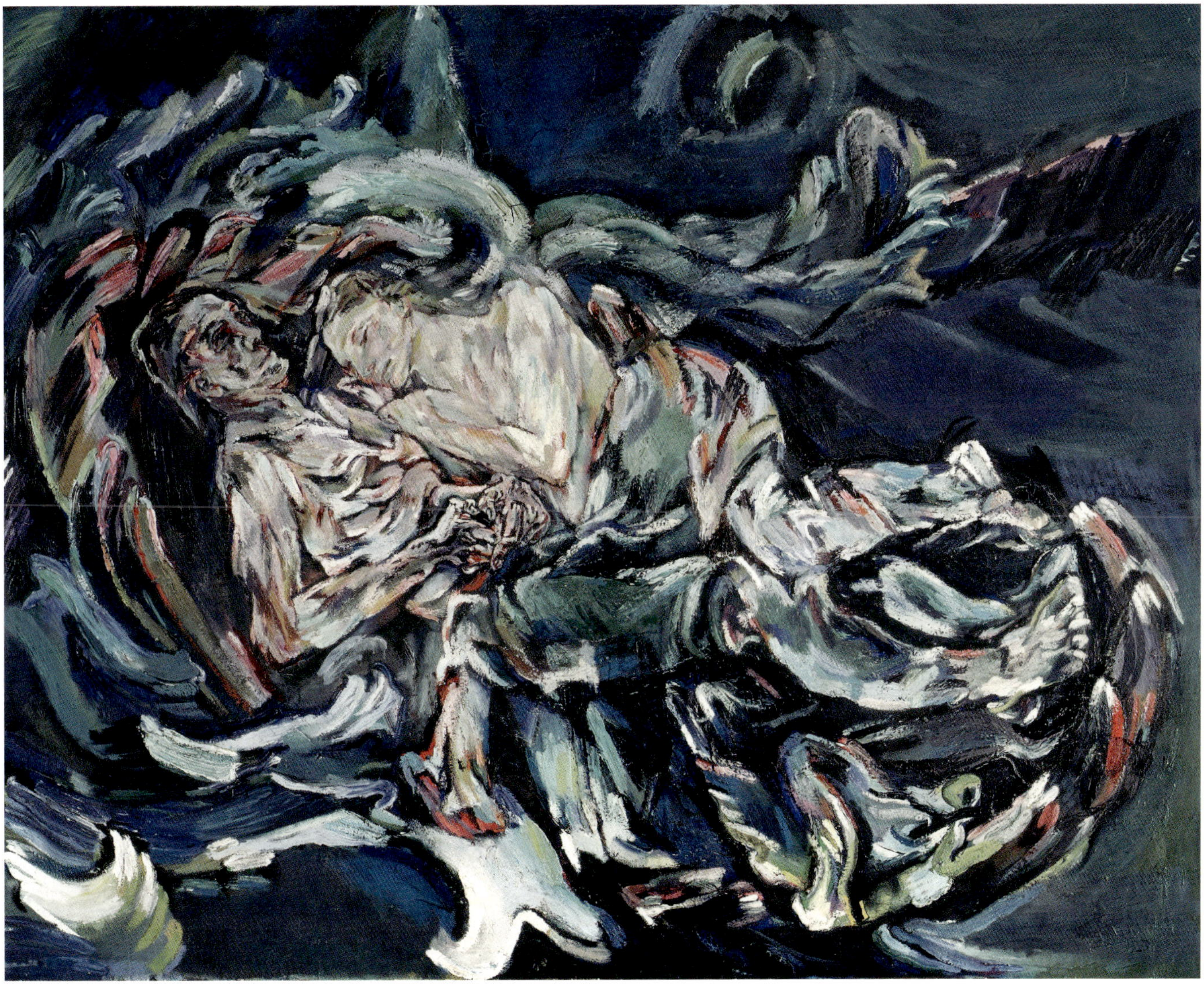

Gustav Klimt

Death and Life, 1910/11, reworked 1915/16

"Death
Nay, not so!
Your wealth was but a loan,
which now, you gone,
Another shall inherit;
and full soon
That other's hour shall strike,
and he in turn
Shall bid farewell to all
and wander forth.
Yea! I come quickly!

Everyman
Just a day! This night!
This hour ere sunrise, that,
in penitence
I may hear holy words
and be prepared
The better to go with you!"

— HUGO VON HOFMANNSTHAL, *EVERYMAN*, DANCE OF DEATH, 1911

The year 1911 was important for Gustav Klimt. The master painter was compelled to give up his studio in the Josefstadt district of Vienna; he moved temporarily into a villa on Hohe Warte, and a few months later he settled in what would be his last studio in Hietzing, another exclusive suburb. In Brussels, the frieze he had designed for the dining room of the Palais Stoclet (ill. p. 56) was installed. And at the International Art Exhibition in Rome he was awarded the first prize for *Death and Life*.

At that time, his large-format, almost square painting with the neutral background had the terse title *Death*. It is divided into two sections: on the left is the haggard main figure and on the right a group of people. Their naked bodies are partly covered; the fabrics and robes are scattered with typical Klimt ornamentation. The subject – the threat to love and to life – permeates Klimt's entire oeuvre, with an early high point in the *Beethoven Frieze*.

In 1912, after its first presentation in Rome, the painting was displayed at the International Art Exhibition in Dresden, this time with the new title *Death and Life*. Further exhibitions followed, always abroad surprisingly enough (1913 in Budapest and Mannheim, 1914 in Prague). After that Klimt began to make major modifications to his danse macabre. We can only speculate about the reasons for this. The First World War had begun and Klimt's mother Anna (1836–1915) had died.

In the original version, Death was looking downwards, holding a red club in his hands as if it were a sceptre; his skull had half disappeared inside the blue robe decorated with black crosses. And he was surrounded by a golden nimbus. Facing him were five figures more or less intertwined, a mother and child, an older woman and a couple, and framed by a meadow of flowers.

Following the reworking of the picture, Death adopted a much more threatening posture. The white skull grins as it gazes with huge, dark eye sockets at the tangle of bodies. The robe is broader and the nimbus has disappeared. The background, originally reddish-brown or gold-coloured, now hovers between shades of green, blue and grey. The flower-covered meadow has become larger and numerous figures have been added to the original individuals. Among them – on the side facing Death – are two young women: one has wide-open, staring eyes. Perhaps she can sense the proximity of the threat? The other figures appear not to demonstrate any fear of Death. And no one is looking directly at him. Life will go on.

In January 1916 the picture was shown in its final version for the first time – at the Berlin Secession. The doctor and art critic Curt Glaser (1879–1943), who had made himself the spokesperson for Expressionism, found the picture highly irritating on that occasion: the subject of Death and Love had served as an excuse for a decorative piece.

The painting was not sold until after Klimt's death, to the painter Hans Böhler (1884–1961). It was on view for the first time in Vienna in 1928 – in a memorial exhibition marking the tenth anniversary of Klimt's death. Half a century later, in 1978, it was purchased by the ophthalmologist and collector Rudolf Leopold for just 225,000 schillings. That would be the equivalent of less than €50,000 today. Since 2001, it has been one of the main works of the Leopold Museum. TT

Death and Life, 1910/11,
reworked 1915/16
Oil on canvas, 180.8 x 200.6 cm
(71¼ x 79 in.)
Vienna, Leopold Museum

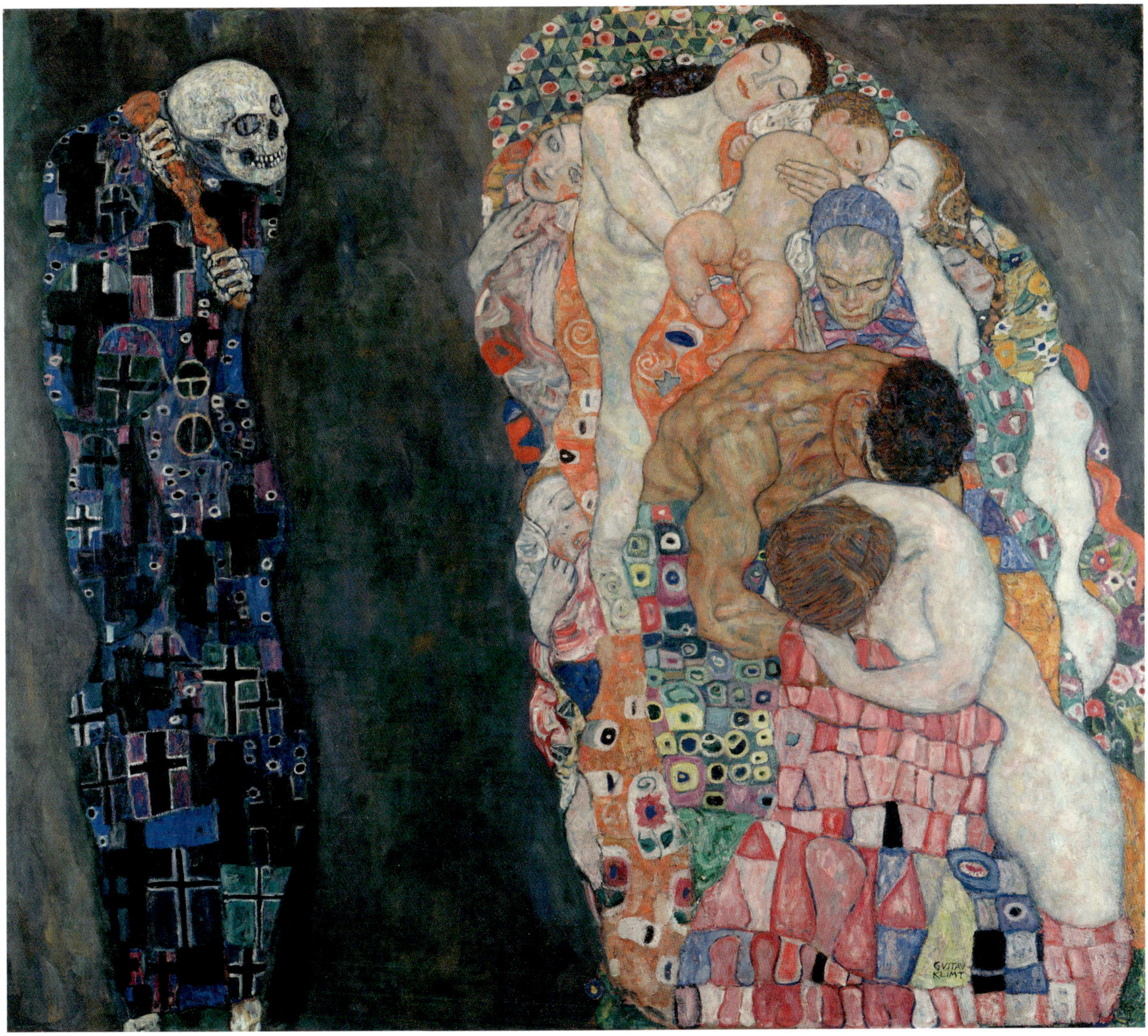
GUSTAV
KLIMT

Madame d'Ora

Emperor Charles I of Austria with His Family, 1917

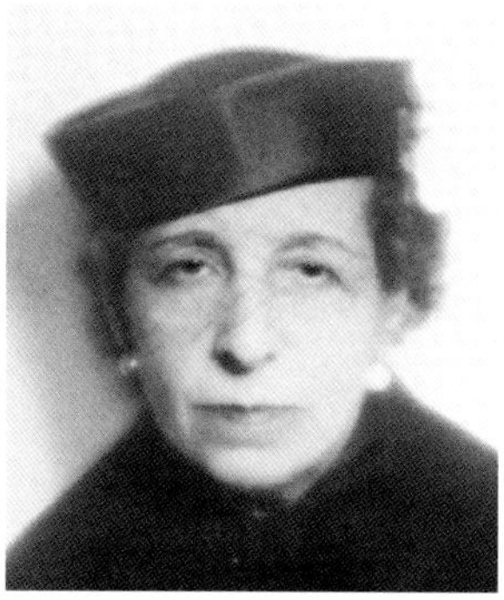

b. 1881 in Vienna
d. 1963 in Frohnleiten

Their appearance is not exac tly distinguished. It looks as though a family has quickly dashed into the photographic studio shortly before their Sunday walk along the main avenue of the Prater. The father is standing slightly to one side of the picture's centre, his hands casually in the jacket pockets of his Hussar uniform as he gazes past the camera lens into empty space. His blond, curly-haired son, aged about five, has been positioned in front of him; he is wearing a spotless white sailor suit with short trousers and white high-laced boots. He seems to be following the instructions that are being issued from the direction of the camera. His mother, also dressed in white and sitting on a striped sofa, has turned towards him so that his little sister is sitting at somewhat of an angle. The little girl is leaned up against her mother, her hand lying in childlike unselfconsciousness between her bare legs; she, too, is wearing a white dress. Although the father does stand out within the group, the scene looks more like a cohesive, almost intimate family portrait of a bourgeois family. However, here we are looking at no less than Charles I (1887–1922), the Emperor of Austria-Hungary, with his wife Zita (1892–1989) and their two oldest children Otto (1912–2011) and Adelheid (1914–1971), who had visited the studio of Madame d'Ora in central Vienna during the First World War for a series of family and individual portraits.

Although she personally never stood behind the camera, Dora Kallmus was the woman behind the studio of Madame d'Ora. Within a short time the studio, which she had opened in 1907, became one of the best addresses for society photography in the fields of art, stage, fashion and aristocracy. Arthur Schnitzler, Hermann Bahr and Karl Kraus were among those who had their portraits taken, as did Emilie Flöge, Berta Zuckerkandl, the dancing Wiesenthal sisters and the hotel owner Anna Sacher (1859–1930) surrounded by her pug dogs. "It was considered sufficient to have permitted me to be the first woman to attend the lectures, but they kept the chemical reagents away from me, as if they were improper jokes", was how Kallmus recalled the difficulties of her training at the Graphische Lehr- und Versuchsanstalt (Institute of Graphics) in Vienna. Before that the society photographer Hans Makart (1870–1946, son of the master painter of the same name) had permitted her to look over his shoulder in his summer studio. She subsequently continued her apprenticeship under Nicola Perscheid (1864–1930) in Berlin. In addition to dealing with customers it was here that she learned to "look and look again", the photographer noted later. Thus she ensured that there was a suitable atmosphere during the photo sessions, as well as optimal lighting conditions, a purposeful arrangement of decor, draperies and details – in short everything necessary for a successful picture. During her time in Vienna the stagings by Madame d'Ora were rarely daring, but they nonetheless possess a highly individual signature. The books of her studio in Vienna record some 90,000 photographs until 1927.

"Her important act as a lady of Viennese society in establishing a photographic studio demonstrated great courage", commented the photographer, colleague and later companion Arthur Benda (1885–1969), whom Dora Kallmus had met during her time with Perscheid and whom she had taken back to Vienna with her. Madame d'Ora also demonstrated courage in her old age, when she took up her camera and visited the slaughterhouses of Paris – alone. DG

Emperor Charles I of Austria with His Family, 1917
Gelatine silver print, 39 x 30 cm
(approx. 15⅜ x 11⅞ in.)

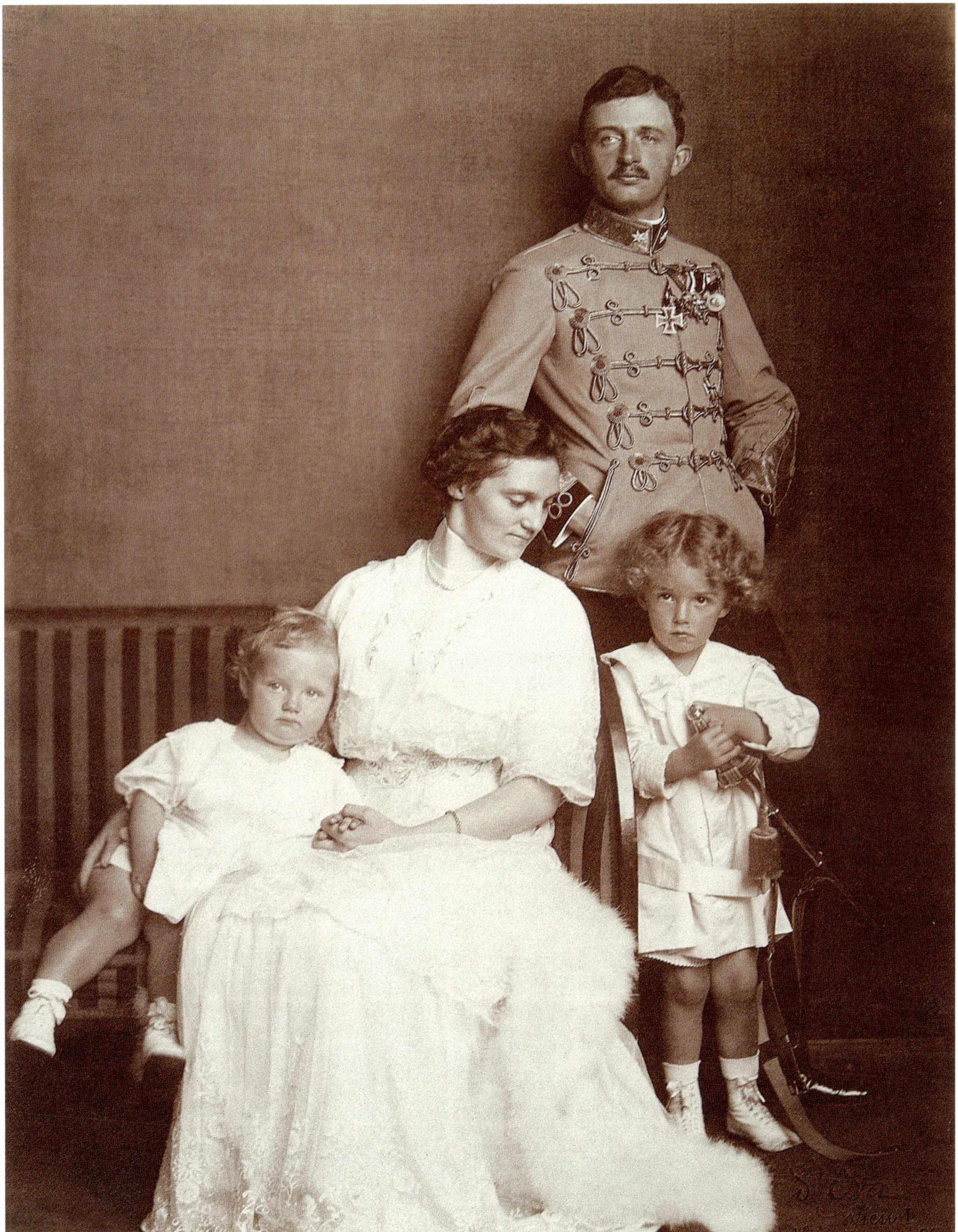

Egon Schiele

The Family (Cowering Couple), 1918

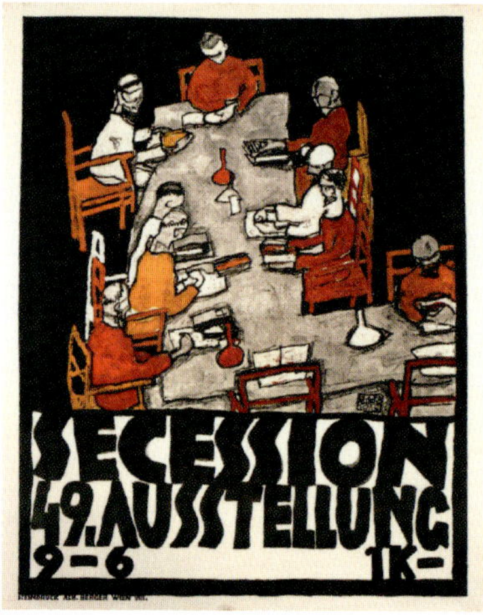

Egon Schiele
Poster for the 49th Exhibition of the Vienna Secession, 1918
Colour lithograph, 68 x 53 cm (26¾ x 21 in.)
Vienna, Wien Museum

In 1918, Egon Schiele positioned himself at the forefront of the "modern department" of the art scene in Vienna. Gustav Klimt had died in February of that year and Oskar Kokoschka was undergoing a radical cure in Germany following his traumatic experiences during the First World War. In spring the 49th exhibition (ill. p. 94) would take place in the Secession, the establishment par excellence for questions of progressive visual art. It would be a triumph for Schiele, who was not yet 28 years of age. One of the outstanding exhibits was a large-format canvas that showed a nude man embracing an equally naked woman in a beguiling manner, completely relaxed and calm; at their feet lays a child. The picture seemed to echo an appeal for a certain order after the overheated excesses of the avant-garde in art and war. The title of the work in the Secession exhibition was *Cowering Couple*.

It would later be renamed *The Family*. The definite article stands for the concreteness of the persons depicted since the artist was very familiar with this family. Schiele portrayed himself here, together with Edith (1893–1918), his wife, whom he had married during the summer of 1915. If Emperor Charles had chosen Madame d'Ora to photograph him (ill. p. 93) informally as a father with his family, wearing his uniform, in a moment in which it looks as though he is just on home leave from the front like millions of other fathers who etched their families into their hearts in this way – then an artist, too, can lean on the happiness of something predictable. But Schiele would not be Schiele were it not for his ardour, eccentricity and weakness for excess, had he not included a considerable amount of exaggeration in his very balanced piece of moral uprightness. We can recognize it in the somewhat too-general portrayal of childlikeness in the baby: there was no child like this in Schiele's family. It was an invocation. His wife would indeed become pregnant, but no baby would ever be born. At the end of October 1918 Edith Schiele would succumb to the Spanish flu, the epidemic which befell the whole of Europe, weakened as it was by the world war. Three days later, Schiele would become ill as well. He died on the eve of his global success. His life story bears some resemblance to that of Mozart.

Of course, the painting knows nothing of this. And yet it is prescient enough, because the man who painted it, Schiele, worked once more on his image of a woman. And in a milieu furthered by Sigmund Freud that revelled in the obsession of the Oedipus complex, the image of the woman is, above all, an image of a mother. Schiele had constant dealings with the woman who had given birth to him. We can read that into one of the numerous notorious letters to her, which went more or less as follows: "Dear Mother, I appreciate all that, and I should like to – believe me, you do me an injustice… I want to enjoy my pleasure in the world; that is why I can work creatively – and woe betide anyone who robs me of that. – I have myself to thank for my existence, and nothing and nobody helped me". In fact, after the death of Schiele's father in 1905, Marie Schiele (1862–1935) had energetically supported the artistic career of her son. That then provided opportunity enough to work away at a lifelong relationship. Pictures visualize the dead mother; they visualize the encounter of the allegorical figure of Death with a girl who then, in turn, is his own wife. And they repeatedly imagine pregnancies. When Schiele paints a family, he also paints the abyss. RM

The Family (Cowering Couple), 1918
Oil on canvas, 150 x 160.8 cm (59 x 63¼ in.)
Vienna, Belvedere

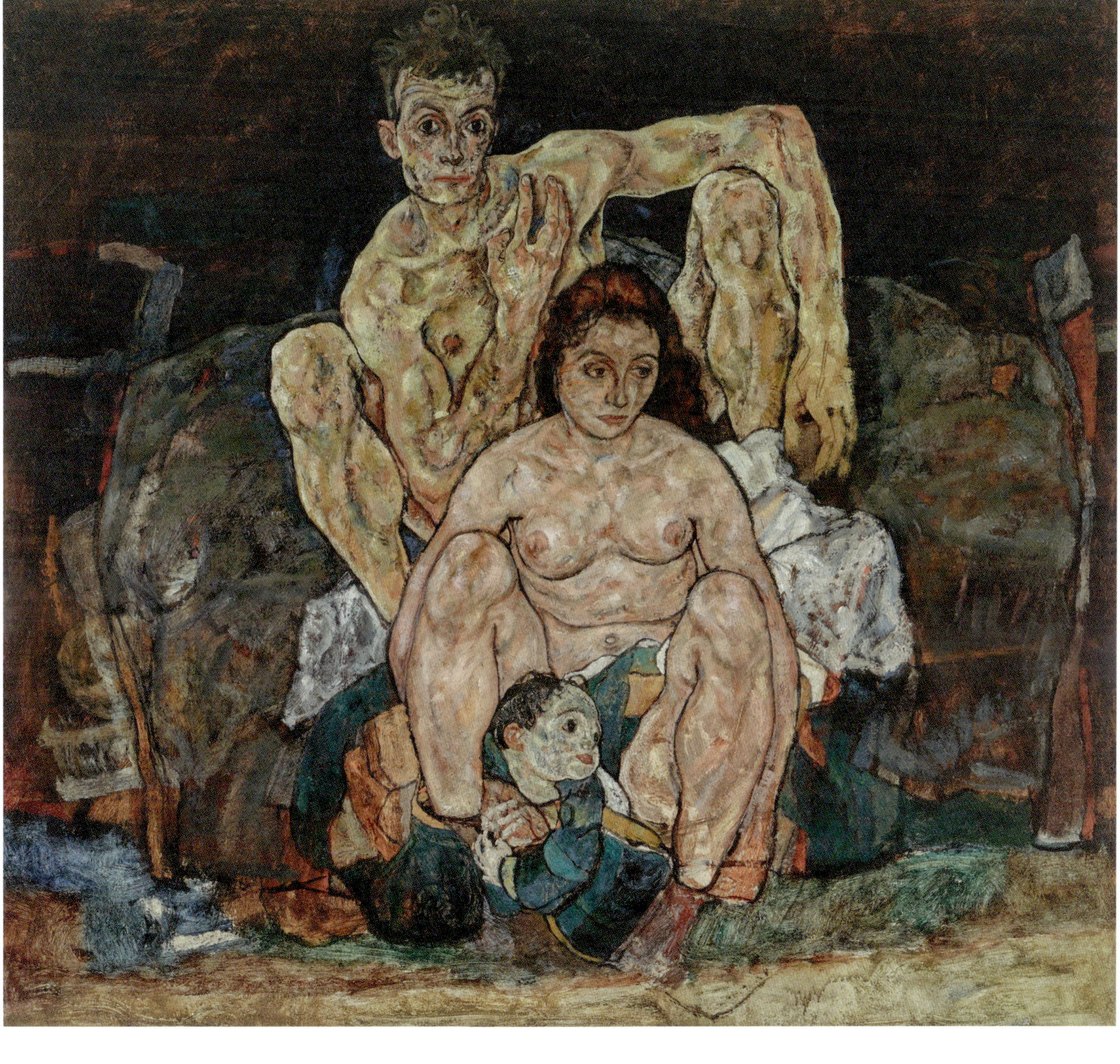

Notes

1 http://depts.washington.edu/vienna/documents/Hofmannsthal/Hofmannsthal_Anatol.htm
2 Hofmannsthal, quoted in Wunberg 1981, p. 353.
3 Ibid., p. 341.
4 *Die Fackel*, no. 400, p. 46.
5 Broch 2001, p. 46.
6 Bahr, quoted in Nebehay 1979, pp. 23f.
7 Herzfeld, quoted in Wunberg 1981, p. 312.
8 Klimt, quoted in Nebehay 1969, p. 394.
9 Bahr, quoted in Wunberg 1981, p. 190.
10 Musil 1978, vol. 6, pp. 46f.
11 Freud, quoted in Alt, p. 272.
12 Freud, quoted in Wunberg, p. 651.
13 Freud, quoted in Alt, p. 283.
14 Mahler, quoted in exh. cat. *Die nackte Wahrheit* 2005, p. 147. / 15 Schnitzler 2006, pp. 279f.
16 Fels, quoted in Wunberg 1981, p. 196.
17 Altenberg, quoted in Fischer 2007, p. 70.
18 *Die Fackel*, no. 389, p. 37.
19 *Die Fackel*, no. 300, p. 24.
20 Loos, quoted in Rukschcio/Schachel 1982, p. 87.
21 Ibid., p. 109.

Bibliography

Overviews, anthologies, overall representations:

Archiv der Schaulust. Eine Geschichte des frühen Kinos in der k.u.k. Ära 1896–1918, exh. cat., Filmarchiv Austria, Vienna 2016
Brandstätter, Christian (ed.), *Wien 1900. Kunst und Kultur*, Vienna 2005
Broch, Hermann, *Hofmannsthal und seine Zeit*, Frankfurt am Main 2001
Fischer, Lisa/Brix, Emil (ed.), *Die Frauen der Wiener Moderne*, Vienna/Cologne/Weimar 1997
Haider, Edgard, *Wien 1914. Alltag am Rande des Abgrunds*, Vienna/Cologne/Weimar 2013
Gustav Klimt und die Kunstschau 1908, exh. cat., Belvedere, Wien, 2008
Die nackte Wahrheit. Klimt, Schiele, Kokoschka und andere Skandale, exh. cat., Schirn Kunsthalle, Frankfurt am Main, Munich 2005
Nebehay, Christian M., *Ver Sacrum 1989–1903*, Munich 1979
Pfabigan, Alfred (ed.), *Ornament und Askese. Im Zeitgeist des Wien der Jahrhundertwende*, Vienna 1985
Der Preis der Schönheit. 100 Jahre Wiener Werkstätte, exh. cat., MAK, Vienna 2003
Schorske, Carl E., *Wien. Geist und Gesellschaft im Fin de Siècle*, Frankfurt am Main 1982
Traum und Wirklichkeit, exh. cat., Historisches Museum der Stadt Wien, 1985
Trotzdem Kunst!, exh. cat., Leopold Museum, Vienna 2014
Vereinigung bildender Künstler Wiener Secession (ed.), *Secession. Permanenz einer Idee*, Ostfildern-Ruit 1997
Wunberg, Gotthard (ed.), *Die Wiener Moderne. Literatur, Kunst und Musik zwischen 1890 und 1910*, Stuttgart 1981

Individual catalogues, biographies, monographs:

Alt, Peter-André, *Sigmund Freud. Der Arzt der Moderne*, Munich 2016
Richard Gerstl. Retrospektive, exh. cat., Schirn Kunsthalle, Frankfurt am Main 2017
Fischer, Lisa, *Lina Loos. Oder wenn die Muse sich selbst küßt*, Vienna/Cologne, 2nd ed., 2007
Kraus, Karl (ed.), *Die Fackel*, reprint Munich 1968–1976
Oskar Kokoschka. Träumender Knabe – Enfant Terrible, exh. cat., Belvedere Wien, 2008
Metzger, Rainer, *Gustav Klimt. Das graphische Werk*, Vienna 2005
Musil, Robert, *Gesammelte Werke*, Reinbek 1978
Nebehay, Christian M., *Gustav Klimt. Dokumentation*, Vienna 1969
Rukschcio, Burkhardt/Schachel, Roland, *Adolf Loos*, Salzburg/Vienna 1982
Egon Schiele, exh. cat., Albertina Wien, 2017
Schnitzler, Arthur, *Jugend in Wien. Eine Autobiographie*, Frankfurt am Main 2006

Copyright

Portraits of artists

P. 72: Franz Setzer, *Der österreichische Komponist Arnold Schönberg* (Detail), Vienna 1922; IMAGNO/Archiv Setzer-Tschiedel
P. 86: Madame d'Ora: *Emilie Flöge* (detail), 1910; IMAGNO/Collection Hubmann
P. 92: Madame d'Ora: *Madame d'Ora* (detail), c. 1925; IMAGNO/Austrian Archives

Photo credits

The publishers are grateful to the galleries, archives and photographers involved for granting reproduction rights and for their help and support in producing this book. The following credits apply in addition to those already mentioned in the picture captions:

akg-images/Erich Lessing: p. 79; Albertina, Vienna: pp. 25, 42, 71, 82; Architektur Bilderservice Kandula, Photo: Ernst Wrba: p. 8; Archive of Auchentaller: p. 36 b.; Archive of Otto Breicha: p. 64; Archiv der Secession, Vienna: p. 49; © Belvedere, Vienna: pp. 20/21, 95; © Martin Bond/Alamy Stock Photo: p. 39; © bpk: pp. 16, 41; © bpk/Nationalgalerie, SMB/Roman März: p. 27; © Courtesy Dallas Museum of Art, The Eugene and Margaret McDermott Art Fund, Inc., 2013.31.A: pp. 62, 63; © Bildarchiv Foto Marburg: pp. 56, 57, 70 b.; Photo: Andrej Hrausky: p. 46 top, 50 top; IMAGNO/Austrian Archives: front cover, pp. 1, 4, 9, 11, 13–15, 17, 21 b., 22, 24, 26, 32, 34 top, 35, 36 top, 44, 58, 59, 60 b., 61, 67, 70 top, 74, 76, 78, 83, 87, 92, 93; IMAGNO/Archiv Setzer-Tschiedel: p. 72; IMAGNO/Christian Brandstätter Verlag: p. 12; IMAGNO/Dagmar Landova: p. 10; IMAGNO/Leopold Museum, Vienna: pp. 30, 53, 81; IMAGNO/ÖNB: pp. 23, 46 b., 88; IMAGNO/Öst. Volkshochschularchiv: pp. 7, 77; IMAGNO/Collection of Hubmann: p. 86; IMAGNO/Wien Museum: pp. 33, 34 b., 45, 80, 94, back cover; IMAGNO/Wienbibliothek im Rathaus: pp. 40, 66; Photo: Michael Jencewk: p. 43; © János Kalmár: p. 47; Leicester Museum & Art Gallery, Leicestershire, UK/Bridgeman Images: p. 31; © Leopold Museum, Vienna: pp. 29 (Inv. 648), 65 (Inv. 651), 75 (Inv. 465); © Leopold Museum, Vienna/Manfred Thumberger, Vienna: p. 91 (Inv. 630); © MAK – Österreichisches Museum für angewandte Kunst/Gegenwartskunst, Vienna: pp. 14, 48, 69; Arnold Schönberg Center, Vienna: pp. 28, 73; Photo Margherita Spiluttini, © Architekturzentrum Wien, collection: p. 18 (Inv. 1591-55), p. 19 (Inv. 1592-42); Svenska Filminstitutet, Stockholm: p. 85; © Keiichi Tahara: pp. 2, 51, 55; ullstein bild: p. 84 top; Universitätsbibliothek Heidelberg: p. 37; © Van Gogh Museum, Amsterdam: p. 8; © White Images/Scala, Florence: p. 89; Wien Museum: pp. 6, 10, 38 b.

The editor

Rainer Metzger studied art history, history, and German literature in Munich and Augsburg. In 1994 he received his Ph.D., on the subject of Dan Graham, and subsequently worked as a fine arts journalist for the Viennese newspaper *Der Standard*. He has written numerous books on art, including volumes on van Gogh and Chagall. Since 2004, he has worked as Professor of Art History at the Academy of Fine Arts in Karlsruhe.

Imprint

EACH AND EVERY TASCHEN BOOK PLANTS A SEED!
Each year, we offset our annual carbon emissions with carbon credits at the Instituto Terra, a reforestation program in Minas Gerais, Brazil, founded by Lélia and Sebastião Salgado. To find out more about this ecological partnership, please check: www.taschen.com/institutoterra.
Inspiration: unlimited.
Carbon footprint: (almost) zero.

Want to see more? Visit *taschen.com* to view our current publications, browse our latest magazine, and subscribe to our newsletter.

Hohenzollernring 53, D–50672 Köln
www.taschen.com

Translation: Jane Michael, Munich

Texts:
Daniela Gregori (DG), Rainer Metzger (RM), Maik Novotny (MN), Thomas Trenkler (TT)

Printed in Bosnia-Herzegovina
ISBN 978-3-8365-6705-3

FRONT COVER
Gustav Klimt
Portrait of Adele Bloch-Bauer I (detail), 1907
Oil and gold leaf on canvas,
140 x 140 cm (55 x 55 in.)
New York, Neue Galerie

BACK COVER
Joseph Maria Olbrich
Poster for the second Secession exhibition (detail), 1898
Lithograph, 81 x 51 cm (32 x 20 in.)
Vienna, Wien Museum